P9-DNE-479

ALSO BY ANAND GIRIDHARADAS

Winners Take All:
The Elite Charade of Changing the World

The True American:
Murder and Mercy in Texas

India Calling:
An Intimate Portrait of a Nation's Remaking

THE
PERSUADERS

THE PERSUADERS

At the Front Lines of the Fight for Hearts, Minds, and Democracy

ANAND GIRIDHARADAS

Alfred A. Knopf · New York 2022

THIS IS A BORZOI BOOK
PUBLISHED BY ALFRED A. KNOPF

www.aaknopf.com

Knopf, Borzoi Books, and the colophon are registered trademarks of Penguin Random House LLC.

Library of Congress Cataloging-in-Publication Data
Names: Giridharadas, Anand, author.
Title: The persuaders : at the front lines of the fight for hearts, minds, and democracy / Anand Giridharadas.
Description: First edition. | New York : Alfred A. Knopf, 2022. | Includes index.
Identifiers: LCCN 2022009611 (print) | LCCN 2022009612 (ebook) | ISBN 9780593318997 (hardcover) | ISBN 9780593319000 (ebook)
Subjects: LCSH: Political culture—United States. | Political participation—Social aspects—United States. | Polarization (Social sciences)—Political aspects—United States. | Democracy—United States. | United States—Politics and government—21st century.
Classification: LCC JK1726 .G56 2022 (print) | LCC JK1726 (ebook) | DDC 320.973—dc23/eng/20220520
LC record available at https://lccn.loc.gov/2022009611
LC ebook record available at https://lccn.loc.gov/2022009612

Jacket image by akinbostanci / Getty Images
Jacket design by Janet Hansen

Manufactured in the United States of America
First Edition

For S. and H., Z. and J., M. and P.,
M. and J., A., and, as ever, P.,
in profound friendship

CONTENTS

CONTENTS

THE
PERSUADERS

PROLOGUE: THE WAR ON PERSUASION

In June 2014, Aleksandra Krylova and Anna Bogacheva arrived in the United States on a clandestine mission. Krylova was a high-ranking official at the Internet Research Agency in St. Petersburg, Russia, an ostensibly private company that was known to work on behalf of Russian intelligence. Bogacheva, her road buddy, a researcher and data cruncher, was more junior. Their trip had been well planned: a transcontinental itinerary, SIM cards, burner phones, cameras, visas obtained under the pretense of personal travel, and, just in case, evacuation plans.

The women made stops in California, Colorado, Illinois, Louisiana, Michigan, Nevada, New Mexico, New York, and Texas, according to a federal indictment issued years later. Beyond that, their activities are not well known, though their mission is: to gather evidence of conditions in the United States for a project to destabilize its political system and society, using the rather improbable weapon of millions of social media posts.

In their long-simmering conflict with the United States, high officials in Russia, like their American counterparts, have a range of tools of sabotage available to them. Many are regularly put to use. But in recent years, the project Krylova and Bogacheva worked on was a marquee effort and a standout success, and that was telling. The investment in the project seemed to reflect a calculation by a highly capable foreign intelligence service that, of all the vulnerabilities of modern American society, the particular civic attitude that the project sought to inflame, writing other people off—assuming they would never change their minds or ways, dismissing them as hopelessly mired in identities they couldn't escape, viewing those who thought differently as needing to be resisted rather than won over, refusing to engage in the work of persuasion—was an Achilles' heel. That attitude had a hundred causes and a thousand expressions and could be found everywhere you looked, taking different guises on the left and the right, showing up among regular citizens and in the marble corridors of power.

Americans didn't exactly need outside help to see each other in these ways. If anything, the culture of the write-off had become a rare point of commonality across otherwise irreconcilable factions. Nevertheless, half a world away, in 2013, in St. Petersburg, the Internet Research Agency, or IRA, was founded, and it would soon begin down the road of amplifying Americans' growing culture of mutual dismissal. It was set up as an industrial troll farm, where workers were paid to write blog posts, comments on news sites, and social media messages. Late in the summer of 2013, a job posting appeared online. "Internet operators wanted!" it read, according to the independent newspaper *Novaya Gazeta.* "Task: posting comments at profile sites in the Internet, writing thematic posts, blogs, social networks." Plus: "PAYMENTS EVERY WEEK AND FREE MEALS!!!"

The initial focus of the agency was swaying Western public opinion about Russia's military intervention in Ukraine in 2014. But that same year, the agency launched a new department called the Translator Project. Its bailiwick was to foment political unrest in Russia's great adversary, the United States. Krylova and Bogacheva embarked on their travels that year to aid the project, conducting their off-line field work for use online.

Though the women's expedition had some of the glamour of traditional espionage, with the throwaway phones and escape scenarios, the bulk of the IRA's work was more mundane. Hundreds of workers toiled in twelve-hour shifts at the IRA offices on 55 Savushkina Street. They received detailed instructions about the messages they were expected to promote. Each worker had to manage multiple fake accounts and produce message after message on each one—reportedly three posts a day if Facebook was their medium, and fifty posts a day on Twitter. Managers obsessed over metrics like number of posts, page views, likes, retweets. The office was organized into groups including the Bloggers and Commentators Office, Rapid Response Department, CEO Department, Creative Department, and Social Network Specialists Department.

Like any workplace, the agency had its discontents. A worker might be fined for arriving late or even for leaving the office one minute early. There were also complaints about the cutbacks. At first, according to workers interviewed by local media outlets, there had been a relaxation room with sofas. One day, the sofas were gone. There had been paper towels in the bathroom. One day, there was a sign to use fewer of them. Then they were gone, replaced by an electric dryer that left much to be desired. Someone told a reporter of a clogged toilet bowl covered with tape for two weeks. Agency employees who spoke to the press generally said they were working there for the money, not out of ardor for Vladimir Putin.

One worker painted this picture of one of the bosses: "Oleg was a funny man. Just imagine, a guy with a belly walks around in a denim shirt hanging out, fiddling with the keys to his car like a taxi driver, and saying, 'If a person knows how to write, he will write about anything.' " He wanted the troll farm to be a place where true artists of discourse toxification could unleash their talent.

Not everyone who passed through the agency's doors found it so amusing. Lyudmila Savchuk, a Russian journalist who said she took a job at the IRA to expose it, later recalled, "One can remain sane in the factory for two months maximum." One of the stresses was the constant toggling among online avatars and their views and voices. But there was also a larger dread: "The realization that you can invent any fact, then watch it absolutely synchronized with the media outlets as one massive information outflow and spread worldwide—that absolutely breaks your psyche."

Savchuk was not overselling the agency's reach. In the years ahead, its posts would attract 76 million engagements on Facebook and 183 million likes on Instagram, and it would send more than 10 million tweets. Some posts were outright disinformation; others sought to whip up anger at the truth.

Krylova and Bogacheva's trip, and the larger Internet Research

Agency project it served, would eventually become public knowledge. At first, an oversimple, if seductive, story line grew up around it: the Russian mission was a plot to plant Donald Trump in the White House. "Yes, Russian Trolls Helped Elect Trump," read the headline on a Michelle Goldberg column in *The New York Times*. The subtitle of *Cyberwar*, by Kathleen Hall Jamieson, director of the Annenberg Public Policy Center at the University of Pennsylvania, was "How Russian Hackers and Trolls Helped Elect a President." Aiding Trump was indeed among the IRA's documented objectives, and this fact gave rise to a widespread public perception that electing Trump was the focus of the mission. Some even believed that Trump himself was a Russian agent.

For many rattled by the 2016 presidential election, the idea was tempting. "For Americans and for American journalists and very politicized Americans in particular, the story of Russian interference was a really damaging crutch for the imagination," the Russian American writer Masha Gessen told me not long ago. "It was something that allowed us to think about Trump as somebody from outer space, or at least from Russia, as a kind of alien body, but also an alien body from which we're somehow miraculously going to be liberated." It was easier to think of the country's problems as being of foreign provenance, an act of war that could be answered by doing something to some electrical grid.

In time, however, a more careful, sobering analysis emerged: the Russian mission, far from dropping something on America from outer space, had been to fertilize behaviors already flourishing on American soil. "The IRA's goals are to further widen existing divisions in the American public and decrease our faith and trust in institutions that help maintain a strong democracy," Darren Linvill and Patrick Warren, scholars at Clemson University who became leading analysts of Russia's campaign, have written. "The IRA has used Trump—and many other politicians—as vehicles to further these twin goals, but it is not about Trump himself." An analysis given to U.S. Senate investigators portrayed similar goals: "to undermine citizens' trust in government, exploit societal fractures, create distrust in the information environment, blur the lines between reality and fiction, undermine trust among communities, and erode confidence in the democratic process."

When I began to read the Russian posts myself, I saw even more clearly how the troll farm had gone about this work. It had done more than fan the flames of anger and division. It had encouraged the view, already on the rise, and not without roots in reality, that the basic activity of democratic life, the changing of minds, had become futile work, which in turn fed the feeling that vital political pursuits—of solidarity across difference, of multiracial coalitions, of united fronts against authoritarianism—and other endeavors to create the conditions for meaningful change were doomed. The troll farm wanted Americans to regard each other as immovable, brainwashed, of bad faith, not worth energy, disloyal, repulsive. "The IRA knows that in political warfare disgust is a much more powerful tool than anger," Linvill and Warren have written. "Anger drives people to the polls; disgust drives countries apart."

In 2018, I published a book about how the superrich corrode democracy by hoarding wealth, buying political influence, and using the guise of do-gooding to cast themselves as the solution to the very problems they continue to cause. The book made a case for meaningful structural change through the organs of democracy and against billionaire pseudo-change.

That work led to my interest in people working to deliver this meaningful change through electoral politics—in activism, community organizing, and campaigning. As I began to follow their work, I sensed they were up against more than just the powerful forces I had chronicled. They also confronted, within their own spaces, the challenge of a pessimistic and factional political culture that threatened their great ambitions. Their work—for racial justice, for a humane economy, for planetary sustainability—required attracting more people to a given cause today than believed in it yesterday. But the reigning culture often discouraged the work of changing minds and sometimes isolated those who pursued it.

It seemed significant that this ginning up of differences and fatalism that I saw activists, organizers, and political figures contending with was the very habit seized on by the Russians.

Crystal Johnson is an actual person. She is a real-estate agent. I spoke to her once on the phone. When I explained that I was looking into how her identity had been stolen and weaponized by Russian intelligence, she hung up and stopped answering my calls.

Johnson was an occasional Twitter user given to a combination of real-estate insights and inspirational quotations.

"Resale homes sales R up," she wrote back in 2012. "As we learned from the recent bubble that burst, a healthy housing market puts many pairs of hands to work."

"Good morning!" she wrote on another occasion. "There is so much we have to be thankful for. Be Blessed and continue being a blessing to others."

Heraclitus, the ancient Greek philosopher, made a cameo: "The content of your character is your choice. Day by day, what you choose, what you think and what you do is who you become." And, as night follows day, the corporate philosopher Henry Ford: "Coming together is a beginning. Keeping together is progress. Working together is success."

There was, naturally, some selling as well: "Interest Rates are on the move: the biggest jumps in months, home prices are on the rise, it's a great time to own a home. Contact me now."

These tweets came from an account with the handle @CrystalSellsLA. Its profile photo shows a Black woman in her thirties or forties, with short blond hair. Crystal is smiling widely in the photo, dressed crisply in a black blazer and white shirt. She looks like someone you would trust to find you a home.

In February 2012, a Twitter account with the handle @Crystal1Johnson began to tweet, and it tweeted precisely what @CrystalSellsLA was tweeting. It mimicked all the tweets mentioned above, to a similarly small audience. It had at the most eleven followers before it took a fateful turn. Someone was digitally cloning Crystal Johnson, without apparent purpose.

On the first day of 2013, the real Crystal Johnson wished the world Happy New Year, as did her clone. It would be the end of its mimicry, though. From then on, the clone account of @Crystal1Johnson unhitched itself and began its career as one of the most influential accounts operated by the Internet Research Agency's troll farm.

More than a thousand days passed with silence from the copycat account of @Crystal1Johnson. Then came the second week in December 2015, a tense one. Trump, still a relatively new presidential candidate, had, during a rally in Mount Pleasant, South Carolina, proposed "a total and complete shutdown of Muslims entering the United States until our country's representatives can figure out what the hell is going on." That drew the first real suggestions from mainstream political observers that his campaign was more than a curiosity or a carnival, that its overt appeals to bigotry recalled the beginnings of some of the most dangerous movements in history.

In the midst of these conversations, on December 10, the @Crystal1Johnson clone was back in action. "#BlackLivesMatter," the account declared around the middle of the day. @Crystal1Johnson would tweet twelve times that day, a major increase in frequency relative to the actual Crystal, and in this noticeably different vein.

"KKK was terrorizing us decades before #ISIS appeared," it thundered. "But in America #KKK still is legal!!"

Crystal1 also weighed in on a television remake of *The Wiz,* a play first staged in 1974 in Baltimore as a remix of *The Wizard of Oz,* with an all-Black cast. "So white people see #racism in an all black cast but not when black people are victims of #policebrutality?"

And, with the Muslim ban in the news, @Crystal1Johnson tweeted: "It's a lie! Muslims will never support Trump!"

A new and different Crystal Johnson had emerged, this one, it seems, run out of St. Petersburg, uninterested in real-estate advice or inspirational offerings, instead offering takes about America's deep-rooted racial injustices. It was a modest, lonely effort at first: on that first day, @Crystal1Johnson received only a handful of likes and appears to have acquired a single follower.

But over the next two years, Crystal1 would write another eight thousand tweets and would garner more than fifty-six thousand followers in the process, putting her in the top 1 percent of Twitter users globally. But even that measure underplayed the triumph that Crystal1 represented. By the vital sign of "retweet count"—the number of times other users passed a tweet by someone else on to their own followers—Crystal1 was the second-ranking Twitter user in the entire, sprawling Russian effort, with some 3,752,129 total repostings, including by other bots and by legions of actual Americans. And, among the millions of tweets the Russians attempted in their effort to undermine American democracy, Crystal1 had four of the top ten, including the top spot, with this tweet: "Daily reminder that the most educated First Lady in American history is a black woman with two Ivy League degrees from Harvard and Princeton."

Linvill and Warren, the Clemson scholars, had put me on to Crystal1 as an exemplar of the IRA's left-leaning trolls. But they also recommended that I look into the tweets of another top performer for the Translator Project, the tenth most retweeted account out of thousands—a right-leaning troll named Jenna Abrams.

Jenna had a different set of preoccupations. Two months into tweeting, with more than six thousand followers already in her camp, she wrote, "Everyone has a beard now and I wonder, is that #beard trend connected with #ISIS or just a coincidence?" In a few words, her imagined audience's contempt for city-dwelling, skinny-jeans-wearing, beard-sporting hipsters was married to its fear of terrorism. The tweet suggested a shadowy nexus of difference: not only were your fellow citizens unlike you; they might be in cahoots with jihadists.

On another occasion, she sought to meld liberal pro-choice attitudes with the aversion to war: "Liberals are brave enough to kill unborn children, but not brave enough to kill our enemies #LiberalLogic." She also tried to frame protest and the measure of accountability it could bring as dependency: "#TamirRice's family to receive $6 million from Cleveland. That's the new era of welfares for the Black people." And she took a swipe at the chorus of arguments in the culture about the systemic nature of racism and sexism and at the "social justice warriors" who make them: "A tip for SJWs: not all things're about sexism or racism, things can be just things, stop turning everything into an argument for equal rights."

The trolls covered and amplified a range of ideological topics. The analysis provided to the U.S. Senate identified "a roster" of social issues that the Russians sought to make even more salient in the public conversation:

- Black culture/community issues
- Police brutality/Black Lives Matter
- Pro-police/Blue Lives Matter
- Anti-refugee/immigration & border issues
- Texas culture
- Southern culture (Confederate history)
- Separatist movements
- Muslim issues
- LGBT issues
- Meme culture/Red Pill
- Gun rights/2nd Amendment
- Pro-Trump/Anti-Clinton
- Pro-Bernie or Stein/Anti-Clinton
- Patriotism/Tea Party
- Religious rights
- Native American issues
- Veterans Issues
- Local News/Journalism/Media

But what seemed even more significant than the subject matter was *how* the trolls chose to talk about these issues. Over and over, they used the discussion of these topic areas to suggest to Americans a certain way of looking at each other: as alien, menacing, and, therefore, unchangeable.

Crystal1's tweets shared news stories that implied, not incorrectly, the endemic nature of racism. But this very real problem was often framed as a lurid and sensationalized story. "Awful! White people used Black Babies as Alligator Bait," she wrote. On another occasion, Crystal1 tweeted about the very real unwillingness of many white people to acknowledge the realities of racism, but framed that skepticism in terms that made it seem essentially unalterable: "White people can see aliens, Bigfoot, the Loch Ness monster but can't see racism, oppression or white privilege." While Crystal1 identified real problems, there was a clear sense of dissuasion from the idea that anything could be done to change the minds of *people like that.*

In a different way, Jenna also turned political disagreements into conflicts over identity, in tweets such as "New study confirmed: Men who are physically strong are more likely to take a right-wing stance, while weaker men support the welfare state." Here, the politics of redistribution was turned into something more: a difference in virility. Men who supported the state's responsibility to help others were weak, flawed in their very being, not merely their politics. In another tweet, Jenna framed support for a candidate as an outgrowth of a laziness that fundamentally separated you from them. "How do you starve Bernie Sanders' supporters?" she asked. "Just put their food stamps under their work boots."

The trolls' tweets imbued existing political disagreements with a sense of physical disgust that made engaging with these other identities impossible. "What a time to be alive! Glitter armpits is a thing now. Congratulations. #FeminismIsAwful," Jenna tweeted one day. The tweet didn't rebut any feminist contention, didn't challenge any feminist logic, but attempted simply to plant a bodily image that might gross out a certain kind of reader. Crystal1's tweets also framed political anger or outrage in terms of disgust. "'Hail Trump' video sickens me! It's simply disgusting to see pure fascism!" she wrote—again, not wrongly in sentiment, but presented in a way that did not exactly encourage the work of political persuasion.

The troll farm's efforts to frame Americans of differing views as being foreign Others seemed designed to make people wonder if their fellow citizens were really even their fellow citizens. "Does #Mississippi Gov. follow ISIS example??" Crystal1 asked, casting a domestic political figure as taking inspiration from terrorists. Meanwhile, Jenna tweeted that President Obama was "risking the lives of Americans to bring his sunnis in," casting the first Black president as someone who wasn't simply a leader with a different political philosophy from hers but someone commanding an army of Muslim Others. She also felt that a certain presidential candidate had views in common with Saddam Hussein and that "Osama bin Laden's letter looks more like a Bernie Sanders speech." A domestic difference about economic philosophy was thereby twisted into a physical threat to your life.

Again and again, in one way or another, the IRA posts were sending the same message: These people are not to be trusted. They will never change. They are who they are. And who they are is a risk to your being.

As tempting as it may be to view the Russian operatives as instigators, to witness these moves is to witness a mission of amplification. They saw the othering and writing off from a distance, recognized the potential, and exploited it. In between griping about the paper towel situation and the missing sofas, the trolls' creators dashed off dozens of tweets a day—often thoughtlessly, often full of mistakes, often copying and pasting words found on the internet. Their talent was not inventiveness but rather the faithfulness of their mimicry. For in America in recent years, this fatalism has been on the rise and the hope of persuasion in free fall.

The ascendant political culture, confrontational and sensational and dismissive, has many causes: the inflammatory incentives of social media; the cynical manipulations of billionaire-owned, divide-and-conquer news outlets; the growing confidence and voice of once-marginalized groups; the very real material crises that beg for solutions and continue to remain unsolved; the frustration with how little milder, kinder, more civil, more hopeful politics has delivered; the sense that, absent a politics of us and them, the them will continue to pillage the us. For these and other reasons, many Americans have grown alienated from an idea at the heart of democratic theory: that you change things by changing minds—by persuading.

This challenge to persuasion has taken myriad forms. Social movements that need to grow to win have often seemed to devote more energy to keeping people out than pulling people in. Political campaigns frequently receive advice to focus on mobilizing sympathetic voters more than winning over skeptics. People have watched as tens of millions of their loved ones mentally disappear into online rabbit holes and cults, but little organized effort is made to bring them back or protect future victims. Leaders who attempt outreach have been attacked by their own as sellouts, chided for centering those who would never ally with them anyway over those who have long had their back, if not their attention.

The tendency to write off is rooted in the assumption that differences of identity are unbridgeable, that people are too invested in their privileges and interests to change, that the failure to achieve change in the past predicts failure in the future, that people and their opinions are monolithic and strong rather than complicated and fragile, and therefore the purpose of politics is to protect yourself from Others and galvanize your own instead of trying to reach across.

In the change-making circles I had begun to follow, the political culture of the write-off had made itself strongly felt. It had helped to open an ever-widening, seemingly unsustainable gap between the ambitions for structural, material change and the utter pessimism about individual people changing. How could social transformation come to pass when so many, even those most thirsting to change things, had written off the very possibility of changing people's minds?

The stakes of this writing off were high: some of the most dangerous and antidemocratic movements of our time had managed, in spite of those features, to make their causes appear welcoming and make newcomers feel at home, whereas some of the most righteous, inclusive, and just movements gave many the feeling of being inaccessible, intractable, and alienating.

I became drawn to a group of activists, organizers, politicians, educators, and others in these change-making circles who dissented from the great write-off and were seeking another way. They were a diverse set of people, but what they shared was a desire for real, far-reaching, system-level change and the realization of the promise of democracy. But, unlike many in their own circles and movements, they wanted another thing, too: to reinvigorate the idea of persuasion. These persuaders found themselves up against outright antidemocratic forces as well as an inflamed political culture, including among their allies, that made it harder to win others over and build and keep coalitions.

This book is about their quest, in a time of great crises, for a politics fierce and unapologetic enough truly to change things *and* smart and expansive enough to change the minds to get there.

1

"THE WAKING AMONG THE WOKE"

I

Linda Sarsour

So the story," the activist Linda Sarsour began, "is an old lady from Hawaii, a retired lawyer, posted, 'I think we need to march on Washington.' "

It was the evening of November 8, 2016, and Donald Trump was emerging as the president-elect of the United States. Millions were in the first hours of a shock that would last for days. Among the anguished was Teresa Shook, the retired lawyer in Hawaii, who suggested the idea of a march on Washington, to protest the incoming president and all he represented, and went to bed. Sarsour, who lives on the other side of the country, in Brooklyn, continued the story of how she came to be associated with Shook's proposal for a march: "She wakes up viral. She's a little old lady; she probably gets six likes usually. All of a sudden she wakes up, it's like . . ." Shook had gotten ten thousand RSVPs. In parallel, a woman named Bob Bland, a fashion designer, had posted a similar idea. "Somebody connected the two," Sarsour told me, "and said, 'Why are two white ladies doing two separate things? Why don't you make this together?' And so they did. And the event was called Million Women's March originally."

It was shortly thereafter that Sarsour saw the post about the now-merged event and, with some incredulity, the name. Her reflex was, "I'm not going."

Sarsour might have seemed like a natural customer for the march. As a progressive activist who works on immigrant rights, criminal justice, racial justice, corporate power, labor policy, and other issues, she has spent much of her life marching. As a Palestinian American, a feminist, and a Muslim, she had a special loathing of Trump, who had spent his campaign degrading people like her. If the worst visions of his presidency were to come to pass, she knew the diverse, heavily immigrant communities she organized in Sunset Park and Bay Ridge in Brooklyn would be among the first to hear knocks and watch loved ones whisked into unmarked vans.

But Sarsour, like many on the activist left, didn't necessarily view her enemy's enemy as her friend. She didn't assume that any formation of women organizing a march to resist Trump were her people, aligned with her values and goals, just because of their common fear. She had been around long enough to know that when the undocumented immigrants, women of color, poor people, and other marginalized groups she represented entered into coalition with other groups, especially those with more power, they could be silenced and shut out, told to focus on what the more powerful groups deemed important and to defer their own most pressing concerns. History overflows with cautionary tales. Black women agitated for women's suffrage, only to see white women secure the vote for themselves with the Nineteenth Amendment and leave Black women out. Sarsour's fellow progressives routinely answered the plea to vote for moderate Democrats ("blue no matter who!"), only to see their concerns sidelined after the inaugural.

When Sarsour looked at the post for the proposed march, her instinct spoke to her plainly: stay away. The first tell was the name, the Million Women's March, which all but appropriated a protest with a similar name by legions of Black women in Philadelphia two decades earlier. That suggested to Sarsour that this upcoming march didn't merely happen to be convened by "two white ladies," as she put it, but was anchored in a kind of white women's feminism that Sarsour had learned to recognize and guard against: a kind of feminism that was big on issues like reproductive rights and equal pay but could be considerably quieter about the needs of women in the marginalized communities Sarsour organized—for workers' rights relative to corporations, for protection against the immigration authorities and the police, for economic redistribution, for environmental justice.

Sarsour might have been loath to join what she viewed as a white feminists' march under any circumstances, but Trump's election had intensified the feeling. Like many, she was infuriated by the recent disclosure that 53 percent of white women had voted for Trump—in spite of the sexual assault allegations, in spite of the *Access Hollywood* tape, in spite of his sexist bullying. (The number came from exit polls, and it was later said by some analysts to have been just under half rather than slightly over. But 53 was everywhere at that moment and a source of anger.) "White women sold out their fellow women, their country, and themselves last night," the writer L. V. Anderson declared. And that 53 number strengthened Sarsour's inclination to keep away from the march, even if its organizers were from the other 47 percent. "You're catching me forty-eight to seventy-two hours after this election," she told me. "I'm not really fond of the women who voted for Donald Trump right now. I'm not feeling like I have any trust, particularly in white women."

The 53 percent statistic reinforced Sarsour's skepticism of the kind of coalition building that comes at a severe cost. What was the point of allying with white women—who suffered from sexism but couldn't help but benefit from white domination—and abiding the sidelining of one's particular needs, if some of those white women were inevitably going to sell you out at the first available chance? "I said, 'Do I have the heart for it, really?' Because I don't organize white people," Sarsour said. "Before the Women's March, this was the community that I organized with: North African, Middle Eastern, South Asian, and, beyond that, the immigrant rights movement, predominantly Latino, Asian American, Pacific Islander, and then, beyond that, Black people. I never organized white people."

Among the great projects of Sarsour's life was the dismantling of white supremacy. But she shared with many in her activist circles a fatalism about individual white people changing as part of that broader transformation. It was almost to be assumed that white people would ultimately side with their own. You didn't fight supremacy by appealing to white hearts and minds. You fought it by organizing your own communities of color, amassing real political power, and changing the rules and structures that upheld systems of white domination. "My mission," Sarsour told me one day, sitting in her small office at the Arab American Association of New York in Sunset Park, "is I want to build power among people of color, knowing that we are eventually going to be the majority and we've got to start building our power. I don't want to just be the majority without power; I got to be the majority with power." That guided the work she did bringing together communities in Sunset Park and Bay Ridge that didn't have much interaction but had common concerns. It informed her pleading with voters of color to be more than reliable Democratic voters, to demand a Democratic Party that pushed for real, structural change and answered their unique needs. And when Sarsour did this work, when she sought to build power for her people, what she often found herself up against was white people refusing to change the oppressive systems that kept them in power.

So Sarsour was wary of the march. But that didn't stop her from doing a bit of constructive prodding. Looking at the event page one day, she noticed that the white women of whom she had been so skeptical had actually inserted some helpful language about standing with Black women, with indigenous women, with immigrant women. That was progress! Except for one glaring problem, in her estimation. "All the stuff, but no one said Muslim women," Sarsour told me. "I'm not going to lie to you. I was kind of like, 'Really? Were you not paying attention to this election?'" Trump's campaign had used his Muslim ban as jet fuel, and now the white women convening this march appeared to forget all about that. Sarsour was mad. And while to many on the progressive left, she is an icon of a fearless, unyielding brand of activism for the most marginalized people, she has the ability to be delicate when she chooses. "I wrote a very nice comment," she told me. "I said something like, 'I really appreciate this endeavor. I hope that you would include Muslim American women as well.' Something very diplomatic. And so my comment goes viral."

Her timing was good. The white ladies, the original pair and others who had signed on, came to realize they had a whiteness problem. One of them, Vanessa Wruble, told *Vogue* that she had written to the others: "You need to make sure this is led or centered around women of color, or it will be a bunch of white women marching on Washington." It was not clear from the outside whether this concern was motivated more by principle or by the fear of bad public relations. But in any event, the women reached out to Michael Skolnik, a white consultant to organizations, who was once described by *The New York Times* as "the man you go to if you are on the left and want to leverage the power of celebrity and the reach of digital media to soften the ground for social change." He suggested some women of color who could combine with their efforts. One of them was Tamika Mallory, a Black civil rights activist and a friend of Sarsour's. Around the time when she volunteered to help collaborate on the march, she called Sarsour.

"I see you, girl, on that page," Sarsour remembers her friend saying of Sarsour's Facebook comment. "Relax, we're about to go in there and fix some stuff."

"Go where?" asked Sarsour.

"Don't worry, I got this," Mallory told her.

For some reason Sarsour couldn't fathom, Mallory believed that a march anchored in white feminism, a march Sarsour wasn't even interested in attending, could be improved by "going in there." Not without reason, this kind of "going in" to struggle with white people to make them less invested in their own power and privileges and more committed to the demands of marginalized groups—such work was regarded by many, especially in the circles Sarsour and Mallory operated in, as a fool's errand. It wasn't even clear to Sarsour what the goal was. Diversify the march's leadership? Take it over? Help the white women see their blind spots and embrace a broader array of concerns? Whatever it was, Sarsour told Mallory she had no interest: "I didn't think that I was made to go in there and just organize with these women who, like the Black women were telling us, all of a sudden are mad about things we've been mad about for a long time."

A few hours later, Mallory called back. "She's like, 'We're going to the Women's March,'" Sarsour recalled. "I said, 'I'm not going anywhere.' And then she gave me the whole 'If it's not us, who's it going to be?'" Sarsour recalled: "Tamika made a point and said, 'Look, this march is going to happen with or without women of color. And they're going to have a march, and it's going to probably be fabulous. And the question becomes for us, if they're going to do this march and it's going to be a great march, do we want our voices in it? Do we want people who look like us in it? Do we want people talking about criminal justice reform? Do we want immigrant rights folks? Do we want the Muslims? I mean, hello, this guy won a whole election on the backs of the illegal immigrants and the terrorists. That pretty much was the whole story.'" The march was a platform, Mallory was suggesting, a chance to center issues they cared about, often portrayed as marginal.

Sarsour was convinced: "I was like, okay, fine." She agreed to join Mallory.

Mallory's bet, and now Sarsour's, was just that, a bet that a lot of their fellow activists and movement allies might not have made. But in this case, Mallory's and now Sarsour's instinct was, if it's not us, who's it going to be? It might be difficult to deal with these white women and seek to enlarge the sphere of their concerns and assume the burden of persuading them of what they could not or would not see, but it was also, Sarsour realized, a remarkable opportunity to raise the visibility of her agenda and recruit a broader array of allies for it. Even if it was unpleasant work, Sarsour said, sometimes you have to "go in there."

In making her decision about the march, from her initial rejection to that eventual "going in," Sarsour was navigating a dilemma often confronted by activists on the left. Those who seek the transformation of society, of its deep structures and power equations, often need a critical mass of the public to be mobilized in order to achieve meaningful change. But if you represent marginalized minority communities, those groups on their own may not add up to a mobilization broad enough to deliver the results you seek. Sometimes a broader coalition can get you gains that would elude you otherwise.

Sarsour's initial attitude to the march was informed by her experience of what can happen in such coalitions. There is pressure to compromise, pressure that falls disproportionately on the least powerful members of the group. The more strident critiques of power and systems tend to be pushed to the side, dismissed as extreme and unhelpful, while moderate, milquetoast, platitudinous ideas that will change little rush to the fore. All too often, the norm in such coalitions is to focus on the common enemy and press pause on any "infighting," even if the "infighting" in question refers to the less powerful members telling more powerful ones that they do not feel represented by the coalition they have entered. It was possible to feel, as Sarsour initially had, that the benefits of a broader mass mobilization were not justified by the costs of having your issues melt into the sea.

But there was an opposite risk, too. Activists like Sarsour could stay pure, keep out of those corrupting coalitions, and end up righteously alone. You could refuse to trust those white women and their brand of feminism, and then, as Mallory had said, they would have their fabulous march, and their brand of feminism would only grow stronger, and you would miss out on a chance to "go in there" and force a change. If, on the other hand, you were willing to make a distinction between those truly bent on keeping you down (MAGA diehards) and those who shared some of your commitments while diverging with you on other things (liberal white women), you might be able to form an alliance with these latter folk, these imperfect allies. And that might give you something closer to a mass movement. So it was possible to feel, as Sarsour ultimately did, that the opportunity to build a vast citizen army against Trump—and even, perhaps, against the deeper afflictions of capitalism, patriarchy, and racism that made Trump possible—justified the risks of coalition.

The Trump era, then only beginning, would raise the stakes of this dilemma for many activists and organizers. It made a unified, expansive, winning left more urgent than ever, the fate of the Republic seeming to depend on whether that unwieldly group of groups could hold. But for those in marginalized groups, the rise of Trump and his turning of the country's ugly subtext into text also made it as important as ever to speak plainly and clearly and not be erased and not dissolve their particular needs into the melting pot of fighting one bad guy. With white supremacy and patriarchy and the discontents of capitalism now front and center in the conversation, how could those groups be expected to put aside their feelings on these matters for the sake of keeping the coalitional peace? For activists in Sarsour's position, it had never felt more important to stand one's ground and, equally, to reach out broadly.

But now Sarsour had decided to go in there, and as she embraced this new challenge, her attitude to this long-standing trade-off was a desire to break it. Could she make her communities part of this mass mobilization without bartering away their voice? Could she and the white women she was wary of work together toward a common cause while being honest with each other about their differences and, rather than dismissing them as "infighting," truly take them on? Could she organize white women into a more capacious understanding of justice and oppression without being co-opted? Could she model the kind of progressive politics she longed to see more of—at once unbending and expanding?

As she chewed on these questions, Sarsour received advice from fellow activists and mentors. To many, this project she was taking on was folly. "I'm not going to lie to you," she told me. "There were people picking up the phone like, 'Are you out of your mind? What are you doing to yourself? Why would you believe that white women are actually in this for you? Or are mad for you? They are mad for themselves. Because everything that they are mad about, we've been mad about for a long time.' And they were right." She recalled, "We were heavily criticized by Black women in particular." Many calls came from "the church ladies and the elders," as Sarsour put it, who were channeling the ideas of thinkers like Audre Lorde, who cautioned years ago against this idea of going in to help white women see the light. "Now we hear that it is the task of women of Color to educate white women—in the face of tremendous resistance—as to our existence, our differences, our relative roles in our joint survival," Lorde said. "This is a diversion of energies and a tragic repetition of racist patriarchal thought."

Even so, Sarsour stuck to her bet. There were many reasons to write off. She chose instead the path of persuasion.

"I went to the Women's March because I thought that I could be the one to do the work that others are saying they do not want to do," she told me.

Then again, she added, the Women's March, for her, "is a failure story."

The story of the march has been told elsewhere and more fully. I took an interest in Sarsour's experience of the undertaking because she was a lightning rod who had made an improbable choice to give some people a chance.

The question of the march's name would provide an early opportunity for struggle—about the rich history of Black organizing that preceded the organizers and the white women's treatment of that history. "Even the term 'Women's March on Washington' didn't just come from the sky. It was a very intentional process that we were putting white women through," Sarsour told me, speaking of her efforts to change the name of the march from the Million Women's March in order to teach white women about how not to appropriate the history of Black-led marches.

There had, after all, been that Million Woman March in Philadelphia in 1997, which rallied hundreds of thousands of people around a theme of what it means to be an African American woman. That march had built on the Million Man March two years earlier in Washington, called by the controversial leader of the Nation of Islam, Louis Farrakhan, and it, too, had mobilized legions of Black citizens. "There should be no reason for us to be starting a Million Women's March without understanding where that came from," Sarsour told me. She, like many of her allies, wanted to change the name.

"It wasn't like they were like, 'Oh yeah, we knew it was a Black women's march; we're just going to name it this.' It's just the lack of knowledge and relationships, just having no idea. So then they were like, 'Okay, well, let's call it the Women's March on Washington.' And of course Tamika was like, 'Everybody back up; there was a March on Washington.'"

She was speaking, of course, of the Reverend Dr. Martin Luther King Jr.'s 1963 March on Washington for Jobs and Freedom. "We have to understand that there's a lot of responsibility," Sarsour recalled saying. She told me later, "All this is new to white women because white women—just white people generally—think that they can just do whatever they want. And there's no consulting; there's no talking to people of color about what they think. So we were putting them through a lot of exercises."

In the matter of the march name, it was decided to call Bernice King, Dr. King's daughter. If she gave her blessing to remix the name of the original 1963 march, then they could.

"We put Dr. Bernice King on a conference call to make a proposal to her," Sarsour recalled, "and said, 'As you know, this is what the march was called, and we wanted to change the march in respect to those women in Philadelphia, and we want to call this the Women's March on Washington. We want to make sure that you know that we understand the great responsibility that comes with doing a march fifty-something years after the march your father led, and we want to make sure it's full of integrity and dignity and intersectionality and that people are seen and heard.'"

King thanked the women for recognizing that responsibility and gave her blessing.

"The deeper philosophy among people of color—and I won't say every person of color, but the majority of people of color, particularly those that are activists and organizers—is that we understand our history," Sarsour told me. "We are very connected to movement history, and we believe that what we do is a continuation of something that came before us. I don't think white people have that same philosophy."

So in the simple matter of naming were lessons that could be taught or could, in the name of coalitional peace, be withheld, and here they were explicitly being taught: don't think you are first to anything; pay attention to what preceded you; trust that you are standing on someone else's ground until proven otherwise; don't Columbus. What Sarsour and others wanted the white women organizers to understand was that the behaviors exhibited in their hasty naming process were distinct from but not unconnected to behaviors exhibited in far greater concentration by figures they despised like Donald Trump. A way of moving through the world that erased others as a matter of course was to be resisted, even when it came from members of the sisterhood of the #Resistance.

The naming episode seemed to validate Sarsour's bet. Yes, it was not her duty to change these white women. Yes, she shouldn't have to persuade them not to erase the work of women of color and instead center those women. But she did make that effort: the work of coalition building required it. She had, in those early days, found a way of joining a broader alliance through teaching. "We went through it," Sarsour told me, "and it was really powerful."

The name change was a prelude to broader changes, including on the question of scope. In its original conception, the march focused on those issues associated with white feminism. As a writer in *Vogue* (herself white) explained, "Where past waves of feminism, led principally by white women, have focused predominantly on a few familiar concerns—equal pay, reproductive rights—this movement, led by a majority of women of color, aspires to be truly intersectional." The essay then explained what that meant in practice: "Women are not a monolith, solely defined by gender; we are diverse, we represent half of this country, and any social justice movement—for the rights of immigrants, Muslims, African-Americans, the LGBTQ community, for law enforcement accountability, for gun control, for environmental justice—should count as a 'women's issue.'"

For Sarsour, this schism was reflected in the fact that many of the white women organizers were die-hard Hillary Clinton supporters. To Sarsour's taste, they could be blind to the ways in which Clinton, while indeed a woman and a feminist, championed a philosophy and policies that had been damaging to many communities, all of which contained women. Her hawkishness had not been good for women in Iraq. Her long-ago remarks about "kids that are called superpredators—no conscience, no empathy" and her advocacy of tough-on-crime policies had had devastating effects on the Black and brown populations Sarsour worked with, including women. Clinton's neoliberal economic philosophy had been a principal cause of an age of yawning inequity, which had made millions of women's lives more precarious.

Sarsour wasn't interested in a women's march that focused only on the issues that influential white feminists thought to be priorities and tabled everything else. Criminal justice and corporate power were women's issues, too, as were union busting and empire and war and wealth inequity. But when everyone met to draft unity principles for the march, some of the organizers didn't see it that way. "They were excited," Sarsour said. "They were like, okay, reproductive rights, women's right to choose, women should get paid the same as men. We started a whole march about women who wanted to do reproductive rights and equal pay, which of course are issues we care about, too. And then it kind of ends there, and you're just like, 'Come on, folks.'" She added, "When you go to a Black woman in Ferguson and you ask her what her priority issue is, she's probably not going to say reproductive rights. She'll probably say, 'I just want my Black son Eduardo to come home to me.' And so we were trying to explain it."

Sarsour and her allies were trying to do what many of her activist friends and so many radical Black writers had cautioned against attempting: trying to reap the benefits of "going in there" with the white women—the platform, the chance of a wider mass mobilization—while trying to educate them and at times call them out, and to do each of these things without undermining the other. They were trying to see if they could push for fundamental change not by working around white women standing in their way but by actively seeking to persuade some of them to change how they saw things.

Sarsour and the other women of color organizers made use of the difficulty of the task to take on more responsibility for the march. They explained to the others that they were risking angering women in their own communities by allying with these partners. They understood the anger; they had made their choice anyway. Now there was a possibility of compromise in the coalition that worried them and would confirm the worst fears in their communities. They cited that worry in arguing for more power on the organizing team. "We came and we said, 'Listen, we are women of color who are going against some of the wishes of people in our community who are like, "Don't go." And we want to be leaders here, and we want to have roles that are important roles, and we want to be able to have decision-making power,' " Sarsour told me.

At the time, the intervention worked wonders. An initiative that a few white women launched had now blossomed into a formal march with a proper organization, and when it named its four national co-chairs, three were women of color: Sarsour, Mallory, and Carmen Perez, a fellow civil rights activist. (Bob Bland was the fourth.)

Sarsour continued to walk a fine line. One tension involved fund-raising. There were weeks to go before the march on January 21. They were up against a dangerous new presidency, and there was an all-hands-on-deck feeling among different groups wanting to come together to fight the threat. Sarsour was willing to ally with some organizers she was skeptical of, but she wouldn't ally with just anyone. So when the question arose of whether to accept corporate sponsors, Sarsour was adamantly opposed. Many of the other organizers were incredulous about her opposition. "They were really mad, and they were like, 'We're not going to be able to do this.' And I was like, 'We're not taking corporate money.' I was just not going to do that." Companies like Coca-Cola and Walmart, she told me, might be very happy to associate their name with a women's march, but were they interested in changing their ways when it came to paying women more or selling them sugary drinks that gave them diabetes? The others relented, and the march ended up raising millions from small donations and philosophically aligned nonprofits like the ACLU and Planned Parenthood.

Sarsour had agonized about whether to ally with other organizers despite the risks, and she had gone in there nonetheless, and then she used the risk she took in doing so to get a hand on the reins of decision making, and now, from within, she played gatekeeper herself, unwilling to let in those who were actively committed to structures and systems that did women harm—in contrast, she felt, to her new white women organizer colleagues, whom she tended to regard as well meaning but still waking up to the systems of oppression that bound and benefited them at the same time.

One day, the organizers had a small blowup over merch. As Sarsour tells it, a white woman on the team whose job was to procure merchandise messed up, and now the organization was going to have to spend thousands of dollars extra to get the merchandise on time. It was another of these issues that would have meant little to some in the coalition and a lot to others. "Women of color, because we organize with so little resources, it was a heart attack for us," Sarsour told me. "The minute I heard $5,700, I was like, 'Are you crazy? Like, what? You know what I could do with $5,700? You know how much that goes for a grassroots organization?'" The dispute soon became one about the procurement person's reaction to the criticism.

"The woman was there and all of a sudden burst out into tears, and she was like, 'I feel marginalized. I feel like I'm being treated like a second-class citizen,'" Sarsour recalled. "So all the women of color were like, 'Mm-mm; like, shut up; like, what? Marginalized? Second-class? Like, what are you talking about?'"

Sarsour and Mallory and some of their allies exchanged glances. This was what Sarsour had worried about, what her friends had warned her about. Was anyone learning anything from anyone about absolutely anything? Was her gamble being ridiculed by events? Sarsour decided she would handle this one. "I gave them that look like, I got this." She thought maybe she could put her social-work skills to use. She recalls saying, "Listen, I'm sorry that you feel this way. But this is also a learning opportunity for all of us. There are some words that you are using that you need to understand implications of. You could feel disrespected, you could feel unheard, there's a lot of things you could be feeling in this moment. They would all be valid. But to sit in a room with indigenous women, Black women and Muslim women, queer women, and to say that you feel marginalized and to say that you feel like a second-class citizen is something you really need to reflect on. Because you actually have no idea what it feels like to be marginalized in the society. You have no idea what it feels like to be a second- and third-class citizen in this country. If you were to walk out into the streets of New York City right now, you would be safe in most spaces that you walk into. You will be served at every restaurant that you walk into. You would go to any social service agency, and you will be treated with dignity and respect. We can't say that's guaranteed for everyone."

Even as she called out during moments like this, Sarsour told me she began to see that many of the white women had taken their own risks to be there in that broad coalition. "Some of them really were very honest," she told me. "They were like, look, I came because my husband voted for Trump. I came because my parents are Republicans from Ann Arbor, Michigan. I came because whatever. I mean, people really came almost feeling rebellious against people in their families who put us in the situation." In coming into this coalition with imperfect allies, Sarsour, Mallory, and other women of color had to navigate relationships back in their communities with people who might not understand their choices. Sarsour now felt that many of the white women had their own versions of that tension.

The coalition's awkward juggle of accommodation and truth telling and challenging and teaching carried the women through the day of the march and produced an outpouring of remarkable events around the world, with several million marching—including, in the United States, at least 1 percent of the entire population.

When Sarsour climbed onstage for the first time, she was bowled over, and perhaps in that moment she could tell herself that the price of reaching for that wider mobilization was worth it. "I just couldn't believe my eyes," she told me. "I couldn't see the last person, and it was ten o'clock in the morning. When I first got there, I didn't go up on the stage, but I was like at the bottom, and it was six o'clock in the morning. And I'm like, 'What the hell are these people doing here? This thing doesn't start till ten o'clock.' So they could have been there since three o'clock in the morning." In spite of it all, the organizers had answered a hunger.

In the days and months after the march, though, the coming together that made it possible wouldn't hold. Not long after the march, Sarsour and some of the other women of color were infuriated to learn that some other organizers had gone behind their backs to establish a permanent post-march organization without telling them. This was what those friends had been warning Sarsour about, that the white women would use the political cover of representation she had provided, the rainbow patina, and, when convenient, would forsake her work. When Sarsour and others tried to hold these women accountable, they defaulted into the familiar defense that those complaining about their behavior were being "divisive." In 2018, Teresa Shook, the woman in Hawaii who had written one of the original posts that led to the march's creation, wrote another Facebook post saying the four co-chairs—three of them women of color, including Sarsour—had "steered the Movement away from its true course. I have waited, hoping they would right the ship. But they have not."

Among the incidents named as responsible for these rifts was Mallory's presence, in 2018, at a Saviours' Day event in Chicago, organized by the Nation of Islam. There, Louis Farrakhan, the bow-tied, charismatic, bigoted leader of the group, referred to Jewish people as "the mother and father of apartheid." He reprised old anti-Semitic tropes about Jews having "control over those agencies of government." As Adam Serwer recounts in *The Atlantic*, he even "surmised that Jews have chemically induced homosexuality in black men through marijuana."

The Anti-Defamation League, CNN's Jake Tapper, and others picked up on the story, and specifically on Mallory's presence at the event. If you were a co-chair of a progressive organization devoted to the intersectional pursuit of justice, how could you sit through such an event? How could you fail to condemn it? Mallory publicly explained that she had connected with the Nation of Islam because of the ground-level work it does in Black communities. Her son's father had been murdered. "In that most difficult period of my life, it was the women of the Nation of Islam who supported me and I have always held them close to my heart for that reason," she wrote in a statement. Eventually, the Women's March put out a statement saying that "Minister Farrakhan's statements about Jewish, queer, and trans people are not aligned with the Women's March Unity Principles." But neither the organization nor Mallory went so far as to condemn him, and for many people that was unpardonable.

"Therein lies the key conflict for Mallory, and her colleagues at the Women's March, going forward," Serwer wrote.

> The Nation of Islam may be essential to antiviolence work in poor Black neighborhoods. It may be an invaluable source of help for formerly incarcerated Black people whose country has written them off as irredeemable. It may offer a path to vent anger at a system that continues to brutalize, plunder, and incarcerate human beings because they are Black. And it may also be impossible to continue working with the Nation and at the same time lead a diverse, national, progressive coalition that includes many of the people Farrakhan and the Nation point to as the source of all evil in the world.

Coalitions were important, and coalitions were hard. Sometimes they required holding the line, refusing to bend. Sometimes they required pleading for nuance, trying to reach this way and reach that way without being torn asunder.

I felt like the Women's March for me," Sarsour said, "particularly in my relationship to white people—that was the line that I crossed. When I was organizing on criminal justice reform, on immigrant rights, that was good. You was good, you were organizing people of color, you were with your people, you were thumbs-up. The minute that I started going from just being able to organize people of color and I went to organize white people, too—whew."

Yet those feelings she had ran up against evidence she saw with her own eyes that many of the white women who got involved with the march really were altered by the experience, by the organizing process, by the changes Sarsour and others fought for. Persuasion had worked. "I've had absolutely hopeful experiences," she told me. "The question is, how scalable is it? For example, I had experiences with white women at the Women's March, many of whom I've met across the country, who are absolutely transformed. I mean women who are using a different lexicon. I've even watched their trajectories on Facebook. I will look up their posts from back around the 2016 election, and then you look at their posts now, and it's night and day." Some women who had once shown a narrow interest in the slogans of the #Resistance, who had not been political before, had gone on a deepening journey and were now neck-deep in the latest voting-rights bill, in the effort to shore up DACA, in issues of taxation.

So the march left Sarsour both wary and hopeful about the possibility of individual white people changing as part of, and as a step toward, the deeper-rooted, system-level change she sought. She remained committed to her theory of change: the building up of the power of her own community as a means of ushering in progress. Yet a part of Sarsour continued to reach for those moments when it felt possible not to overwhelm the forces opposed to the future she sought but rather to invite them into it.

Not long after the march, Sarsour went to speak at the University of Massachusetts at Amherst. Before she did, her hosts at the Women, Gender & Sexuality Studies program warned her that they were expecting some college Republicans to be in the audience. "It's in this auditorium, and they come in. It was so cute," Sarsour recalled. "They were like little nineteen-year-old white boys wearing shirts that said 'Pence-Trump.' And they sat in one row all together." She gave her talk. No disruption. Then she was standing outdoors after the talk, chatting with students, taking selfies, when one of the young men wandered over. "It was like the sea parted and everyone was like, 'Oh,' because they're wearing these shirts," Sarsour said.

Sarsour extended her hand. They shook. "I was like, 'I'm very happy that you came today.' He was like, 'I'm Jonathan.' And I said to him, 'What's up? I heard word on the street was you were coming to protest me. What happened?' And it was really profound. You know what he said to me? He said, 'Listen, I started listening to you, and I made a decision to give you a chance.'

"That's it," she said. "That's all he said. And I thought it was one of the most profound things I've ever heard. That's all I want from people.

I tell people all the time, 'I just want you to give me a chance. Let me share with you who I am, where I come from. And I will guarantee you there will be disagreements. But the question for you is not whether you disagree with me. It's whether you think that I'm a threat to your humanity. And that's the question I want you to answer.' "

On another occasion, on another campus, at a discussion of the question of Israel and Palestine, a student stood up and made a case in defense of Zionism, and she countered him forcefully, and then as it grew clear that they were not getting anywhere, she remembers telling the student, "I'm not asking you to give up anything about yourself. I just want you to know that you have to figure out how to exist with my story."

Sometimes Sarsour worried that many of her allies in the progressive movement had grown too comfortable writing off people they needed, and could win over, for their cause to succeed. For reasons she understood all too well, they refused to make the kind of choice she had with the march. "Even the question in every election about whether we want to go get those white voters in these different states and whatnot," Sarsour said. "There will be some people who will tell you, 'No, we don't need those white people. We've just got to expand our electorate, and we've just got to get more people of color, more young people to the polls, more women to the polls, and then that's how we're going to win.' Other people will tell you, 'Yes, we do need those people, but I'm not the one that's going to go get those people. You go get those people. I'm going to build power in my own community. I'm going to focus on the African American vote and Latino vote and whatnot.' I'm in the boat of we definitely need those people in swing states for sure. There's no doubt in my mind."

Sitting in her office, Sarsour told me a story that still haunted her. Most of her work isn't national limelight work but rather ground-level organizing in the highly mixed communities of Sunset Park and Bay Ridge, helping community members escape abusers, find employment, navigate the police, and build bridges of solidarity. One of the things Sarsour seeks to do as an organizer is bring together populations that are fundamentally on the same side but don't know each other well and don't have a bedrock of trust. A lot of these people are just everyday people living in the community, and Sarsour worries about whether activists like her are winning those people over or instead keeping them at bay.

Not long ago, Sarsour arranged a meeting in the community for some immigrant women, mostly Middle Eastern, to meet with a Black mother who had lost her son to police violence. It was a classic coalition-building effort. The immigrant women had their concerns about life in the neighborhood, and perhaps police violence was among them or perhaps it wasn't, but she sensed that it wasn't at the top of their list. For the Black woman who had lost her son, it very much was, whereas concerns about immigration policy might have been less of a focus. If you could put people from these different communities together, perhaps you could give them empathy for each other's struggles and put them into alliance with each other. So the Black mother and these immigrant women all met in a space. Very quickly, things grew awkward.

The organizers whom Sarsour had partnered with—they had arranged for the Black mother to speak, and Sarsour had brought in the immigrant women—began asking the immigrant women their preferred gender pronouns. Now, unlike some right-wing person who would criticize this moment, Sarsour is a big believer in asking people's pronouns. It is an important feature of life in a diverse movement. But there and then, in that room, with women who had come to America within the last few years in many cases, who didn't speak English well in many cases, who had never heard of the concept of pronouns in many cases, the request by the organizers erected a barrier. "They felt really out of place," Sarsour said, "and then they were looking at me like, 'What do we do?' "

Sarsour turned to the organizers. "I said, 'I appreciate what we're doing here, and everyone's pronouns should be respected. But these women who are here, English is not their first language, and this is a very new concept for them. So I would ask for forgiveness, and I would ask if that would be something that maybe we'll do next time when we're together as we get these women through this process.' " She was confirming the legitimacy of the request while pleading for mercy on behalf of the women she had brought in.

"The thing about our movement is that we're too woke," Sarsour told me, "which is why we don't have mass mobilization in the way that we should." In choosing the word "woke," she was using a term that once had real meaning in a Black radical tradition—"Today our very survival depends on our ability to stay awake, to adjust to new ideas, to remain vigilant and to face the challenge of change," Dr. King once said—and had since been co-opted by the political right as a catchall label for the more pluralist, egalitarian future that many white people feared. I took Sarsour to be claiming the word consciously, to name her fear that some elements of the movement go beyond recognizing difference to fetishizing it and beyond clarity to purity. Sarsour's concern wasn't that the future her allies wanted was wrong. She was making a case against a superhighway to progress with too few on-ramps. She was conflicted about the matter, because she deeply believed in where the superhighway was going, believed in these efforts to make the society more inclusive. She just worried sometimes that the way of going about it created barriers to entry for a movement that, in fact, needed growth if her communities were to be safe and to flourish.

"When we're like, 'The heteropatriarchy . . . ' If my immigrant mom in Sunset Park doesn't know what that is, that's not going to move her. Or we talk about cisgender people. I get it. I get what you're saying, and I understand that it's an important concept that we need to get through, particularly to make sure that people who are trans and people who are gender nonconforming and others feel whole in space. And they deserve to feel whole. But I also believe in this idea of mass mobilization and meeting people where they're at. And a lot of people in our community are not there yet. And a lot of white people are not there yet."

Sarsour's concern with these barriers was pragmatic—that they turned away potential customers of the future she wanted to live in. "A lot of people sometimes don't even come to our spaces because they don't feel equipped," she said.

But it is one thing when it is immigrant women who don't speak English, I suggested. Most people would probably give that a sympathetic hearing. But if we were talking about a fifty-year-old white guy in Michigan, I wondered if the same principle would apply—that he would have to be given a ramp, some way in, even though he possessed greater privilege. Here, Sarsour surprised me.

"Oh, yeah, I do believe that," she said. "This idea that we expect people to be good and right about things is just not realistic. And that's why I always struggle with whether I should be the one reaching out, or who are the other people that could be on this journey with us to get people there. But you have to meet everybody where they're at. Twenty years ago, you had to meet me where I was at."

She was speaking of her upbringing in a conservative Muslim American family and community. "In my community, the positions on things like homosexuality—if it wasn't for me venturing out into the world, meeting people, building relationships with people, and really questioning so many things that were around me, if you would've met me twenty years ago, only God knows what my positions were on things."

For all her frustration with the white women, she identified with them, too—or could identify with them if she dug deep and remembered to. She had a way in to empathy for them if she wanted it.

I asked if she felt an analogy between her own political evolution and what millions of white Americans are struggling with in a changing country.

"Oh, absolutely. Because, you know, I grew up in this community, and at that point it was a very insulated community. I went to school with a lot of people of color, but there were a lot of Muslims here, and I lived in a Palestinian community. I went to events about Palestine with my people. I went to Arabic school on the weekends. A lot of my friends that we would go to each other's houses were people from my community. And these were people born and raised outside the country. These were people that didn't have exposure to certain issues and certain things. And so I was growing up learning whatever my parents were teaching me at the time.

"For example, I went through my own anti-Blackness at a very young age because my father owned a store in Crown Heights. After school, we would go to my dad's store, and after doing our homework—my dad had a little living room in the back of the store—we would go out into the neighborhood to play. And the kids that we played with were Black kids. There were no other kids to play with. And so, for me, I was able to get through that at an early age where I was able to see, 'Oh, those kids I'm playing with in the streets—fun, great.' But other kids in my community didn't have that. I came from Sunset Park. There were few Black people in Sunset Park. Most of the people in my community were Puerto Rican, Guatemalans, Hondurans; there was a couple of dark-skinned Dominicans in my neighborhood. But overall there was no African Americans in my community. So other kids that didn't have the privilege I had of being able to have a father who owned a store in a different neighborhood, they probably grew up with a different type of experience around Black people. And until people venture out and go to high school or even college, until they get to meet people they didn't otherwise have relationships with—for me, transformation comes from relationships. And so sometimes it may not be that the white person has to have a relationship with me, but they have to have a relationship with someone."

These stories gave a greater understanding of why Sarsour had been willing to try with the Women's March. Seen from one angle, she represented the future that terrified and discomfited many. But seen from another, she, too, had once needed to evolve. She, too, had to learn new values, new terms, purge the prejudices of custom by forging relationships.

She told me a story about her mother. Her mother had become interested in the campaign of a local elected official named Carlos Menchaca. Sarsour had known him for years and knew that he was gay, but she didn't want to say anything to her mother, whom she feared might have a problem with that. It wasn't her place to get involved, she felt.

When Menchaca announced he was running for New York City Council, something clicked for Sarsour's mother. She threw herself into door knocking, signature gathering, phone banking. "My mom's a little immigrant from Palestine," Sarsour said. "She never door knocked in her life. She never was involved in politics. I mean, she would go vote, but she would vote for whomever I told her to vote for. But because she had a personal relationship with Carlos, she got heavily involved." All this despite her mother having retrograde views on homosexuality that reflected her upbringing.

Menchaca won his race in a stunning upset of an incumbent. Not long afterward, he stopped by Sarsour's mother's home, and they took a selfie together. "My mom's beyond," Sarsour told me. "My mom thinks she just won this election." Sarsour said to herself, I've got to tell this lady. But she found herself scared to let her mother know Menchaca is gay. And she felt hypocritical for feeling scared to tell her. "I forgot that I'm a progressive, that I believe in these things," she said. "Why am I scared to tell my mom?"

Finally, she went for it. "I want to tell you something about Carlos," she remembered saying.

"Yeah, what?"

"He's gay."

Her mother stopped talking. It felt like a lifetime to Sarsour, but it was probably ten seconds. Sarsour began to gird herself for what was about to happen. "Then my mom just looks at me, and she's like, 'He's wonderful. He won the election.' And she just went back to talking about what she was talking about."

Sarsour didn't know that her mother had evolved on the issue, she told me, that she had ended up in "a whole other place." She had grown in the shade. She had allowed her mind to be changed, as millions had in recent years on the question of homosexuality. A few days later, Sarsour went over to her mother's home, wanting to talk about the evolution she had missed. "We're dining room people," Sarsour told me. "We just sit at the dining room table and eat nuts, drink tea, and that's like a congregating place for two hours." So they sat and did these things, and Sarsour told her mother about her work on LGBTQ issues in their own community and about the problem of hate crimes. Without any prompting or tutelage, her mother found the language to connect the struggle of a Palestinian immigrant who was once homophobic to the struggle of a Latino politician who is gay. "My mom says, 'Look, this is a country where we all get to live here.'" In that sentence of revelation was the dream Sarsour kept chasing—that instead of the movement for progress turning people away, it drew them in, and educated them, and people began to notice the ways in which their distinct struggles could flow together.

Perhaps it worked in this case because Sarsour had given her mother space to grow. "I'm not saying that it's about accommodation," she said. "It's really this concept of meet people where they're at and bring them along. A lot of people in the movement don't want to do the work."

As she admitted, sometimes that included her. Without Mallory's prodding, she wouldn't have messed with the Women's March. Your mother, on the other hand, is your mother. It was hard to imagine Sarsour, or many people of her political orientation, so patiently talking through the homophobia of a white guy she didn't know. But sometimes when in those situations, on a lark, something in her would tell her to try where she didn't have to, to go in there for the future's sake.

One of those times was a trip to Kalona, Iowa, a heavily Amish town of a couple thousand people. The local school district had gotten a grant to add two languages, and one of them was Arabic. Sarsour was a guest speaker in celebration of the expansion. She visited multiple schools in the area, and what she remembers, above all, was the overwhelming whiteness of the place.

"It was all white, white, white everywhere," she said. "But the people were very lovely people. Everybody was lovely, and I got to eat Amish food, and it was great, and they were so hospitable. The woman who picked me up at the airport basically told me the minute we met, 'I want you to know you're the first of your kind that we've ever seen here.' Her point was if anyone treats you weirdly, it's because of that."

She was there a few days. It became a big deal in town. The kids went home and told their parents they had met a real, live Muslim lady. Sarsour's host called her in her hotel room. Would she be open to tacking on a parents' night? The curiosity had spread through town. Sarsour agreed.

At the event, she spoke to the parents about who she was, where she came from, her family's immigrant story. Afterward, several locals came up to her and began to touch her hijab—"Oh, this is too beautiful!" And her Brooklyn-tough instinct was to do what was more than within her rights, to shout, "Get your hands off me!" And on another day, she might have. But on this day, for whatever reason, another part of her came to the fore. She looked past their Orientalizing and tokenizing and thought to herself, "They're trying."

"It was worth it," Sarsour told me. She tried to imagine that there was a hopeful trajectory that would justify her forbearance. Why had she gone there in the first place? Because far away in Iowa, a school district was adding Arabic to the curriculum. Yes, they touched her hijab. Yes, it was completely uncalled for, inexcusable. But wasn't the trajectory toward a more open and just country, a country with greater space for the communities she represented back home? Wasn't the fact of being invited proof of that trajectory? And something in her decided to extend what she didn't need to but was glad she did.

She was also quick to acknowledge that it was harder for some than for others to extend this kind of civic grace, and that it wasn't anyone's duty: "Especially for Black people, in particular, who have had historical dehumanization, people whose ancestry goes back to people who were seen as property and sharecroppers, and the continuous, public, everyday, in-your-face dehumanization, the killing of people that look like you in the streets on video every day, every day—I feel like the types of experiences that Black people in particular have when it comes to sitting with white people who dehumanize them is a different burden to hold.

"For me, I cannot claim that my oppression in America is anywhere near the oppression of Black people. So maybe I'm carrying a lesser load, and I'm willing to sit with someone who's like, Muslims are bad people. And I think that we need to keep each other safe." What I took her to mean by that last idea was that the "going in" should be defended, as should the staying away.

After the trip to Iowa, Sarsour continued to hear from the host who had picked her up at the airport with that stark warning about being the first of her kind. The host would send pictures of the kids writing in Arabic and updates like how the mothers had gotten together and created a recipe book to accompany the new language classes. Sarsour would have been justified in demanding to be treated differently while in town. But she had to wonder if that would have threatened the broader change that she celebrated.

Toward the end of our conversation, I asked Sarsour if she thought the movements she was part of had an evangelical spirit, a hunger to win souls. She surprised me by speaking of her religion.

"As a Muslim, I am missionary. That's what I want to do. I want to evangelize," she told me. But in her professional identity, as a progressive activist, the attitude was different. "Our movements are oftentimes extremely self-righteous and very stringent. There's like four doors. It's like when you're going into a prison. You have to go through this door, and then that door closes, and then you go through another door, and then another door closes. And my thing is like, if we're going to do that, it's going to be one person at a time coming into the movement versus opening the door wide enough, having room to err and not be perfect. I'm not perfect. And there's a lot of people that need a space for people to make mistakes in our movements." It was an unexpected comparison, the evangelism of her faith and the prison doors of her movement.

Now she said another thing that stayed with me. It had to do with people in the movement giving each other more space to pursue different theories of change. "My thing is like, 'You just got to take the risk of opening your heart as much as possible and getting as many people in here as possible, and respecting those in the movement that don't want to do the hard work.' But then letting the people in the movement who are willing to do the work do the work without being criticized for wanting to do the work and getting the white woke, folks that are in the movement that are genuinely the transformed white people who have come along and have evolved to be part of doing that work with us. And I think that we haven't figured out a coordinated way to do that.

"So that's kind of where I'm at," Sarsour said.

II
Loretta Ross

One day back in the 1970s, Loretta Ross received a letter from a prisoner she didn't know.

Ross—who is now in her late sixties and a pioneering activist, theorist in the Black radical feminist tradition, and co-creator of the theory of reproductive justice—was, at the time, working at the D.C. Rape Crisis Center in Washington. The center provided direct support to women via a hotline and pursued system-level change in parallel, using street theater to move public opinion and lobbying to influence public policy. Its mission was a world free from sexual violence.

A letter arrived from the Lorton Reformatory, a prison complex in Virginia that housed inmates from D.C. It was signed by a man named William Fuller who was more than a decade into a long sentence for rape and murder. The gist of his letter, as Ross remembered it, was this: "On the outside, I raped women. Now on the inside, I rape men. I want to stop raping. Can you help me?"

When the letter arrived, it befuddled Ross. For all its activities helping rape victims, the center had never conceived of its work as encompassing helping men not rape. "First, it sat there on my desk for a couple of weeks as I tried to figure out, 'What am I going to say to this guy?'" Ross recalled in a twenty-three-hour-long oral history recorded by Smith College. "My first immediate visceral reaction is, 'We don't even have the money to help rape victims. How dare a rapist ask us for help?'"

It was an understandable impulse for Ross, who knew the pain and the enormity of sexual violence all too personally. When she was eleven, after visiting an amusement park in San Antonio with her Girl Scout troop and losing track of the group, she was raped by a man who offered her a ride home. Years later, an older cousin sexually abused her, which led to pregnancy, which in turn cost her a coveted scholarship she had earned to Radcliffe. Later, as a student at Howard University, she was gang-raped. At that university, she had immersed herself in books and ideas that explained the deep, endemic nature of sexual violence in a male-dominated world, the vastness of the societal affliction of which William Fuller was but a small symptom.

At first, Ross rejected the idea of investing her time helping one random man rape less, and when she raised Fuller's request with her colleagues, they agreed. But the decision somehow didn't settle the matter. Something about the dilemma they had been presented hung in the air. "We talked about it at the staff level," Ross recalled, "and we talked about it and talked about it with the board, talked about it and talked about it and talked about it. What should we say to this guy?" If Fuller's question wouldn't go away, it was perhaps because, in a few words, it had planted a doubt about the center's theory of change. Its mission was a world without rape, and its daily work was to support women at the personal and policy levels. But now the letter prompted a question that Ross felt hadn't been considered: "You could bandage women up all you want to, but if you don't stop men from raping, what's the point? Better bandages?"

So Ross decided that she would go check Fuller out. She drove to Lorton, subjected herself to the searches of her person and bags, and was asked whom she wished to see. Ross remembered holding up a brochure and telling them, "I'm from the D.C. Rape Crisis Center, and I want to talk to your rapist." (In fact, there were several rapists in the prison.)

She was led into a room with Fuller and a handful of other male prisoners. Fuller struck her at once. He was six feet four and ripped. "They beef up in prison to keep from being victims, and he was the master rapist in this prison," Ross said in the oral history. "I mean, everybody was scared of William Fuller. I was scared of William Fuller. Gorgeous, though, very good-looking Black man. But apparently when he was eighteen, he raped, sodomized, and murdered this woman."

Now in his thirties, with time on his hands, he had become a reader—including of feminist texts. The feminist analysis of rape had influenced him, Ross realized, with some measure of shock. "His argument was that 'I believe that rape is a form of power and control, and I want to know how not to be a rapist.'" He told them rape for him was not about gender, because he would rape men or women; it was about his ability to dominate.

The meeting took Ross and her colleagues aback. Fuller somehow changed the women's minds about the possibility of changing him in turn. But now, having crossed that threshold, they confronted new questions. The risk of not doing this kind of work is leaving a problem to fester. The risk of doing such work is that the work would end up capitulating somehow, being co-opted. "We didn't want to be used," Ross recalled in the oral history. So Ross and her team drafted some guidelines.

Rule No. 1: "Nothing we could do could help them get out of jail, because nobody wanted these rapists on the street again. Not us." That meant no letters, petitions, parole requests. That wasn't the point. They weren't teaching prisoners not to rape so that the prisoners could get off earlier. They were teaching them not to rape to have fewer rape victims. Rule No. 2: "We weren't bringing anything into this jail for you. I don't care if you're dying. We couldn't bring you bandages, shoes, cigarettes, nothing." Rule No. 3: The only exception to Rule No. 2 was feminist literature.

They brought feminist texts into the prison, where Fuller organized a reading group—"five guys, all rapists, like this little clique he controlled," Ross recalled. A rotating contingent of Ross and her colleagues drove down to Lorton every Friday afternoon for a discussion circle with the rapists. They stuck with it for two years.

Eventually, other programs around the country would emulate the model—all because Ross overcame that initial, justified instinct to focus on those hurt by the problem, not those perpetrating it.

Several years later, she was walking around Washington, D.C. "I hear this big, booming bass voice hollering out my name," she said in the Smith testimony. "My head whips around, and walking towards me is William Fuller. I didn't know whether to run, to cry, to holler, or what, because I never thought this guy would get out of jail in my lifetime." He was indeed out and working—in construction. He had continued to read—in fact, had gone back to school. He looked whole.

"He was a transformed man," Ross said in the oral history. "But he did that himself. I mean, we did not do that for William. He did that himself. Because he came into prison barely literate, and he taught himself to read, and it was through his practice, process of teaching himself to read that he had encountered this feminist literature. And so he was his own mentor. He was the source of his own determination and genius."

Fuller had done something improbable, but it was hard to imagine his doing it without Ross's gamble. She had made a considered decision that if one were serious about ending the phenomenon of rape in the world, one might try to work with people who perpetuated that phenomenon and whose minds were the least likely to change. Just as Sarsour thought of her work as being to build power around white domination rather than coax people away from it, until with the march she decided to try, so, too, Ross thought of her work as being to protect women from rape, until she opened herself to the possibility of helping men not rape. It wasn't her duty, wasn't her mission as she had understood it, wasn't likely to succeed, wasn't deserved, wasn't a justifiable diversion of resources from women, wasn't her theory of change, wasn't, wasn't, wasn't. She did it anyway. She sought to change a mind, on her terms, in her way.

Ross spoke of the episode as an early, instructive moment in the storied career she would go on to have as an activist, thinker, and institution builder. After running the Rape Crisis Center, she worked for the National Organization for Women, ran programs for the National Black Women's Health Project, served on the D.C. Commission on Women, led research on the Ku Klux Klan and other right-wing groups for the Center for Democratic Renewal, and founded the National Center for Human Rights Education. She wrote several books. She was best known as a leading activist in the reproductive justice movement, which, with echoes of the future fights over the Women's March, challenged a pro-choice movement dominated by white women and focused on abortion rights, to the exclusion, Ross argued, of "the necessary enabling conditions to realize these rights," including "issues of economic justice, the environment, immigrants' rights, disability rights, discrimination based on race and sexual orientation."

As Ross fought these fights, the questions she had confronted when she opened William Fuller's letter would resurface again and again: When fighting for justice and change, how do you bring others along—those who are not there yet, and those who are actively complicit? In the movement to end oppression, is there space for imperfect allies? How imperfect is too imperfect? Do people who are part of a problem have a place in the search for solutions?

Like Sarsour, Ross was a persuader. She wanted her movement to be bold, unapologetic, ambitious, fearless, and, at the same time, more inviting than it often was. And, just as Sarsour had come to that idea of a movement with more bridges because of the bridges she had crossed, so, too, Ross's ideas seemed to flow from her own spanning of worlds.

Ross was born in 1953, to a family that wore the identities of Black, immigrant, and military. Her father had come to America from Jamaica and was a military man who moved the family constantly—Texas, Oklahoma, California. Ross did first grade at three different schools, in three different states. In most of these settings, Ross recalled being surrounded mostly by white people. She had little exposure to a Black community and only a faint awareness of race until she was older. "All my dad ever wanted to do was to assimilate," Ross said in the oral history. "All he ever wanted to do was to be the best G.I. he could be. He was a hyperpatriot. I mean, we were the ones that, you know, flew the American flag on Memorial Day. We were the ones that went to the gun shows."

Ross credits her childhood with shaping a comfort with navigating difference. "It wasn't something I had to learn," she recalled in the oral history. "It was something that I grew up with that I can now apply, that it wasn't like, 'Oh, now I've got to learn how to get along with white people because I grew up in an all-Black environment.' That's not true. Nor did I have to learn how to get along with Black people because I was living in an all-white environment. That's just not true. And so I was drawn to work that brought people together."

Ross's parents also shaped the persuasive instincts she would bring to her activism. Each of them was politically complicated, a vessel of clashing ideas, and she grew to understand that you could win them over by pitting one thing they believed against another thing they believed. Her father was highly conservative, "the classic immigrant who was more conservative than other African Americans," she said in the oral history. He was a member of the National Rifle Association. Ross's mother was a born-again Christian, "probably against every progressive value I tend to stand for." But both parents also supported Jesse Jackson's campaign for president in 1984, presumably because he was a minister. In fact, Ross said, her mother supported Jackson even as she sent money to another, differently oriented pastor, the right-wing fundamentalist Pat Robertson.

Growing up this way shaped an attitude in Ross that was realistic but never fatalistic about the difficulty of changing minds. She and her parents saw the world differently. But sometimes there were cracks that let a new thought in. "With the right words, with the right persuasion, I could convince them to join me," she told me. "Like when my father retired from the military and he found out that the government had privatized his health care, when they had promised him that he'd have health care for life—except when he needed to go into a nursing home. Then he was more than willing to listen to me about a human right to health care, probably in a way that he wouldn't have listened when he didn't need health care."

Ross developed more awareness of racism as a teenager, attending a high school named after Jefferson Davis, the president of the Confederacy. The school actually held mock "slave auctions," Ross recalled, "where you bid on your classmates and they got to be your slave for a day." She protested that. The school also held two separate proms, one white themed and one Black themed, though anyone could attend both. But it was only later, at Howard University, that Ross's racial and political consciousness truly blossomed.

She read *The Autobiography of Malcolm X,* by Alex Haley, and *The Black Woman,* by Toni Cade Bambara, and felt transformed. "It was like a whole new world had been opened up to me," she recalled in the Smith testimony, "because I had not thought of myself as—I don't want to seem silly as saying I hadn't thought of myself as Black or a woman before I read those books, but the politics of being Black, the politics of being a Black woman, I hadn't really thought about up until my freshman year in college."

She got involved with Black nationalist politics and tenant organizing in Washington. She was part of a Marxist-Leninist discussion circle called the D.C. Study Group and an antiapartheid organization called the South Africa Support Project. She became an informed and fierce critic of capitalism and patriarchy, white supremacy and imperialism.

Ross's growing immersion in theory and activism gave her new frameworks for processing the sexual violence she had experienced as a young woman, as well as other systemic cruelties. While at Howard, she was sexually harassed by a professor demanding sex for a better grade. While trying to focus on her studies there, Ross had to struggle with her mother over custody of her own son because of family laws stacked against women. And she was rendered infertile by a flawed contraceptive implant called the Dalkon Shield, which inspired her work on reproductive health.

So Ross had experienced the brutalities of living on the wrong end of power, and she had acquired, in time, a theoretical structure to make sense of those experiences. She also had, from her youth, an ability to negotiate a diverse array of people and their attitudes and an instinct for helping people evolve. All of this shaped the particular approach she went on to take as a professional activist to changing systems and changing minds, being more resistant than most to writing others off—a resistance that had been tested when she received Fuller's letter.

As Ross approached seventy, she had become a mentor to many young activists who reminded her of earlier incarnations of herself. And something that had come to worry her as she observed their battles was the phenomenon of callout culture within their movements and beyond them.

She first noticed it when, trying to connect with her grandson, she finally joined Facebook. (It didn't work. "Once I got on Facebook," Ross told me, "he decided that was for old folks.") As she scrolled, she was taken aback by the rage and hostility she saw, especially from those ostensibly working to win other people over to their visions.

"People just say anything that they want to each other," she recalled telling a young organizer who worked with her.

"Oh, you mean calling out?" the activist replied.

"You named it?"

"Yeah, we talk about calling out all the time."

"Well, what do y'all do about it?" Ross remembered asking.

And, Ross told me, "she just kind of shrugged like, 'Ain't nothing we can do.'" (This answer didn't satisfy Ross, who began to research a book about the problem.)

The culture of callouts took her back to the 1960s, when the FBI, through its notorious COINTELPRO program, infiltrated leftist organizations and sought to destabilize them by, among other things, spreading gossip and lies. The goal, she said, was "to try to splinter us apart, to make us turn on each other. So the calling-out tendency has been there as long as I've been conscious. The question became, what do you do with that?"

Back in those days, Ross and her comrades would have SCCU sessions—for self-criticism, criticism, and then unity. In a meeting, before you could call out someone else, you had to explain how you had contributed to the situation. Before calling out, you looked in. You were compelled to take a broader view of complicity and fallibility. Then you could air your criticism. Finally, having aired things and hopefully cleared the air, the goal was unity. "This is an activist practice that we had to engage in to withstand COINTELPRO," she said.

So Ross had been thinking about the callout problem for a long time, and in recent years she had devoted time and research to investigating a term long used by activists but with a lower cultural profile—"calling in." She defined it this way: "For me, calling in is a callout done with love. You're actually holding people accountable. But you're doing so through the lens of love. It's not giving people a pass on accountability—like you don't have to pay attention to the fact that they said something racist or that they caused harm to another person. No. It's not ignoring it. But it's about seeing a pathway or multiple pathways for addressing accountability through the lens of love."

To Ross, calling in was far from the dominant approach these days.

The callout was ascendant in the political culture. It was not lost on Ross that an earlier connotation of the phrase "calling out" was challenging someone to a death duel. She was especially concerned by the problem of calling out in her own movement spaces. She worried about the threat to power building. She had fought on behalf of the marginalized for all of her adult life, and she was worried about lost occasions to come together and mobilize a broader coalition.

In her writing and activist work, she had developed a theory called "circles of influence," which was a guide for navigating these kinds of coalitions and alliances of the imperfect without blowing it all up. It was about how a political actor should deal with differences with people she called their 90-percenters, 75-percenters, 50-percenters, 25-percenters, and 0-percenters.

Ross defined her 90-percenters as people who shared most of her general worldview: "that capitalism is problematic, that racism and homophobia and transphobia and anti-immigrant bias are bad," and so on and so forth. The problem she observed with one's 90-percenters is that instead of focusing on the vast area of overlap, they fixated on the 10 percent divergence. "I might work on reproductive justice, while someone else works on immigrant rights or trans rights or whatever," she told me. "I think that the 90-percenters spend too much time trying to turn people into 100-percenters, which is totally unnecessary. I mean, there's certainly enough oppression to go around that we can all work on it in our own different ways and never run out of oppression."

Ross was speaking of those who say things like "If you're not working on my issue from my angle, then you're erasing my issue. If you're championing economic justice, you're problematic for minimizing race. If you're championing racial justice and fighting white supremacy, you don't post enough about the ills of capitalism. If you're focused on long-term climate change, you're neglecting the here-and-now needs of poor communities." She found this compulsion to make others into one's clones "totally unnecessary." "Why," she asked, "are we trying to get everybody to work on the thing we think is most important when there's a lot of stuff that needs to be changed?"

Outside that inner ring of the like-minded (if often fractious) was Ross's next circle—an activist's 75-percenters. "These are people who probably share a good portion of our worldview, but not totally," Ross told me. "For example, I work on abortion rights. I work with the Girl Scouts, which probably doesn't talk about abortion a lot, but they talk about women's and girls' empowerment. So they would be my 75-percenters. I would not spend my time trying to persuade them to become a 90-percenter, since there's enough common ground for us to work on."

For an activist who works in coalition, 75-percenters require a further skill beyond what 90-percenters do. You don't merely have to tolerate others focusing on different things, attacking a broadly similar vision of the problem in their own, distinct way. You have to accept large islands of disagreement in a sea of assent. With your 75-percenters, there is still so much you can get done together. But Ross observed an excessive interest in that nonoverlapping 25 percent. It was a scab people wanted to keep picking instead of doing the things they could do. Or, just as often, a couple of 75-percenters, like, say, Ross and the Girl Scouts, would do something together, successfully bracketing their differences, only to have one of Ross's 90-percenters call her out for collaborating with a group that wasn't properly vocal on abortion rights. In other words, two people almost in perfect lockstep with each other would fall into a schism over one of those people finding common cause and getting something done with a near ally.

Next in Ross's schema was one's 50-percenters. The circle of agreement has shrunk drastically. "They're my people who share values with me, but what makes them 50-percenters is that they could use these values to go to the left or the right." Ross hadn't had to look far for her first 50-percenters: they were her parents. They shared core values around hard work, taking care of one another, and how you ought to treat people. But, depending on the issue of the day and the circumstances of their lives and what information sources they were taking in, those values could drive them to Jesse Jackson or Pat Robertson, to libertarianism or a view of health care as a right. You approach such people by first accepting they don't want the world you want. Their vision is different. But if you can understand their values and needs and look for openings, as when Ross's father fell into dread about his health care, you can, in addition to helping them, pry open a closed mind.

Then, in Ross's schema, came your 25-percenters. In the realm of electoral politics, these are people on the diametrically opposite side from you. They don't share a vision with you, nor even a basic worldview, nor even necessarily fundamental values or language. They may use the exact same words and mean completely different things by them. "When I talk about patriotism and wearing a mask to keep my neighbors safe, they talk about liberty or their freedom to go get a haircut," Ross said. "We don't have enough common ground."

You may or may not need your 25-percenters; it depends on the situation at hand. If you do, there is, in Ross's schema, one valuable thing you have to work with: your 25-percenters still want to be seen as, and see themselves as, good people. "One of the things I learned in working against hate groups," Ross told me, "is that most of them start off every conversation with a Black person saying, 'I'm not a racist, but . . .' Internally, they actually do think they're good people, even though they're standing there in Klan robes. Part of my calling-in strategy for them would be to help them lean in to that internal exploration of themselves and show them how to bolster that self-perception of them being good people by walking them through examples: 'Well, if you saw a Black person that needed a kidney donation and you were a match, would you do it?' That kind of thing. Make them really question that interior set of values that they think they have and see if they're willing to actually go down that path of exploring those values. I find you don't make a lot of headway trying to convince them that they're racist, because they're just not willing to accept that about themselves at that time. But you can convince them, 'Well, if you want to be a good person, you've got to do good things.' "

For this group, there was one further prerequisite for success, Ross said. You had to take the fears of your 25-percenters seriously, even if you were appalled by those fears. "You have to spend a lot of time on the concept of fear, because a lot of people, particularly in that 25-percenter category, operate from platforms of fear," she told me. "Fear of immigrants, fear of queers, fear of this, fear of that. And so you can have really productive conversations talking about their fears, but you have to take their fears seriously for them to even be able to listen to you. If you dismiss their fears, they don't listen. They don't think you're taking the fact that they're afraid seriously enough."

Technically, there was one other group in Ross's analysis: the

0-percenters. "I don't think I have any common ground with them and do my best to overpower and overwhelm them," she said. She had a simple term of art for them: "fascists."

The kind of outreach and engagement Ross was calling for could feel like a lot to ask. And she wanted to be clear: it wasn't for everyone. But she worried about an ever-more influential view of movement work as therapeutic, which set unrealistic expectations about the slog of it.

"The movement is not therapy," she told me. "It is not going to be your healing space. The job of social justice activism is to end oppression, not to make you feel safe, comfortable, and loved. You need to get that somewhere else, preferably in a therapy session."

She partly blamed herself and her peers. "I think as part of the movement to end violence against women, we made some over-promises. We told people, particularly rape survivors, that we could create safe spaces, when in fact all we can do is create spaces to be brave together." To call people into a brave space was to summon everyone to try something together. To promise people a safe space was to make everyone a promise about everyone else that was impossible to keep. Somehow, Ross felt, the idea of the safe space, the worthy idea of it, grew out of hand into the idea "that social justice work by definition should be safe spaces."

A similar evolution and distortion of a term had occurred, in Ross's view, with the notion of "identity politics." It was coined in a statement by the Combahee River Collective in 1977, a Boston-based collective of Black women who identified as lesbians, feminists, and socialists and who said that "no other ostensibly progressive movement has ever considered our specific oppression as a priority or worked seriously for the ending of that oppression." The group wrote that many of its members had been part of, and been shaped by, the civil rights and Black nationalist and Black Panthers movements. However, the statement said, "it was our experience and disillusionment within these liberation movements, as well as experience on the periphery of the white male left, that led to the need to develop a politics that was anti-racist, unlike those of white women, and anti-sexist, unlike those of Black and white men." This led in turn to the vision of a politics rooted in one's particularity: "We believe that the most profound and potentially the most radical politics come directly out of our own identity, as opposed to working to end somebody else's oppression."

In Ross's view, that genuine insight had in later years often come to be misrepresented into something unhelpful. "The whole question of identity politics has become so distorted that people are obsessed with not only who they are but who everybody else isn't," she told me. "You are not like me. You don't share my identity, so, therefore, you can't understand where I'm coming from. And I'm only going to work with or coalesce with people who have the same identities that I have." That feeling contradicted the Combahee statement, which described its members' ambition plainly: "organizing Black feminists as we continue to do political work in coalition with other groups."

There was a fine line between "here is what you'd see if you were me" and "you will never get me because." Both flowed from something Ross admired about the new generation of activists. "The thing that they get the best is intersectionality," she told me, "because they refuse to be boxed into categories that sometimes we were trapped in. And so I really love the fact that they are pushing the boundaries of definitions and identities, and self-naming themselves." Still, there was an approach she saw around her that was fundamentally additive and coalitional. And another approach, angled slightly differently, that was fundamentally subtractive and fatalistic about the possibility of anyone ever knowing, let alone changing, anyone else. Ross was interested in ways that a diverse group of people could revel in their kaleidoscope of identities and still coalesce. She was interested in a kind of coalition that had struggled to establish itself in the past—a coalition that represented everyone in the coalition, that didn't erase, that honored difference, while reaching broadly.

Sometimes Ross feared that the insights of identity politics were being construed to make coalition of that kind harder rather than easier. For example, on the campuses where she taught, Ross worried about a tendency toward lumping the awkward together with the truly dangerous.

Like many who teach today, Ross has had the experience of getting students' pronouns and/or current names wrong, often students who are gender nonconforming, nonbinary, trans. "If you don't get someone's gender pronoun right or their changed identity name, or you accidentally use what they call their dead name, you can get in a world of trouble," she told me. Like Sarsour, she was not claiming to be right when she messed up. She considered herself a fierce advocate for the rights of gender-nonconforming people and allied struggles. Her concern was that an episode like that could quickly descend into a place of anger and calling out instead of rising to the plane of justice. "There's no process for forgiveness with accountability," she said. She wasn't asking for people not to complain—on the contrary. She was suggesting that in the absence of a process to deal with an episode like that, outrage was the only tool available, and not a very useful one.

"Yes, I should make an effort to learn your preferred gender pronoun and your preferred name and all of that," she continued. "But, at the same time, I'm not going to be crucified because I made a mistake and you're doing a bad threat assessment: you can't tell the difference between someone who misgenders you and a fascist who's trying to kill you.

"Every hurt is not trying to exterminate you," Ross said. "Matter of fact, why you're hurting may have nothing to do with the person standing in front of you, but from restimulated past pain that just got triggered, but you dump on the person accessible to you because you can't get at the past hurt that's inaccessible.

"My particular talent, if you can call it that, and certainly my gift, is an incredibly thick skin, so I don't react to comments that other people would call racist," Ross said. "I really don't care, for the most part. I try to see into the heart of individuals because I think that none of us will ever learn the social skills to be appropriate interracially all the time, because they're not taught."

Because of Ross's long record, she had a chance of being heard on this advice. But even coming from her, there was risk in this line of suggestion. Yes, it might make for a better, less fractious society if everyone gave each other that grace, if some smilingly endured the asking about the hair or the touching of the hijab or the where-are-you-fromming. Yes, as Sarsour had, you had to remember the long trajectory. Even so, it could also feel unfair to ask the most put-upon members of society to be the ones with a sense of humor, the ones to let things go, to surrender their hair and hijabs and their right to be identified properly and not to have to show their metaphorical papers. Even with Ross's threat-assessment point, the same people being merely misrecognized by some were indeed being targeted by others, and the toll of dealing with these others, even at times ruled by them, made it harder to tolerate the misrecognizers.

This burden was now described by a term originally coined by the sociologist Arlie Russell Hochschild to describe relations between employer and employee. When you asked marginalized people to smile through being misrecognized or objectified or Orientalized or dead-named, when you asked them to use such moments to educate or strengthen the civic fabric, what you were demanding of them was "emotional labor." Hochschild had been referring to the corporate use and management of human feeling, but here the labor in question was civic. What was being asked of people was, in a sense, a kind of emotional voluntarism.

Ross was attentive to the burden of that work. It formed an important caveat in her ideas. She believed that for the country to survive this perilous era and realize the ideals of democracy, some would need to do what no one should have to; some would have to be given indulgence they didn't deserve; and some would have to make what was not their fault their problem. But the caveat was this: no individual person had to do this work.

"The point I make around emotional labor is that you have to be at a healed enough space to be able to offer it," she told me. "If you're still raw with your own emotional healing, then you're not going to be in any space to help somebody else do theirs. That's why the whole concept of emotional labor has to be voluntary, because you'll actually make things worse if you do it involuntarily." To do that work was a choice. Ross respected people who refused to do it, and she respected those who gave it a shot.

"Calling in and calling out exist on a continuum," she said. "They're not binary. They're not an either-or concept. They're very situational, and they have to be very voluntary. You have no obligation to see to someone else's consciousness. It's a choice you get to make, and you have to make the choice with love and respect.

"I don't expect every Black person to be ready to have a conversation with a white person about racism," Ross went on. "Hell, they may have been so brutalized by it that they just want to tell them to talk to the hand. And that's okay. But some of us are in a different space. And, like I said earlier, there's enough work in the movement for us all to do different work. So you don't have to do the work I do. Do the work that works for you."

Ross had recently been teaching a course about white supremacy in the era of Trumpism. As she spoke about calling in and coalition and winning people over, the first thing many of her students wanted to know was, how do I reach out to relatives on the right? They wanted, she joked, "calling-in strategies for not blowing up the Thanksgiving dinner conversation."

She told them that before they worry about those they were trying to win over, they should look at themselves. "You have to be in a loving, healing space to call anybody in," Ross told me. "You can't do it from anger, because it's just going to end up badly. So you have to assess why you're doing it. What's your motivation? Are you trying to help this person learn, or are you actually trying to change them?"

It was a striking distinction—helping a person learn versus trying to change them. When we speak of changing someone's mind, winning someone over, aren't we attempting both at once?

Not for Ross. "You can't change other people," she told me. "You can't even change the person you're married to. You can help people. You can expose people to different information and help them learn—if you do so with love."

She offered an example from her work in reproductive justice. She often dealt with doctors who fretted about women who have access to contraception but have repeated unintended pregnancies. "She is a bad contraceptor" is a phrase Ross has heard more times than she cared to. Ross tried to persuade the doctors to go deeper to understand the experiences of their patients.

"I'll push back on that and say, 'How much time have you spent with this person trying to understand what's interfering with her ability to use contraceptives? Does she have a violent partner? Could getting the prescription from her provider be a problem? Could she have so much going on that her fertility is not at the top of her issues? Or does she feel a warm, fuzzy feeling every time she's pregnant? Maybe that's the only time she feels human. I mean, there are a whole bunch of things going on with people that are beneath your medical radar as you're saying, "She's a bad contraceptor." ' "

Ross said she wasn't trying to change the doctors, which could backfire. "I'm not trying to change them in terms of rethinking their worldview, but to add additional information that they may not have considered."

With the doctors, she assumed that their heart had once been in the right place. "I find that most people don't enter the medical profession because they want to fuck over people," she said. "So, generally, there's something there that you can reach that re-stirs their empathy and reconnects them to why they became doctors in the first place."

Had she come at those doctors with "You're just a racist, insensitive provider who's making judgments about a woman because she has multiple pregnancies," she said, she might have been on solid evidentiary footing. The data bear out that many doctors minimize the experiences of less privileged patients and Black women in particular. But would it work? "I don't think the conversation would go really far," Ross said.

Ross said she had found more success in seeking—and, crucially, seeming—to displace beliefs rather than replace them. Approaching someone and wanting to jumble up their ideas and make them think and learn again was one thing. Approaching them with what felt like an agenda to remove one thought and supplant it with another—that read very differently. It put people off. It was hard to get people to dump their beliefs and fill the void with yours. But it was possible to make people curious again, raise the ratio of their questions to answers. You couldn't necessarily make them certain of what you knew. But you could try to make them less certain of what they knew.

"Really, it's about taking people seriously where they are," Ross told me. "And letting them stay where they are, thinking new thoughts, instead of trying to pull them up the mountain."

III
Alicia Garza

Another activist grappling with these questions about broadening the circle was Alicia Garza, a longtime community organizer in Oakland and a major figure within the Black Lives Matter movement.

In Sanford, Florida, on the night of February 26, 2012, a seventeen-year-old Black man named Trayvon Martin had been walking down the street when a self-styled neighborhood watch vigilante, George Zimmerman, shot the teenager to death. It was not the first, nor the last, killing of an unarmed Black person by police or by people who play police in their heads. But it shook the country. Zimmerman was charged with second-degree murder several weeks after the killing. And then, more than a year later, on July 13, 2013, a jury, having taken some sixteen hours to think it over, pronounced Zimmerman not guilty.

Across the country, Americans, especially Black Americans, reacted with horror and rage and anguish and resignation. The pain was all the more acute because, at that moment, the country had its first Black president, who had come to office amid airy talk of a new post-racial America. The old realities, though, seemed to have no plans of disappearing.

One of the disconcerted was Garza. Sitting at a bar in Oakland, she reached for her phone and posted, "I can't breathe. NOT GUILTY?!?!?!?!?!"

She walked outside and, ten minutes later, posted again:

> Where those folks at saying we are in post-racial America? Where those folks at saying we have moved past race and that black folks in particular need to get over it? The sad part is, there's a section of America who is cheering and celebrating right now.
>
> And that makes me sick to my stomach. We GOTTA get it together y'all. Our lives are hanging in the balance. Young black boys in this country are not safe. Black men in this country are not safe. This verdict will create many more George Zimmermans.

Garza was reeling. This was a gut punch of a case. Yet there had been so many. Garza wasn't even sure why this one was stirring so much in her. Five minutes later, she posted:

> Black people. I love you. I love us. Our lives matter.

Twenty-three minutes later, Garza posted again—this time directing her words to those who sympathized with her view of things but who had succumbed to fatalism about change. These were the people posting at the very same hour that the verdict didn't surprise them, that it was always thus, always would be.

> Btw stop saying we are not surprised. That's a damn shame in itself. I continue to be surprised at how little Black lives matter. And I will continue that. Stop giving up on Black life. Black people, I will NEVER give up on us. NEVER.

In the coming days, friends and colleagues of Garza's saw her posts and offered their collaborations to amplify the message. A friend named Patrisse Cullors, a fellow activist and an artist, helped to distill and popularize the message using the hashtag #blacklivesmatter. Domains were purchased; logos were sketched. People were picking up on the phrase online. A manifesto emerged:

> #Blacklivesmatter is a collective affirmation and embracing of the resistance and resilience of Black people. It is a reminder and a demand that our lives be cherished, respected and able to access our full dignity and determination. It is a truth that we are called to embrace if our society is to become human again. It is a rallying cry. It is a prayer. The impact of embracing and defending the value of black life in particular has the potential to lift us all. #Blacklivesmatter asserts the truth of Black life that collective action builds collective power for collective transformation.

Garza, along with Cullors and her activist friend Ayọ (formerly Opal) Tometi, who had a background in immigrant rights, began talking about building what would eventually become the Black Lives Matter Global Network, an organization within a larger movement, building on work already happening on the ground in local communities across the country. And after another killing of another unarmed Black man, the movement took off in the national consciousness.

In the town of Ferguson, Missouri, on August 9, 2014, a Black teenager named Michael Brown was shot dead by a white policeman named Darren Wilson. This time, even before the failure of accountability that felt inevitable, massive protests erupted. Riots spread. A great many Americans mobilized by the everyday brutality visited upon Black people flocked to Ferguson. The governor, Jay Nixon, called in the National Guard.

Garza was among those who went to Ferguson, to bear witness and to help organize. She knocked on doors. She advised local organizations on strategy. She tried to resolve internecine conflicts. And as Ferguson throbbed with fury, on the ground and online #blacklivesmatter became an organizing mantra of an emerging movement. Groups popped up calling themselves local chapters of Black Lives Matter. On Black Friday in 2014, the day after Thanksgiving, Garza joined a group of protesters wearing the hashtag on their T-shirts in occupying the West Oakland BART transit station and shut it down, disrupting one of the biggest shopping days of the year to raise the profile of their struggle. Just days earlier, Garza's earlier plea to stop saying one wasn't surprised had suffered another blow when a grand jury in Missouri unsurprisingly decided against indicting Wilson.

Thus was born a movement whose story has been well and fulsomely told elsewhere. I was interested in how the experience had shaped Garza's thinking about persuasion and change. It has often been said that the approach taken by Black Lives Matter, as the dominant face of the racial justice struggle in this era, differed somewhat from the approach of the mainstream, religiously led, nonviolent civil rights movement of the 1960s. "Black Lives Matter has been described as 'not your grandfather's civil-rights movement,' to distinguish its tactics and its philosophy from those of nineteen-sixties-style activism,"

Jelani Cobb of *The New Yorker* has written. For one thing, it combined on-the-ground protest with online organizing and moment making in a way that was novel. Its adherents also rejected the hierarchical leadership of the older civil rights movement. "The model of the Black preacher leading people to the promised land isn't working right now," Garza has said. Instead, Black Lives Matter was defined by decentralization and local sovereignty. And whereas the civil rights movement of the 1960s had been male dominated, the new movement was full of women leaders, queer leaders, and committed feminists. Garza, who identifies as queer, has spoken of having "this experience being queer Black women in a movement for Black freedom that really isn't shaped in our image" and of demanding to change that.

Above all, Black Lives Matter, drawing on the example of more radical movements in the 1960s, seemed to represent a different relationship to establishment power from that of the mainstream civil rights movement with which it was often—perhaps mistakenly—compared. It called white supremacy "white supremacy." Many of its biggest voices championed ideas like defunding the police. It seemed more at home outside, arguing for the dismantling of structures, than inside, corralling votes in marble corridors. When the country's first Black president invited three of Black Lives Matter's leaders to the White House during Black History Month, along with icons of the civil rights movement like John Lewis and Sherrilyn Ifill, two went and one turned Obama down, calling the event "a sham that would only serve to legitimize the false narrative that the government is working to end police brutality and the institutional racism that fuels it." Jelani Cobb would later argue that the controversy "reflected a larger conflict: while Black Lives Matter's insistent outsider status has allowed it to shape the dialogue surrounding race and criminal justice in this country, it has also sparked a debate about the limits of protest, particularly of online activism." There was no question that the movement was able to change the conversation and force reckonings and compel introspection about racism. But could the largely online movement also do what its 1960s forerunners had done in translating that reckoning into action and policy changes like the Civil Rights and Voting Rights Acts?

That debate was what led me to Garza. I had heard from people in activist circles that Garza cut an interesting path through the debate, within Black Lives Matter and in progressive organizing more generally. She was, on the one hand, as committed to these fights against structural oppression and for greater justice as anyone you would find. But in many of the spaces she worked in, she had a reputation as someone who championed the need for a greater emphasis on expanding.

"Many of my teachers, trainers, and mentors have fallen into a pattern of making the political circles smaller and smaller rather than bigger and wider," she wrote in her memoir, *The Purpose of Power.* But movements, Garza says, "cannot be cliques." She understood the fear that motivated that insularity. Building broad always carried the risk of hindering your ability to achieve real change and real justice. What Garza was seeking—long before Black Lives Matter came about, and long after it became something infinitely bigger than she—was a way of building broad without undermining your own pursuit, with greater magnanimity toward those not yet where you are.

"This is, I think, the crux of it," Garza told me in one of our many conversations in recent years. "We can keep talking to each other and becoming a narrower and narrower slice of this country, or we can actually fight for power."

Alicia Garza was raised as the daughter of a Black mother and a white Jewish stepfather who owned an antiques business. The family bounced around tony Marin County, just north of San Francisco, during Garza's childhood, exposing her to some of the very different worlds she would seek to organize, and challenge, as an adult. Until four or five years old, Garza lived in the town of San Rafael, in its mostly Black and Latino Canal District. Around the age of seven, she moved to an upper-middle-class, considerably whiter neighborhood of San Rafael, near Gerstle Park. In seventh grade, the family moved to Tiburon, which she has described as a "wealthy, mostly white enclave," where the median income was more than double the national figure and where the views of the Golden Gate Bridge and San Francisco were gorgeous.

To be Black in so white and moneyed a setting was to straddle contending realities and be both exposed to privilege and arbitrarily deprived of it. Garza had the fortune of going to a private school, but only, she says, because her mother failed to get her precocious daughter into public school early. ("School after school wouldn't take me," she has written. "Many didn't believe that I could read, even when I'd do it in front of them.") Her classmates superficially venerated what they perceived to be Black culture, she writes, with their "flat-billed baseball caps" and "baggy clothes with expensive underwear peeking out from sagging pants." But even as they partied without fear of being caught, she was the one in middle school called out for smoking marijuana when she never had. Later, when she did actually smoke weed and was pulled over by the police with half a pound in her trunk, she was let go with a lecture—a fate she grew to realize was unimaginable for many others who looked like her. Her Black mother, who came from the working class, met Garza's budding independence with "fierce resistance." Her white stepfather, who came from a wealthier family, was, Garza suggests, "more interested in being my friend than being my parent."

These contradictions continued to shape her as an adult, as she has written:

> I'm a writer who doesn't know (or much care) about "literary society." I'm a radical who doesn't care much for the doctrinaire distinctions among leftists. I'm a Black girl who didn't grow up around a lot of other Black girls, except for my mama, who is the Blackest woman ever and who loves Black people fiercely. I'm a queer person who struggled more to out myself to the strangers and friends in my everyday life than I did with my family, who largely just kept it pushing when I came out to them. I'm a Black girl who came up mostly middle class, who had to work for everything I've ever had but was also given the world by my parents.

Garza studied sociology and anthropology at the University of California at San Diego before returning to the Bay Area and working for AmeriCorps. She taught in a middle school. She worked part-time in her parents' antiques business. Eventually, she found her way into community organizing in the Bay Area. It was in that work that she began to forge her own vision of change.

Her formative organizing experience was in the San Francisco neighborhood of Bayview Hunters Point, working for an organization called People Organized to Win Employment Rights, known colloquially as Power. It was an outfit that combined door knocking and on-the-ground mobilizing with political theory education and a focus on Black communities, and for Garza it was perfect. Bayview was a small, insular, everyone-knows-everyone neighborhood, a hamlet in a big city. It had been ravaged by decades of neglect, by drugs and crime, by a lack of chances. It had a greater fraction of residents living in public housing than anywhere else in the city, but it also had the kinds of neighborhood bones that realtors can sniff, with its own microclimate of sunshine in an otherwise gloomy city and stunning hilltop views of the bay.

Power set itself the mission of resisting the tide of gentrification that was coming for Bayview, by helping residents stay in their homes and fighting for more affordable housing.

Garza walked around, knocking on doors, reading questions from a script:

"How long have you lived in this community? What do you like about it?"

"Do you know that Bayview Hunters Point is now a redevelopment project? How do you feel about the changes happening in the community?"

"Who do you think these changes are for?"

Garza's first campaign in Bayview swung into motion when the city announced it was requiring every resident in the area to pay for the airborne electrical wires in front of their homes to be moved underground, presumably in the name of "development." The cost of this "undergrounding" was $1,400 per household, a staggering sum in a neighborhood where that was roughly the amount collected in a two-week paycheck for many residents. Further, the city threatened that those who failed to comply risked having a lien put on homes they owned. There was, in theory, a program to help residents who couldn't afford the change, but it had hardly enough money for the number who would need it, and it was tricky to access.

Garza and her colleagues organized Bayview residents, educating them about the issue and making demands of the city to cover more of the conversions out of its coffers. When none of that seemed to be working, Power staged a direct action at the municipal office overseeing the project. Ultimately, Power won.

It was one kind of organizing victory, with particular lessons. Power's members had raised consciousness among voters who were busy working multiple jobs and tending to their families and juggling budgets. They had forced a conversation with the people in authority. They had confronted those actors and caused them to back down.

Then Power was presented with another opportunity for another campaign, this one with its own, rather different lessons. It was asked to join a larger, if slightly unwieldy, coalition of organizations hoping to introduce and pass a ballot measure requiring half of all new housing in the Bayview redevelopment zone to be made affordable to people at or below the median income of $40,000 a year. The idea was compelling, innovative, and ambitious. But for Power it was also a difficult call. Gathering eight thousand signatures to secure a ballot measure, and then rounding up forty thousand votes, wasn't exactly Power's thing. It was a radical organization that kept a slight distance from traditional electioneering, in part because that was not the skill it had cultivated but also in part because that was not its theory of change. The group was better known for protesting and publicizing accusations of developer corruption than it was for wooing middle-of-the-road voters and playing nice in a big tent. Being a dynamic activist organization and being a good coalition partner are two different things, and Garza and her colleagues had reason to be wary of those they would be in bed with: the Nation of Islam, the Sierra Club, and faith groups like the St. John Coltrane Church.

In this case, given the establishment forces it was up against, Power decided to go for it anyway. And, though it eventually lost that campaign, Garza's work on it laid track for much of her later organizing: this was where she learned the art of seeking radical outcomes by working with those who are not radical and of being simultaneously at the back and at the throat of your allies.

"We built a really broad coalition, and we had a lot of disagreements about all kinds of things," Garza told me. "There were environmental groups that really wanted to focus on environmental impact. And so, in some ways, they were like, 'We don't want housing at all. We want less housing, and we want less impact on the environment.' Others felt pretty strongly that the income threshold for affordable housing should change. And we felt strongly that we didn't want people to get edged out of their ability to afford a home that was being built in their community that they had been struggling in for years. We were coalition partners with religious institutions and faith-based institutions. And we had a bunch of disagreements about how to get things done.

"We were more in favor of direct-action tactics when we were getting the runaround from the city and from bureaucrats," she went on. "Others were more in favor of what I think they would have considered decorum. I remember one time we did some direct action, and it really pissed off people in our coalition. We really had to figure out how do we employ multiple methods, multiple tactics, within a broad strategy to get what we wanted? Ultimately, what we were trying to do is pass this ballot measure. In the end, it wasn't about do you protest or do you have a sit-down meeting? It was about how broad can you build this coalition?"

The meaning of the Bayview campaign, Garza has written, is not that "we had to be less radical. It meant that being radical and having radical politics were not a litmus test for whether or not one could join our movement." After the loss, Garza found herself wondering if she and her colleagues could have gone even broader, stomached even more uncomfortable alliances, to get the measure passed.

"Winning," she writes in her memoir, "is about more than being right—it is also about how you invite others to be a part of change they may not have even realized they needed."

I began a series of conversations with Garza in February 2020, just before the pandemic hit the United States in earnest, a few months before George Floyd would be murdered by a police officer. The second time we spoke, in August of that year, the world felt severally changed: in addition to the health calamity and its economic fallout, America was in the grips of a racial reckoning that impressed Garza. "Never in my lifetime," she wrote, "have I seen this country have the kind of epiphany around race that it is having now."

This period coincided with big transitions in Garza's personal life:

her mother's passing, the end of a long-term relationship, and the publication of her first book. She was in a liminal space as she approached forty, no longer quite a young activist grasping at the future, en route to being a mentor of the struggle with lessons for a rising generation. "I find myself at thirty-nine not being an elder in any way, shape, or form," Garza told me one day. "But, having been in movement for a long time, I have a longer perspective. My charge at this point is to figure out how I become a bridge to help people orient in a moment that I'm also orienting in. Bringing a level of perspective, but also learning new ways of being." And this is how we began to talk about the lessons she had learned and her vision for the movements she was part of.

During the summer protests of 2020, Garza was still processing the sudden surge in popularity of ideas she and so many others had been pushing for so long. At that moment, it might have seemed as if white Americans were really engaging with the ideas of the movement, reading *White Fragility* and *How to Be an Antiracist* and discussing them in book clubs over Chardonnay in plastic cups. Poll after poll was claiming evidence of sizable changes in white public opinion. In recent years, Monmouth reported, the percentage of Americans who agreed that racism was a "big problem" had leaped from 51 percent to 76 percent. Another poll reported that white Americans' support for the idea of police violence as a very serious problem had doubled since 2015. "There has never been an anti-racist majority in American history; there may be one today," Adam Serwer wrote in *The Atlantic* in a moment that to many at the time felt both fraught and full of potential.

Garza was trying to make sense of what had made these shifts in opinion possible. In her practice as an activist, she said, "you have moments you create, and you have moments you take advantage of." A protest or direct action is a moment you create, like Power's storming of the municipal office back in the day. But people coming together in the wake of George Floyd's murder fell in the second category.

"Moments that you take advantage of are moments where everybody's eyes are on something, but meaning hasn't been made for them yet," she said. Using George Floyd's murder as an example, she explained: "The whole world watched a man be choked to death on camera by somebody who was sworn to protect and serve. What was so eerie about it—and it's actually an image that haunts me, and I think it haunts a lot of people—is that the officer looks directly into the camera while he's killing this man.

"There's a space afterward where people go, 'Whoa, what the fuck just happened here?' What usually happens in those moments is that police unions and other actors fill the space immediately afterward. They make meaning. So they start to put out things about the past of the person they have killed, their record. They start to project images of the person in a less sympathetic light. And that helps people make meaning about where they stand on what just happened.

"If, however," she continued, "directly after that moment, that space is filled with something else—protests, interviews with the young woman who filmed it, or other things—people make different meanings.

"My story of how this movement gets to be where it is," she said, "is that there are people all over who have been determined to make meaning of things that don't make sense, and to shape that meaning, and to engage people's imagination around why things are the way they are, whether or not they agree. And, if they're really successful, it gives you something to do about it."

Those who sought to make meaning out of the Floyd case were helped by all the groundwork that had been laid in recent years, all the institution building and network formation that activists and organizers had undertaken. And the context of the moment helped. That summer, people were trapped indoors by the virus, growing restless and frustrated. The killing of George Floyd came on the heels of other killings, including those of Ahmaud Arbery and Breonna Taylor earlier that year. Then there was the white nationalist ascendancy in national politics, with the country now run by a flagrant racist, a few years after Americans were promised, in the guise of his predecessor, a post-racial society. There was, according to Garza, a "confluence of anxiety about the political state of the world, anxiety about the economic state of the world, anxiety about your own health. And you have to stay in place, so there's not really a way to take the pressure out of the valve." And then Floyd's murder did just that.

A year later, with the outrage having cooled somewhat and some of the once-hopeful polling numbers having regressed, but with a sense in the air that certain things had indeed changed durably, Garza reflected on whether Black Lives Matter could already be judged a success.

"It's undeniable that this movement is successful," she told me. "Has it achieved Black lives mattering? No. Absolutely not. In eight years? No. Absolutely not. And it's probably going to be another fifty years before we're able to look back and say, 'Oh, wow! Yeah. Look at how far this has come.' But there are some significant developments." Garza asked, "Would there be a voting-rights law being debated in the way that it is right now without this movement? Absolutely not. Would there be a police reform bill in Congress without this movement? No. Absolutely not. Would there be widespread concern and shifts around police violence without this movement? Absolutely not. Would you be able to flip on the television and see an entire season of your favorite show talking about 'defund the police' and what that might look like in practice? Absolutely not. So it is undeniable that this movement has been successful."

She also pointed to what she saw as the turning in white Americans' attitudes. "This is the first time in my lifetime when white folks are having to grapple with racism," Garza said, "and pick a side, decide where you're at." She added, "Whiteness, as the foundation of this nation, what established it, and what continues to be its driving engine, not just here, but around the world, is deeply entrenched." What gave her some measure of optimism is that "there's a context that has been developed that is requiring whiteness to account for itself."

Garza was far from the victory-lap kind. She had the activist's eye for all that remained to be done. And as she looked out on the world and looked back on her work and looked inward at the struggles she had been part of, she was thinking about what it would take to build movements capable of doing all that needed to be done and addressing so many grave, connected crises.

Garza celebrated that the progressive movement had grown more strident, more self-confident in its demands, more determined to hold leaders accountable. But she wondered if, in the bargain, the movement had acquired a narrowness that kept it smaller than it had to be.

She wanted an expansionary progressivism that followed the example of Power fighting gentrification in San Francisco: being unflinchingly radical and, at the same time, making space for the non-radical.

"Because crisis is here now, and because we haven't done the work we've needed to do over the last thirty years to actually build a left in this country that is viable, even as we pursue that, we are going to have to figure out who else can we work with in order to get a little bit closer to where we're trying to go," she told me. "That doesn't mean we abandon the project of building the left, and in fact it actually brings into focus how necessary it is. But in the meantime, we can't just continue to be small." She often repeated a line picked up from a fellow activist about how the left had to stop trying to be the god of small things.

"We have to be a lot more selective about who *can't* come," Garza said. "You would think, listening to certain people, that every-fucking-body in this country is on some organized left. It's just deeply not fucking true. We are so small in relationship to the breadth of where 300-plus million people are politically. We need to understand that in a deep way."

With that assertion, Garza distinguished herself from a certain strain of her fellow progressives who argue that their policies would be overwhelmingly popular and readily received among those who would obviously benefit from them, but for the corporate media thwarting them and the powerful lobbies blocking their policy proposals, along with the legislators they buy. Garza saw it differently. The ideas in many cases had both a powerful-enemies problem and, partly because of the exertions of those enemies and partly because of primordial realities of American political culture, a lay-public-opinion problem.

For Garza, this was a hard-earned lesson going all the way back to Bayview. It was true that powerful developers and their allies in the city's power structure wanted to gentrify the areas as precipitously as possible. And one could casually assume from that that regular people in the area wanted to resist what was being done. But Garza and her colleagues realized that they had *both* a special-interests problem *and* a popularity problem. Many of the residents, particularly older Black people who deplored the area's descent into drugs and violence, were open to the promises of those heralding change. It wasn't enough to push back against the powerful. You had to be hard on yourself about just how popular your ideas were, assume they were less rather than more popular, and work like hell to make them popular.

In her memoir, she writes that too many of her political allies seem to enjoy the cozy homogeneity of their ranks, instead of viewing that as a problem of smallness. They believe

> that finding a group of people who think like you and being loud about your ideas is somehow building power. . . . And while I feel most comfortable around people who think like me and share my experiences, the longer I'm in the practice of building a movement, the more I realize that movement building isn't about finding your tribe—it's about growing your tribe across difference to focus on a common set of goals.

"There's a purism that can come with social justice work," Garza told me in one of our conversations, "and that purism, unfortunately or fortunately maybe, is actually pretty detrimental to getting things done." But it was also complicated, she hastened to add. There were bridges too far. You probably don't want to end up in a partnership with Jared Kushner just because you favor prison reform. When it comes to coalitions, she said, "you do have to assess at any given moment the amount of risk you are willing to take and the potential impacts of those risks. And if the impacts of those risks are not just about being scared or about what people are going to say about you, because you're making unconventional relationships, but actually that you are enabling a really nefarious and dangerous set of values and principles and people, then you do need to say no to those things.

"For me, this isn't about catering to the middle," she said. "And it's also not about beating up on the left. It's just a longing that I have for us to be more effective and to actually want to win, really want to win. And be willing to do what we need to in order to get there. And so much of what I think is missing is a smart assessment of the landscape that we're operating in.

"I am somebody who spends a lot of time talking to people who don't eat, sleep, and shit politics every day," Garza continued. "And it's really fascinating the way that people who don't do what I do make their decisions about what they're going to do and what they're not going to do. And a lot of it has to do with 'Does this make sense? Can I see it? Do I think it's possible? And how do you make me feel? Do I trust you?' And a lot of times, I have been in political organizations where it almost functions like a clique as opposed to a place where we win shit." She wondered what it would look like for her own movements to focus more on building that sense of trust, painting that vivid picture of the future they sought, providing the comfort of a welcoming community, not a hard-to-join club.

For Garza, a striking instance was the 2020 Democratic primary. For the first time in memory, there were two seriously progressive candidates in the race in Elizabeth Warren and Bernie Sanders: longtime friends, ideological allies, with some minor and some major differences on policy and philosophy, but profoundly synced on the big questions of the moment. It was, Garza writes, "an important opportunity to defeat the more moderate and conservative candidates in the race." The opportunity was squandered, she says, because

> our movements were energized around Sanders and Warren, but in a way that was insufficient to build power, because that energy was largely focused on ideology rather than base building. Rather than focusing on defeating moderate and conservative candidates by building the largest coalition possible and energizing more voters to turn out—including those who did not consider themselves to be activists or a part of any movement—the left became focused on litmus tests around ideology and labels that were and are largely irrelevant for millions of people who are trying to decide where they are going to place their votes.

In the end, the moderates were able to coalesce, and the progressives were not.

Progressives, Garza said, too often seek out united fronts when, in fact, they should be forging popular fronts. Drawing on Marx, she defines popular fronts as "alliances that come together across a range of political beliefs, for the purpose of achieving a short- to intermediate-term goal, while united fronts are long-term alliances based on the highest level of political alignment." And make no mistake: popular fronts get funky. When Garza and Power allied with the Nation of Islam to beat back gentrification in San Francisco, she relished that group's organizational skills but didn't much enjoy the norm of having to sit on the women's side of the local mosque. So she refused to sit on that side. Popular fronts can require a meticulous avoidance of what will blow up the coalition and a total focus on a singular goal. But there may be a way to respect their rules at the mosque *and* decline to comply.

That progressive movements were struggling with these issues in the first place was a positive development, Garza felt. They had grown more comfortable with calling out injustice and calling out half measures. Now, as the Princeton scholar Keeanga-Yamahtta Taylor has written in *The New Yorker,* "Garza and other organizers are grappling with how to raise a level of accountability while also opening doors to new people who are not schooled in this kind of political culture. They are asking different kinds of questions, such as 'What will it take to expand our ranks and build our movements broadly?' "

Social media made that harder, because it rewarded the hunt for apostates more than the conversion of nonbelievers. Garza observed many of her political allies spending more time online calling out their ideological cousins than the very real enemies of democracy. "Most of what they do is create performance," she said, "and they expose our vulnerabilities, weaknesses, challenges, gripes, grievances, and jealousies to the people who want to use them against us."

What masqueraded as a culture of brave stance taking was, Garza argued, often just showboating. Politicians and other public figures have long put out statements getting themselves on record about the bombing in Kazakhstan or the verdict on that shooting or the death of that singer. But now regular people felt a similar need to register their take on any number of passing events—a kind of democratization of statement making. But, Garza said, "being on record only matters if there are people who depend on you, follow you, need you to be on record. Most of the time, people go on record with no audience. You know what I'm saying? I actually think it's ego. The thing we haven't really addressed on the movement side is, where does ego get in the way? And where does ego force us to cut off our noses to spite our face?

This isn't actually moving anything forward. Going on the record for who, exactly? I find it to be strange. It's another version of creating smaller and smaller circles, when actually what we're trying to do is grow and expand our ranks."

To be clear, Garza said, there was a place for internal criticism in the movement. But, she said, "it works best in the context of an organization where there's shared values and relationships and accountability. And that's not what social media offers." Somehow the culture of taking someone aside or getting on the phone to deal with a minor disagreement had faded, and the reaction expected of people was a public callout—even of people you knew and were friends or colleagues with. "I really long for more organization on our side," Garza told me. "And I don't mean have your pens in one place and pencils in another. I mean people used to meet and talk to each other about shit and hash stuff out.

"Critique is important," she went on. "It can make us sharper. It can make us more effective and better. But criticism is also a skill. It's not just about throwing out the first thing that makes you mad or that you thought about in your mind. It requires skills. The skill to boil it down to the essence and not make shit personal. The ability to make room for growth and assume that growth is possible, and really be grounded in a desire for growth and not just a desire for punishment or revenge. And it requires the ability not only to give it but also to receive it."

Garza had been thinking about how the movements she was in could make themselves more hospitable to people whose political consciousness was new and evolving, who were curious but not committed, and how to welcome them without bartering away one's dignity or wasting energy on people who wouldn't change.

Not long ago, Garza attended a work dinner. The purpose was to bring together frontline activists with wealthy donors to encourage the latter to donate money to the cause and get their many-homed friends to do the same. The softly spoken context of the dinner was that the right-wing machine has abundant support from billionaires and these activists wanted donors on the left to step up and equip them for battle.

At one point in the dinner, one of the wealthy donors, a woman, made a slightly ill-phrased comment that was, Garza recalled, "well intentioned and indicative of someone who is developing their political consciousness." Another attendee "jumped on her and rode her for the entire dinner," she told me. This person called the wealthy donor out and, Garza said, "basically went on to devour her. Running her down for why what she said was wrong and why it has impact."

As the dinner rolled on, the wealthy donor became withdrawn. Eventually, she slipped out. She probably wouldn't come back. "Here was the challenge with that," Garza said. "This woman had generally progressive politics. She has a lot of resources that she wants to give, and she was trying to find a place that she could do that from. So the moral of this story is how you make people feel matters. And sometimes part of our purist culture can be not having room for the waking among the woke. And because of that, we just kind of keep circulating among the woke. Forgetting that the whole point is not to be cliques."

Garza wasn't suggesting letting moments like that go, but rather using them to educate, lovingly but firmly, instead of sending a signal that people should develop their consciousness on their own time and only then show up. "What I've learned in twenty-something years of doing this work is that nobody wakes up super-conscious," she told me. "Everybody who develops a consciousness or a passion about something starts off at a place where they don't know. They don't know what they don't know. It's through the process of being engaged, through the process of being educated, being debated—or even just having compassion for somebody's perspective even if it's something that you disagree with—that's the process that people go through in order to get to a particular place." She worried about "this dismissal of people who are perceived as not being far enough along in their understanding of the thing." Those weren't foes. They were potential allies.

"The only way you get people to a different place is by walking with them," Garza said. "I have never seen an instance where, because somebody was deeply shamed or called names or ignored, they changed their mind. I just haven't. I haven't seen that in my own life, and I certainly haven't seen it in organizing. There is often just a lack of understanding of the methods needed to create change."

That said, it was important to assess who was entrenched and who was open and therefore capable of that kind of growth. "There are some people who are really, deeply committed to what they believe, and you're not going to move them," she said. "It may not be a good use of your time to spend twenty years trying to undo thirty years of conditioning." But others who espoused the same views as the entrenched may be persuadable, because they felt contradictory things on a topic, because their ideas and experiences hadn't yet been arrayed into some definitive meaning. This is where trained organizers dove in.

Garza recalled a woman she met in one of her first organizing projects, knocking on doors in East Oakland, in a heavily working-class, Black, and immigrant community. The campaign was around the relationship between safety and economic security. Garza knocked on the door of a Black woman in the area and got into a conversation about policing.

"Fuck that," Garza remembers the woman responding. "I like police. I think police are good for the community. I have called the police on my own kids when they are acting up and acting crazy. I'm not for anything that is quote-unquote antipolice because I like the police."

The obvious move in that situation might have been to leave. Garza and the woman were pretty much on opposite sides. But Garza decided to dig in. She didn't try to do it all in a day. Rather, she kept coming back. This was not persuasion as a transaction. This was organizing close to home, in the context of a community.

As her visits accumulated, Garza learned more about the woman's life. She learned that the woman's experiences with the police and feelings about them were more complicated than her initial reaction. At the door that first time, she might have sounded to certain ears indistinguishable from rural white police supporters on the far right. But Garza, being anchored in the community and rooted in relationship, knew there might be more going on.

One day, as they spoke, the woman opened up about an episode with the police that still haunted her. Out of nowhere, they blazed into her apartment complex and broke down her door. They raided her home. She had no idea what was going on. It turned out to be a case of mistaken identity. It was traumatizing.

Now, as she spoke, the woman's feelings grew more complex and layered. "What she was telling me was both what she's always been told about police *and* trying to navigate that experience of also having been terrorized by the police," Garza said. "She was telling me, 'I've always been told police keep you safe. When I have a problem in my family, I'm calling the police because they're also supposed to solve problems. Yet they also have created problems for me.'" The woman had had the very kind of run-in with cops that motivated Garza's campaign, but she also had been acculturated in a different story. The organizer's task was to resist the temptation to dismiss the woman, and instead to walk with her and cultivate her dissonance as grist for the persuasive mill.

But the progress that occurred in the story was only possible through sustained organizing anchored in community. Garza first built a relationship strong enough to withstand her mining of the woman's dissonance and her attempt to reconcile it. "The more that we root in relationship, the more that we realize that our ideas about how the world works get shattered by the humanity of people," she said. "That is a fundamental tenet of organizing, and it's a fundamental tenet of how we find room for the waking among the woke."

Though in casual speech she identified as both, here Garza drew a distinction between the organizer and the activist. "As an organizer, you know that your role is to recruit people who may be looking for you, but they don't know it. You become a bridge for people who want to be a part of making change but don't know where to start, don't know how to do it. And they carry with them the problematic ideas that you're trying to change." Their problematic ideas are the whole point.

"An organizer," she continued, "builds a base and understands that in building that base, you're actually bringing together people who may agree on one thing, but they might not agree on a lot of things. Your job is to figure out how to keep those people woven together in order to accomplish a goal. Part of that weaving is making space for the waking among the woke. That's important. That's actually, I think, the locus of change."

An activist, in her definition, focused more on galvanizing in the short term, manufacturing attention-getting moments, marshaling a protest, but then moving on. The goal was more to attract millions of people to an idea or cause than to build connections among them. "An activist's perspective is different," Garza continued. "An activist's perspective is fundamentally individualistic in that they speak to a collective that is wide but not deep. An activist's perspective is necessarily confrontational, but not necessarily visionary or clear about how to bridge the gap between where we are and where we want to be. That's not to throw any shade at people who are not a part of something that's more organized. It's to say that there's a role for it. Cancel culture, to me, is a function of an activist's orientation to movement versus an organizer's orientation to movement."

"Cancel culture," of course, meant different things to different people and to Garza herself. On the one hand, she used it, as above, to speak of the trigger-happiness that she saw among her own cohorts when calling out allies. "There are nice ways to help people make different meaning, and there are ways that maybe are more forceful or aggressive," she said. She wasn't in favor of the kind of "cancel culture" that meant people piling on to people who might potentially evolve if given space to grow. But a lot of the time, she said, "cancel culture" was used as a "euphemism for ideas that are changing and consensus that's being built around them." It used to be more acceptable to be flagrantly racist and sexist and homophobic and transphobic and ableist than it is today. The consensus has moved. New norms have elbowed in. When some spoke of "cancel culture," they were, Garza said, describing "the process of the discomfort that comes with being socialized into a new way of being." If that was cancel culture, sign her up.

These questions became especially thorny for Garza on the subject of white Americans in an era of swelling nationalism and authoritarianism. Garza's work focused on organizing Black people and other people of color, immigrants, and others on the margins of power. I asked her whether and when she found it worth it to try to organize white Americans to beat back the dangerous currents pulling tens of millions of them in.

"If I was going to prioritize being in a struggle with white folks, I'm going to prioritize being in a struggle with white folks who are in struggle," she said. "I'm not going to prioritize somebody sitting in a place I've never heard of watching Fox News and talking about the Blacks and the Mexicans. But some people will do that, and I believe they should be supported." A division of labor.

"With white people, I have a lot of filters," Garza continued. "One of my filters is, what is their level of commitment to these ideas, and what is their relative level of power? I am probably not going to spend a lot of time trying to awaken Mark Zuckerberg. I am probably not going to spend any time on that. The reason for that is because, one, he has endless resources to access to get him on a better page, but, two, he actually materially benefits from his worldview. It's actually how he gets to where he is, in addition to the fact that that worldview also shapes our economy and our politics."

If, instead, we are talking about "a poor white woman who really feels like immigrants are taking her job and taking jobs from this country or a middle-class white woman who knows all the right things to say but does the wrong things," as Garza put it, there was more potential. But another filter entered the picture: Was she actively in relationship with the person in question, as she felt she was knocking on that door in Oakland, or not? "If I'm in relationship to you," she said, "I'm much more willing to struggle with you than I am if you're just a random person who is spouting off at the mouth."

Now she brought up her own story of the Women's March that Linda Sarsour had helped organize, and her own experience of the question of organizing white women and dealing with those conflicts. For Garza, the Women's March was an example of a setting where it *was* worth expending energy and time and frustration to engage with white women still waking up to injustices and oppressions beyond their own as women. Her reasoning was that these women "generally understand inequality conceptually. They understand how they feel unequal relative to men, and they also struggle with their level of understanding of inequity of other people in relationship to them." These white women met Garza's standard of people "waiting to be organized," as she put it. "The way to organize them in my opinion was not to berate them about all the terrible shit they've ever done," she said. "It was to invite them into a home where they could learn about all the terrible shit they've ever done. And also see themselves in common cause with others who have experienced terrible shit and who continue to experience terrible shit."

What Garza recoiled at, she said, was certain suggestions at the time from some fellow activists that "white women just need to come here and shut up and support women of color. I think that that's a reductionist view of power. When I think about reorganizing power, I actually think about reorganizing it. I don't think about just having women of color on top and white women on the bottom. I don't think that that is structural change. It's demographic change. My goal is not to create an elite class of Black people who dominate and oversee white people."

When she walked around the march on January 21, 2017, she saw a sea of women, many of whom felt newly politicized. "It was an entry point for people who were not already politically engaged but maybe had liberal views," she said. "Maybe some of these people even thought that Black Lives Matter was a little too radical for them, right? But, through this angle of electing a fascist dictator, they are able to get exposure to all of these other movements that maybe they were unfamiliar with, maybe they were unsupportive of, but they start to see the connections and relationships between them."

Trump voters and their ilk were another matter, as Garza saw it. And when the Democratic Party, in her view, conflated the persuadability of previously apolitical white women in pussy hats with that of MAGA diehards, it doomed itself: "The strategy that Democrats have employed, which is 'Let's get Trump voters to be Democratic voters'—that seems like a big fucking waste of time to me, because there's no indication in a lot of these cases that there's an awakening happening. There's an indication of entrenchment.

"Maybe a third of this country is going to continue to be extreme, is going to continue to be extremely susceptible to fascist tendencies and desires, and I don't think we need to be spending a lot of time on folk like that," she said. "This notion that everybody has to come along is completely ridiculous. Sometimes you've got to cut your losses and move on to the person who still has questions.

"I am spending time these days trying to figure out in a real way who is actually persuadable," she said, "who is trying to make sense of what's going on right now and trying to figure out how to make their lives better for real, for real, not in a fantasyland. Those are the people that I'm going to spend my time on."

Garza was also thinking about language in the movement. The struggles she belonged to had, happily, become blunter, and movement terminology—"white supremacy," "patriarchy," "prison abolition"—had moved into the mainstream. But she sometimes felt that these breakthroughs risked lulling activists into a false sense of being understood.

"The term 'white supremacy' is much more mainstream now than it ever was in my lifetime," she said. "And that doesn't mean people know what it means. Just because someone's saying 'white supremacy' on CNN doesn't mean they're using it correctly."

The practical question is whether you use a term like that with less politically conscious audiences. Is it worth the risk? And here Garza made a distinction: do change your language for comprehension, but don't change it merely for comfort. "I might not use the term 'white supremacy' with somebody who I'm quite sure has never heard those words before," she said. "But I would not *not* talk about white supremacy to white people because it makes them uncomfortable. Not using the term 'white supremacy' with white people because it turns them off defeats the whole fucking purpose of fighting this shit in the first place." She was wary of those who treat "message effectiveness" as "a substitution for having uncomfortable conversations."

Tempering language to be understood mattered especially in the electoral context, and here Garza had a further concern. She empathized with the bottom-up approach taken by many in movements now, the aversion many of her allies had to working inside the electoral process. She wanted to hold on to some of that rebellious spirit and iconoclasm, even as she would tell anyone who listened that elective politics is where the power is, and if you're not there, you're not building durable power.

She wasn't lecturing kids not to protest. She was one of America's leading protest orchestrators. But she aspired for the movements she belonged to to have a savvier relationship to power and to translating rage into programs. In her memoir, she engages in clear-eyed reflection about the early days of Black Lives Matter, musing about what might have been had she and her peers had a clearer set of demands to bring to meetings with leaders like Hillary Clinton. "We have to protest," she writes, "and we also have to step in to lead and govern."

"People are afraid that engagement means you're watering down your values or your position," she said. "That's not what it means at all. If my landlord won't fix things in my house, it does nothing for me not to engage my landlord. If I'm employing a range of strategies to try to convince them to fix my house, that's beneficial to me. If it doesn't work, it doesn't work. It doesn't mean that my values have changed. I mean, I'm trying to get something done so my roof isn't leaking."

Even when the movement left did engage with electoral politics and pursue this kind of power, Garza said, it often fell short of the right at a crucial element of persuasion—giving citizens more than arguments from reason, providing a kind of emotional shelter. "People want to find a place that they call home," she told me. "Home for a lot of people means a place where you can feel safe and a place where someone is caring for your needs. In a political sense, when we look at the infrastructure that the right has built, I think we see lots of political homes. We see homes on university campuses where the question of who's to blame for the anger and disillusionment that you feel gets answered in different ways. We see homes in places like churches and religious institutions that end up taking political positions and aligning it with a message of duty or destiny. We also see it in the organizing that the right has done in communities. They do a very good job of making people feel like they can be a part of something.

"The right deeply understands people," Garza continued. "It gives them a reason for being, and it gives them answers to the question of why am I suffering? On the left, we think a lot about facts and figures and logic that we hope will change people's minds. I think what's real is actually much closer to Black feminist thinkers who have said things like 'People will forget what you said, people will forget what you did, but people will never forget how you made them feel.'"

2

CAN LOVE CHANGE A MIND?

In a seminar room on a farm in rural Ohio, the race trainers took the floor. Erica and Adele ran workshops on diversity, equity, and inclusion. They consulted for organizations, often teaching overwhelmingly white audiences to become aware of privilege, open up systems, and gain visibility into blind spots. They were somewhere along the continuum between activists and coaches, persuading people to rethink their identities and choices.

Erica, who is Black, told the group, seated at rows of desks, that she had dreamed of being a public relations mogul before ending up in the field of racial training. She was wearing a T-shirt with the names of unarmed Black people killed by the police. As she introduced herself, she said she was happy to be among this particular group—a collection of white parents who had adopted children of color, most of them Black—because she believed they played a special role in society. "At the same time you're living in your privilege, you are uniquely positioned to have a bird's-eye view into the challenges associated with being in a Black body," she said. Then Adele, who is white, introduced herself. After her name, she said, "And I have the honor and privilege of being here thanks to waking up to my own whiteness."

The demand for race trainers had been exploding in recent years. The trainers played a curious role, hired to come in and make people feel uncomfortable, for a fee. This was their métier—the careful fostering of discomfort. Throughout the seminar at the farm, they would repeat the mantra of discomfort. Adele: "Growth is uncomfortable."

Erica: "A comfort zone is a beautiful place, but nothing ever grows there, right? So it is going to be uncomfortable and it is going to be hard, and you can't quit because it got hard." Discomfort was vital to their persuasive method.

And in the particular case of these parents, the trainers said, the discomfort had a payoff, if the parents were willing to stomach it. "You're in a really unique position as white folks who walk in the world with whiteness, with children who walk in the world very differently than you do," Adele said. "And so we want you to really use your privilege to take action in a way that has some urgency underneath it, given where the world is right now." In Adele's vision, these white parents of children of color could be some kind of vanguard for racial progress, propelled by the fuel of family love.

And yet, this pair of professional persuaders warned, change would indeed be hard. Erica provided a sobering statistic to that effect. After people got heart attacks and were told to change their diet, only a small fraction were able to. So here the parents were being told that the country—which was plunging ever deeper into political crisis, a crisis driven in great measure by white backlash to racial progress—needed these parents to change in order to show that it could change, even as they were being told that change is so hard that people were usually incapable of doing it even to stay alive.

In their own ways, Linda Sarsour, Loretta Ross, and Alicia Garza had spoken of where white America fit into their visions of change. As activists, they sought more than attitude shifts; they worked toward new laws, structures, material conditions. But they had no choice but to think and strategize about resistance their movements met from white Americans wary of the future they sought—resistance that could take the form of electoral backlash, flare-ups at school board meetings, even the picking up of arms. Was it possible, they wondered in their respective ways, to persuade some white people, who still constituted the majority of Americans, to be part of a change that would decenter them? I had traveled to this farm in Wakeman, Ohio, to witness the difficulty of changing minds on race and privilege, even among those who profess a desire to be changed.

The Transracial Journeys Family Camp had been founded several years earlier by a woman named Barbara, a white mother of two adopted Black children. She and her husband, Marshall, were well-meaning white liberals who knew a lot of other well-meaning white liberals. But parenthood offered reminder after reminder of what they and their kids were up against, in the hostility of the outside world and in their own limitations. When Marshall crossed the street to avoid an oncoming Black pedestrian, only to realize he was carrying his Black son on his shoulders; when he and Barbara failed to notice for the longest time that the white kids on the playground had chosen their child to throw sand at; when flight attendants, seeing the kids misbehave, barked, "Who's the parent?" until realizing that the parents were white—in these and a hundred other moments, they came to accept that they would need help raising Black children well as white parents.

When they still lived on the West Coast, Barbara found a local camp for transracial adoptive families. The camp offered trainings, workshops, placement, and various other services, and it was guided by a particular doctrine: the perspective of adopted children of color had been all but ignored in the past, and now it ought to be centered. Barbara generally enjoyed the sessions, but sometimes she recoiled at what she saw as a political agenda. One session you were getting parenting tips, and the next you were being told that white people are inevitably complicit in white supremacy. "The tone and tenor of those conversations was sometimes a callout culture, not call-in culture," Barbara told me.

When Barbara and Marshall moved to Ohio, she couldn't find a similar camp. She started her own. From the start, she wanted Transracial Journeys to offer a better balance, from her standpoint, between calling out and calling in. "Our camp was always designed to be more inclusive while also educating," Barbara said. She paused for a moment. "The criticism of that would be we're just trying to educate people within their comfort zone." Like a growing number of white Americans, Barbara claimed to believe white supremacy had to be broken down if children like hers, and the country itself, were to thrive. But she had strong feelings about how this change should occur, how it should address her, how it should bring her along. Barbara also said she knew that letting white wariness set the rate of racial progress is precisely what had kept things the way they were for so long. Barbara believed these contending things, although balancing them at the camp was no longer her responsibility.

A couple of years earlier, Transracial Journeys had undergone the transition so many start-ups do to new leadership not present at the founding. But Barbara's successor, April Dinwoodie, represented more than just a new generation of management. April is Black and a transracial adoptee herself. The camp was now run by someone whose experience of the question at hand was from the vantage point of the children of color at the camp, not of the white parents. Her motivation, April said openly, was to avenge the wrongs of her own childhood, but for the benefit of today's kids.

April had grown up in the lily-white town of Westerly, Rhode Island, the lone Black child and lone adoptee among her family's four children. She often told groups of parents like this one that her parents' sin hadn't been overt racism. It was, rather, their blindness to difference. They didn't think of her as "less than," in her experience. They just didn't think about race at all. They watched *Hee Haw* and listened to Fleetwood Mac and Engelbert Humperdinck and John Denver. In high school, her peers would ask, "April, can you break-dance?" "Can you do the moonwalk like Michael Jackson?" And she began to realize the difference between how the world perceived her and how she had been raised. When certain R&B songs came up, she would pretend she knew what everyone was talking about. "We ate white food—shepherd's pie and just regular white-people food," April said. "There was no Black culture. They adopted me and kept doing white things." It never occurred to her parents that maybe they should take her to a Black church from time to time, not just their overwhelmingly white Presbyterian one. When April took longer than everyone else in the shower, the family's preferred brand of Breck or Prell shampoo taking forever to come out of the thick coils of dark hair for which they were ill-suited, April recalled, "they'd be like, 'Why you taking such a long shower?' They had no clue."

April came up during the heyday of a once-influential mantra given to white parents who adopted children of color: "Love is enough." "My parents' whole philosophy was just, 'We'll just love her. She'll be part of our family,'" she said. "There was no conscious thinking about raising a kid that was a different race or that was adopted. They just put me into the fold."

But in recent years, as the country reckoned with race and white domination in ways big and small, the world of transracial adoption had experienced its own upheavals, not unrelated to those broader shifts. Transracial adoptees had published memoirs of their misery growing up in a false color blindness that was really just whitewashing. Activists had pushed successfully for changes to international treaties and domestic laws, to require parents adopting transracially to receive some basic education on race. Researchers had published heartbreaking studies of what so many transracial adoptees went through, feeling cut off from themselves, wishing they were white.

April, now in her forties, had been too old to benefit from this turning as it happened, but now she had the chance to help another generation of adoptees get what she hadn't. So in addition to the workshop on hair care that weekend, and the family meals and games and evening shows, April had made sure the parents got this experience of sitting in a seminar and being guided through the idea that simply doing nothing, loving their kids and ignoring race, wasn't good enough given the realities of the racist systems that encircled them. If they wanted to be good parents, they needed to change how they thought of race and how they lived.

Before the trainers had gotten started, April had tried to put a positive spin on what was being asked of the parents. "I just think what inspires me the most," she said, "is knowing that if my parents did have this, I might be president." The parents laughed. "If I'm doing okay and my parents didn't have any of this, imagine how your kids might be."

As Erica and Adele worked the seminar room, the parents responded with various levels of agreement and defensiveness, engagement and dejection. Over that weekend, I took several of them aside to try to learn what had brought them to seek this intervention and how they experienced the attempt to convince them of avowedly uncomfortable ideas about race. Even as the country engaged in shrill arguments about the content of racial trainings like these, I was interested in how a group of people who had signed up for edification on these subjects both accepted and resisted ideas that asked them to account for their identities in often painful, destabilizing ways.

Joan was a longtime Republican political operative from Michigan. She spoke in the well-worn rightist dialect of economic freedom and low taxes and excessive regulation, though she claimed to find Donald Trump a bridge too far. Her up-by-the-bootstraps ideology was vital to her, immovable even in the face of all the contrary reality she had confronted raising her Black son.

She had come to camp because parenting Mikey made her aware of limitations, doubts, and blind spots she had on race. She confessed that she had never realized how white her neighborhood was until she had to fill out the adoption paperwork asking that question. She had put him in a mostly white school at first, only to realize that it would probably be good for him to be around some people who looked like him. When she switched him, he suddenly thrived. "He came home the first day listing every Black kid," she said. When she took him to a swimming class at the YMCA with mostly Black children and was confused about whether to let a Black teacher throw Mikey into the pool as a teaching tool, or whether to overrule as a mother who felt it wouldn't work on him, she felt profoundly confused about her position.

"I came here this year knowing I'm going to sob the whole freaking time, because I have now realized everything I don't know," Joan told me. She had become someone April, Erica, and Adele could work with: a person with questions. Yet she was also someone with deep ideological commitments that seemed to rein in her answers.

I asked if her growing awareness of the structural barriers Mikey was up against had altered her politics of rugged individualism in any way.

As if to avoid the subject of race that I was raising, she spoke of her white Jewish grandfather. His family had come from Europe with little. He became a truck driver. He bought his own truck, then a second truck. Before long, he had a business. Like her son, she said, he faced prejudice—in his case, as a Jew. But her point was he overcame it. He got a contract from no lesser anti-Semite than Henry Ford, she said, "because he basically camped out at his office and said, 'I'm the best one to do this. I'm going to be here every day, and at some point you're going to give me the contract.'"

But had Mikey revealed any limits to the philosophy that anyone can defy anything? Had raising him shaken any of Joan's assumptions?

She said that his treatment in school had made her realize that the playing field wouldn't be level for him. Even in the more diverse new school, a teacher seemed to dislike Mikey, kept confusing him with the other Black student in class. But when I asked where her experiences with schools had left Joan, she quickly pivoted from mistreatment to a statement of ideology that seemed to disappear any lessons from the experience.

"I believe he can do and be anything, but he's going to have to try harder, and he is going to have to be so above contempt in any regard," she said. "I mean, he is going to have to be Caesar's wife." A moment later, she added, "The reaction to something not being fair isn't to level the playing ground. It's to rise to what it is and fight harder."

It was hard for Joan to let go of her worldview, in spite of Mikey. She was experiencing the dissonance of someone who had come to camp seeking to change herself but who also had a deep investment in not changing. She tried to explain what she was saying another way. "I come from a family where the story of Anne Frank was not revered," Joan said. "Well, by my father. My father always said to us, 'I'm sure Anne Frank was a lovely girl, and she wrote a very nice diary. But her family hid. And what about the families who fought?' That's the perspective I grew up in. That all the Jews walked in straight lines onto the trains. There were a few guards. What if a couple of people took out a guard? What if they didn't walk in a straight line? What if they acted differently from the society around them and effected major change? We have to be the people who fight."

Freddy's problem was different. He was attending as the grandfather of two adopted Black children. He caught my ear when he talked about his difficulties in peeling back the layers of his own privilege. He was a ruggedly built white man in his seventies, maybe, wearing a firefighter's T-shirt. He wasn't the stereotypical privilege-checking type.

He had worked for thirty-three years as a firefighter in Cleveland—"a fairly strongly racist environment," he says. Before his grandchildren arrived, he didn't know what white privilege was. When a topic like that came up, Freddy says, "I did the typical resistance/not-me thing."

That wall actually started to crack before the children came. Partway through his career as a firefighter, Freddy had gone back to school, completed a doctorate in psychology, and become a psychotherapist at the Cleveland Clinic. He specialized in treating first responders. And he had joined a men's emotional literacy organization called the ManKind Project. In discussion groups, some of the Black men had called out their white peers, saying they needed to go deeper on race, to educate themselves. Freddy took that to heart and tried. So when two adopted Black grandchildren came into his life, he felt he already had some resources available to him to do right by them.

But he, too, realized after a time that love wasn't enough, nor was his rudimentary racial education. There were in his case, too, incidents on the playground he failed to notice, episodes of possible racial bullying undetected. There was the jolt when it occurred to him that his grandchildren would have to be taught a different way of interacting with police than their relatives exhibited.

Unlike for Joan, this budding racial awareness, this sense of what he didn't know and couldn't see, didn't repel Freddy. He found himself interested in this newfound sense of his limitations. But it drove him into a deep sadness, a real low point. It fostered a kind of paralysis. He started to feel as if he were as trapped in his privilege as others were trapped in oppression. Though it is surely easier to escape the former than the latter, he felt stuck.

"I came to this moment of 'Fuck, I'm never going to be any different,'" he told me. He was stuck "being a white guy trapped in this fabric of entitlement and privilege. When I came to that understanding, it horrified me." It was another flavor of dissonance: knowing that one had to change, and being debilitated by that knowledge. "Just because I don't like it, and I realize how unhealthy and dysfunctional it is, when everything around me is about white privilege, where do I go?" he asked. He agreed that everything needed to change, but he had grown fatalistic about his ability to be part of that change. The pain Freddy felt in "swimming in an ocean of privilege," as he put it, had come to be its own avenue of evasion.

Then there was Roger, a father who came up to me one evening after the sessions, wearing flip-flops and a backpack. He used a striking word to describe his experience at the camp over the years. He felt he was being "radicalized" here. But he meant it in a good way. He thought Barbara, and now April, had used the basic hunger parents had for tips and tricks to smuggle in a political agenda—one that he had come around to appreciating.

"If you talk to Barbara, I think she does see this as a reeducation," Roger said. The word took me aback, especially given that Barbara conceived of the camp as a break from the California camp's calling out. What he meant was that the camp was "an extension of an overall human rights issue" for some of the founders and the parents who attended. Roger recalled some of those moments that had jarred him at first and then educated him: "Having people come in and teach us how to call out and attack racism in the workplace. How to call people out for microaggressions. How to take stances, how to be the one intervening if you're in a grocery store and someone's being yelled at because they're being called a Muslim when they're a Sikh or whatever. Of just stepping in, of going to marches."

Roger said the camp gave him a productive discomfort that was changing his values, changing how he lived, forcing a greater consistency. It was, he said, why he came to camp: "to challenge those aspects of ourselves that are still kind of hiding in that safety of white privilege."

But then he brought up his father-in-law. "My father-in-law is the kind of person who is like, 'The white male is the most under-threat person in the country,'" Roger said. The things Roger had come to appreciate, his father-in-law saw as the unraveling of the country. So how did Roger think about the task of persuading someone like his father-in-law, who didn't have what he had—a Black child in his home—to change his mind?

It was a challenge he and his wife thought about often, he said. He put it this way: "We're woke. How do we wake them up without going too fast?" What he meant was that he saw some risk in him and his wife changing too quickly, drinking camp Kool-Aid, acquiring the new antiracist terms, and then being so far ahead of everyone in their community not in their situation that the gulf became too forbidding to cross. What if he and his wife became vanguards of a new way and left others in their social world behind, or even turned them off and drove them toward those who told them they were great as they are and that the efforts to change them were the issue?

In his worry about his father-in-law, Roger pointed toward another source of resistance for those who would change minds on race: By his own account, Roger was totally down, persuaded by the imperative to change. But he wanted you to consider that, just over there in the distance, were people not as down as he, and that you might want to slow progress down lest you lose them.

Then there was Kurt, who thought of himself as embodying the great hope of the experiment Barbara had started many years ago. He was one of her first campers. At the time, he and his wife were like Barbara and Marshall—the white parents of an adopted Black child. Kurt hadn't thought a lot about race before camp, as many white people have not. In raising his daughter, his goal was less nurturing her identity development than not being his own dad. "It was probably driven by my story of my dad being twice divorced, and growing up with that," Kurt told me. "I wanted financial security in my family. Number one reason for divorce is financial issues. I'm like, I'm not going to let this stuff happen in my family. So I was chasing really hard at those things."

That first camp hit him hard. The program dealt with systemic racism and the breadth of what Black and brown people faced in America. "I didn't feel called out," Kurt said, "but I definitely felt like an idiot. I felt like I should have known more already, and shame on me. And I felt incredible guilt, I guess, of sort of being in the white male category."

Kurt's family had come back every year since. In the second or third year, some trainers came in from Cleveland and did an exercise. The parents stood side by side. They were asked about their background, and if a statement was true for them, they were to step forward or backward as the case may be. Did you have two parents growing up? Did your family have financial trouble? After twenty or so questions, there was a lot of dispersal. Kurt ended up right up front, beside one other man.

It was just an exercise, but it shattered Kurt. "We had a breakout session afterward, and I remember the emotions coming up in me, because I always felt like I just worked really hard to get where I'm at. So it's hard for me to accept that, yeah, I worked hard, but I was also advantaged." It was "just a shock," he said. He felt he had lost an idea of himself. He had thought he was what he was now realizing he wasn't: a self-made man, a product of merit, not a man given a leg up. "I went from oblivious to denial to a little bit of shame and guilt," he said. "Maybe I wasn't so special, and maybe I'm part of this category that helped create this."

Kurt's initial reaction was avoidance. To acknowledge all that he had not seen before was to surrender the right to look away, and in those first years Kurt didn't feel he had space to add the pursuit of racial justice to his plate. "It was like, wait a second, I haven't done anything wrong. I've worked hard, I've done stuff. I want to keep doing that for my family. So if I take time to try and help over here, I'm sacrificing something else." That was a sacrifice he felt unwilling to make.

By the time I met Kurt, it was his seventh year at camp. He and his wife had since adopted a second child, who is also Black. He had become chair of the board of Transracial Journeys and a mentor to many of the white parents. In the seminar room, he hovered in the back, looking out over people who he said reminded him of the defensive, blinkered man he had been, ready to tell anyone who would listen that he knew what they felt, he had felt it, too, but he knew, and they should know, that it was possible to change, to surrender an idea of yourself, and that you might find things to replace it.

In the seminar room, Erica and Adele were moving past the pleasantries. Adele was offering the parents a definition of racism that was on the rise in the culture but might have struck many of them as provocative: racism is a system that ensnares everyone in the society, more than just an individual act that takes place at a discrete moment. And a corollary: it is impossible to be free from racism if you are white, socialized by this society. In recent years, the idea had been popularized by writers like Robin DiAngelo and Ibram Kendi. But now Adele added another idea to the mix, to make the callout more of a call in. She turned to the language of pop science and pop psychology—with an emphasis on pop. She told the parents thoughts lead to feelings, which lead to actions, which lead to results. Erica added that stereotypes lead to prejudice, which leads to discrimination. "The thoughts are happening in the mind, and the feelings are happening in the body," Adele said. Our subconscious thoughts form our "paradigm." And it is really our paradigm that is racist.

What the deployment of dubious scientific language did in situations like this was soften the blame the audience might feel. It was a way to be both more sweeping—all white people are racist because they have been raised in a racist paradigm—while toning down the charge, because racism wasn't a choice; it was the air we breathe in the United States of America. *I'm not racist. The atmosphere is racist.* Racism in this account became more ubiquitous, more unshakable, but less malicious. It wasn't a sin. It was a culture, a structure, a regime.

"This is why I refer to myself as a recovering racist," Adele said. "Because I've walked in the world as a white woman, and I grew up in this country. There is no way that this paradigm is not living in my subconscious."

Erica noted that white people often rebutted the charge of racism by invoking their personal goodness. But it is possible to be a good person and racist, Adele argued. "We can consciously say we're a good person and have been working on these things, and that does not always mean on our subconscious level that we are not holding beliefs that have been programmed into us," she said. It was important, according to Adele, to hold two rival truths in one's head: "I did not create this system," and "I'm responsible, moving forward, for the way in which I show up and the impact that I can make." It wasn't enough to be against the idea of racism, because the system you were caught up in was racist. You had to be actively devoted to purging racism from your system to be an antiracist.

Erica and Adele opened it up for Q&A. A white parent named Megan, sitting up front, wearing a T-shirt that said, "White silence equals white consent," lavished praise on Adele for describing herself as a "recovering racist." "I want to say that I just had a completely blown-away moment," Megan said. "As a single mom, being my son's champion, I mean he's the love of my life. And his biggest fan is a recovering racist. I finally figured it out." Megan was embracing this notion of being actively antiracist. It gave her strength to think of herself as a recovering racist. She could hold that idea alongside the idea that she would do anything for her son.

But it wasn't so easy for everyone. In the back of the room, one of the fathers, Dave, now piped up: "Can I share a dissenting view?"

"So I'm having a hard time not shutting down with this whole conversation," he said. He wanted everyone to know up front that he didn't have a problem with the idea of the paradigm and of racism as a social system. "But, for me, it's very difficult to remain open to the conversation when the starting point is 'You're a racist.' And I appreciate what you said about blame. But when you start by saying, 'I'm a recovering racist,' and you throw that word around, these words are very powerful. And when you start by basically saying, 'You're a racist, and we need to fix you—' "

"Did I say that?" Adele asked. Pin-drop silence in the room.

"I think it's implied when you say you're a recovering racist because you, to me, seem to be someone who's very thoughtful and has been working on this quite a bit," Dave said. "You, I would have to say, probably are more woke than I am. So starting with that doesn't give me much encouragement to engage."

Now Dave made a version of the argument Roger had made about his father-in-law, a profession of agreement undercut by concern about winning over other people: "We've got a group of very open-minded, progressive people in this group. I can only imagine, if you were presenting this information to people who are a little more to the center or even to the right of the center, how they would react to this. I know you want us to be advocates and agents of change, but there are people we need to get to, and this message would not go over well with them, in my opinion."

Dave was raising an objection of hearability, rooted less, supposedly, in his own ability to hear and more in the fear that if he feels X, imagine how Y over there will feel, imagine how hard it will be for these important ideas to spread.

Adele at first commended Dave for being "courageous to speak your truth." Doing so, she said, is "a really, really heartful place to stand." She had heard this feeling before. "This is where we will dissent from your closing comment: we do not believe in converting people," Adele said. "Our work is with the willing."

Erica chimed in now: "It is not that that is not work to be done. It is that it is not our work."

"We're clear," Adele says, "that that's not our work."

Erica now explained why converting white people skeptical of these ideas wasn't for them. "I will submit to you that our biggest challenge is not the people that are making the news every day," she said, referring obliquely to the white nationalist president then in the White House and his followers. "I saw somebody's T-shirt: 'White silence equals white consent.' " She looked over at Megan. "I think the bigger challenge is the people who believe that this is important and are not acting. Not actively doing something."

Erica knew some might hear this and say she and Adele were, therefore, just preaching to the choir. "When people say this is a choir," she said with a laugh, "it's like, have you *been* in a choir? A choir is a hot mess, okay? Like there's a lot going on in the choir that needs to be addressed."

Another comment from the back. It was Marlene, who was the aunt of an adoptee and lived in Tampa.

"You talk about language as power," she said. "If you don't want to call a slave owner a 'master,' then do you want to call a white person 'racist'? If they're trying to be good and they believe they're good and they're open-minded and they're working on paying attention . . . I think words have power, too. If you say I'm a racist, I don't believe I'm racist. Do I understand what it's like to be Black? Do I understand what it's like to live in your world? I don't. And that's part of the reason I'm here. I want to understand, but I'm not a racist."

"Adele called herself a racist, not you," Erica said.

"But if you say, 'I'm a recovering racist,' then are you implying that because we don't know what we don't know . . ."

Adele tried to appease her. For years, she had been using this language of "recovering racist." But recently she had taken to saying "I'm recovering from racism," recovering from a system that ensnared her. Maybe, Adele told Marlene, she should have put it that way.

Then Adele said something else, to answer Dave's concern about changing the minds of those even more resistant than these parents. There is an institute in Colorado that has done work on "consciousness shift," she said. Apparently, it takes only 3 percent of the population changing to catalyze change in a society. That's because, she says, "emotions have literally a mathematical, vibrational, quantifiable frequency." And, apparently, love is at a frequency of 500 megahertz and fear, 100 megahertz. "Essentially, love is five times as powerful, mathematically speaking. So it only takes a small number of people—that's what the theory is—to facilitate a great shift."

I was less than confident in the science Adele was presenting, but the trainers' sociological theory was on firmer ground. They believed, as they had said earlier, that the country needed to change and that these parents, with their experience of being white but loving their children of color, had a special opportunity to help change it. They also had a motivation to "do the work," to "get uncomfortable," that most Americans would never have. This was a room full of white people who probably would never subject themselves to this exercise but for the love of their own children. And this was, in Adele's telling, enough, because these parents could be a vanguard for change. They could be part of that 3 percent of Americans who change the 97 percent. Their love, throbbing at 500 megahertz, would out-throb fear—and, perhaps, self-interest.

Now Kurt, the veteran of the camp, hovering at the back, interjected. "I'm sorry. I'm going to take some of my white male privilege and try to be the last one to go," he said, causing a ripple of laughter.

He wanted to address Dave's misgivings, to say I was once like you, and then I changed. "I woke up. I'm at the top of the food chain, top of the system. Took me a while to awaken to that. It was a ton of bricks when it hit. And I was very defensive." He felt Dave had a point: people beyond this room who don't have the vested interest of a child they love are, he said, "going to get defensive right away, and that term 'racist' will get them there."

"But," he went on, "in this room I also see white males in the system, and we actually, unfortunately, probably are the ones who, at a broader scale, are going to be the ones to actually change the system, because white males who are likely to feel shut down will not listen to Erica, probably, might not listen to April. They will listen to us." He was making a case for antiracist ideas while taking it for granted that people will probably listen only to guys like him for the time being. He was walking a fine line between ally and savior.

He told Dave and the other parents that the camp had changed him. After several years, he had begun to see what he had not before. Nowadays, when he was in a meeting and everyone was a white man, it bothered him as it didn't used to. As with Megan and her "White silence equals white consent" T-shirt, for some in this room antiracism could be taken up not as a threat but as a new way of life. Though it implied a certain loss of status, a surrender of power, the sharing of resources, it could also be, for some white people, its own new kind of status currency, a life-giving project, and a deeply American kind of self-reinvention.

Kurt said he knew most people in his place did not feel as he did. Not Dave, who would be part of your racial progress on the condition that you exempt him from any blame for the status quo. Not Marlene, who was happy to learn some tips and tricks but thought the term "racist" was as pernicious as "master." Not Joan, who loved her son but whose love for him wasn't enough to shatter her well-worn narratives about justice and success. Not Freddy, who, like Kurt, did not shy away from the idea of needing to grow but had been paralyzed by the immensity of the task.

Kurt kept asking what it would take to change these parents' minds. At times, the asking of that question became its own brake on progress.

A year after camp, amid the Black Lives Matter protests of the summer of 2020, I received a text message from Kurt:

> Anand, it may have taken me years but I've finally accepted that I need to even do more! Silence is oppression. Can white male America awake and change? I hope so. I'd at least like to see a dent made in my lifetime. I've never been the social media posting type other than fun fam pics. That changed this week. I'm aiming my messages at White Males. I'm approaching from a place of love, faith, and hope. White males collectively need to (1) wake up, (2) understand and be approached that it is looooong systematic and almost unnoticeable to them most days, as to not just shut down immediately and open their minds to their inherent biases and (3) commit that we need to do better. The

last one will require white males to give up (at least some to be realistic) their collective advantage in the system to correct it towards equality. That will be the most challenging of the 3 steps. If you follow me on FB, I would love your feedback on anything I post or others do especially if I unintentionally and mistakenly say something stupid 😳. I'm not used to posting like this so will be a journey. God called me to do it though and it is no longer a choice.

A few days earlier, the country had been convulsed by the revelation of yet another gruesome instance of the persistence of white supremacy up and down the system. Ahmaud Arbery, a twenty-five-year-old unarmed Black man, had been shot and killed while jogging after being chased by three white men in a town in southern Georgia. The case had flipped a switch for Kurt. He wanted to speak out more. I went to his Facebook page to see the post about which he seemed both proud and nervous. It read,

I wept. I mourned. I prayed. Ahmaud Arbery, you didn't deserve it. Countless others before him didn't deserve it. I weep for the family. I weep for this country. I weep for my children. We can do better.

We all should strive to embrace faith, hope and love at all times and in everything. Love, Love, Love the most important. No one is perfect. We all struggle to apply these.

Yet, I can see why many Black Americans could exponentially and often struggle with constant anxiety wondering "when will we (collectively) feel the love?" The painbodies are strong, deep, loooong rooted, and constantly fed to constantly remind. Faith and hope constantly shaken and tested.

The system in which we live was built unfortunately to perpetuate bias so ingeniously that it often isn't even noticed by those doing it . . . we can do better. We need to do better.

After reading Kurt's text message, I had been expecting something more strident, more pointed. A few days later, I talked to him about it. I asked about his goal. He said there was a segment of white men—the ones who at that moment were showing up at state capitols across the country wielding guns, urging reopening after the pandemic closures—whom Kurt figured he couldn't reach. The people he was targeting were more moderate guys "who have already awoken a bit. They realize they have privilege, they realize there's an issue that's systematic. They just maybe are living their lives, and they're not necessarily figuring out how can they help."

The advantage Kurt thought he brought to this work was the memory of what it had felt like to encounter these challenges for the first time and have your defenses go up and babble all the usual things: *I'm successful because I've worked hard. Do we really want to punish success in this country? You don't need to pull me down to lift others up. It's bringing up race that is racist!* He thought he knew how to answer these talking points and reflexes. That was one way of explaining the gap between how he felt about his Facebook post and the text of the post itself. "I think I'm trying to do it in a somewhat subtle way and a way for that audience to process it," he said.

Yet in attending to white people's defensiveness, in making sure not to shut them down, Kurt diluted his message. The comments on his post were revealing on that score:

> "Totally agree. Love you."
>
> "Though many gains have been made, we have so far to go. Thanks, Kurt, for your wisdom. Sadly we have stepped backward rather than forward. I respect you."
>
> "so true 🖤"
>
> "Well thought and written, completely agree. So disheartening. We can do better 🖤🙏 love you, thank you for sharing."
>
> "Such a sad story . . . truly hope justice prevails!"

It was a parade of white innocence. Friends and family commenting on the beauty of his post, on the sadness of it all, on their broken hearts, without any sense of being involved—not them, not their vanilla suburbs and schools and company boards, not their political preferences—and a great deal of sentiment about Kurt himself, with little recognition of all the ways in which Ahmaud Arbery's death implicated their own privileges and immunities in American life.

One comment in response to Kurt's post took a different tone, however, and it was from a Black friend of his. "Justice has already failed," wrote Blake, a race educator and a transracial adoptee himself whom Kurt had connected with through Transracial Journeys.

> 2 men hunted and killed a man and went home and slept in their beds, deleted all social media and went on with their lives as if nothing happened.
>
> I am doubtful they will be indicted. We've been here before and we will be here again because we allow this injustice instead of shouting from the roof tops that this life mattered.
>
> The change will only come when we put action to outrage. Just as we needed ALL to chip in for civil rights changes we need that type of movement NOW!

On Facebook, Kurt praised Blake's "passion." But Blake's comment bothered Kurt. "I had texted him before," Kurt told me. "I said, 'Hey, man, I don't usually do this, but I kind of feel a need here to speak up a little more, and I don't know how I'm going to do it, but I'm going to approach it from love, faith and hope.'" Blake had promised to engage with the message to help it spread. Then Kurt saw his comment. "If you saw his reply, it was just like, 'No, we need action; we need to rise now. We need to march on Washington.' And, at first, I'm like, 'Well, you could give me a softball here on my first post around this.'"

Kurt's memory of Blake's reply was an exaggerated likeness of the original. When I asked what put him off about it, the discomfort seemed to be on two levels, one easier to speak of than the other. Kurt framed his reaction as strategic. He was afraid that Blake's "change and rise up" message, as he put it, would drive white people away.

"They're like, 'Whoa, wait, what have I done wrong? Why are you rising up against me?' It doesn't resonate as much. It'll shut them down."

But the sensibility Blake was violating was also Kurt's own. Kurt had positioned himself as a moderate white man making a case for going slow on the road to justice as a way of running interference for Black America. But Blake's post showed how that very position meant that his people, not white people, kept getting blocked and tackled, with fatal consequences.

I asked how Kurt had developed his ideas about how to change minds to change larger systems, and a surprising answer emerged: his work in sales. He had honed his approach on dentists. He worked for a big company that took over small dental practices and consolidated their back offices—functions like accounting and scheduling. The dental profession tended to be entrepreneurial, with thousands of small practices across the nation.

When he started out, Kurt said, he typically came on strong and couldn't understand why many dentists never called him back. Over time, he came to see that he was asking the dentists to do something more complicated than he had understood at first. He was asking them to undergo not just a business change but also a change of identity. Asking them to let go of one story of who they are and try on another. He began to lead with questions about their ideas of themselves and long-term goals beyond the job. He began to manage the psychological shift he was asking dentists to make.

This new understanding demanded slowness, he concluded. It could take a year or two after the initial contact for a dentist to bite. Kurt came to conceive of that period as a time of mourning. For the dentists who went for it, it was a savvy business decision they had chosen. But it was also a kind of death. "Think of it as a grieving process," he said.

"It's like they've lost something," he added a moment later, "or they realize they need to lose something." And this brought him to what he had been trying to say: the dentists were like white males, like him that first time he did that step-forward exercise and realized how many advantages he had had and felt ashamed and angry and defensive and unmoored. "It was kind of a grieving, emotional moment," Kurt said.

The approach Kurt was taking with white men grew out of this experience with the dentists. For justice to be done in America, white guys like him needed to be dethroned, their privileges curbed, their power diminished—about this, Kurt agreed. But he also believed that the passing of that old regime would need to be mourned. "When you hit those grieving spots," Kurt said, "you've got to let people grieve. You can't attack them. You got to go, 'Okay, you're grieving.' You can't come in and go, 'Come on, let's go.' No, let them grieve and process it, and they'll appreciate it more."

But amid the present political convulsions wrought by white backlash and the very real threat of authoritarianism it had brought upon the country, it was hard to argue that privileged white men needed help surrendering white male privilege. Kurt understood how he could sound. If white males were to say, "Okay, we agree, the system needs to change, but give us a second, we're grieving our privilege," how would that go? "I think the Black community will go, 'Great, big deal. We've been grieving for hundreds of years. So yay! Congratulations. Nice work. Suck it up. Change. Let's go.'" And Kurt understood that feeling; that would be the natural reaction. But what would come of it? "You know what that'll do? Take the turtle and put it back in the shell."

Kurt seemed sincere about wanting to end white male domination in America. It was more than virtue signaling, more than a language he was putting on. It was a project that consumed his mind now. He seemed aware of how hard change would be, the many sources of resistance he would be up against. But when he wanted the Blakes of the world to hold back, give it time, not rise up just yet, be patient, all to avoid white alienation, Kurt seemed to be weaponizing the idea of persuasion against the pursuit of change.

The killing that spurred Kurt's new mission had been in February of that year, though it was not until May that the case came into public view and set off a furor. Kurt's Facebook post came on May 12. In between that killing and Kurt's post, on March 13, 2020, police officers in Louisville, Kentucky, smashed into the apartment of a twenty-six-year-old Black woman named Breonna Taylor, in the course of serving a warrant on an ex-boyfriend, and shot her dead. Weeks later, just thirteen days after Kurt's post, a Black man named Christian Cooper, bird-watching in the Ramble area of Central Park in Manhattan, complained that a white woman named Amy Cooper had kept her dog off leash in violation of the rules, prompting her to make a false report to the police: "I'm in The Ramble, and there's a man, African American, he's got a bicycle helmet. He's recording me and threatening me and my dog." On that same day, police officers in Minneapolis arrested a forty-six-year-old man named George Floyd for allegedly spending a counterfeit $20 bill. One of the police officers kneeled on his neck, according to CNN's account of the prosecuting attorney's opening statement, for "4 minutes and 45 seconds as Floyd cried out for help, 53 seconds as Floyd flailed due to seizures and 3 minutes and 51 seconds as Floyd was non-responsive." And then Floyd died.

That last episode ignited a wave of protests in every state in the Union and around the world. In those fever days a video began to circulate, one in which James Baldwin, from the grave, asked a pointed question of Kurt and white America at large: "How much time do you want for your progress?"

In the months that followed, the kind of seminar the camp had hosted became the subject of a ferocious national debate. As the protests of 2020 spread, white readers hastily one-click-ordered antiracism books, organizations took to hiring more and more trainers like Erica and Adele, schools began to rewrite their curricula. The subject grew so heated that the president of the United States made a point of condemning what he called a "radical revolution that was taking place in our military, in our schools, all over the place." He was referring to the growth of antiracism trainings, including in agencies of the federal government he ran.

In September 2020, Donald Trump's budget director, Russell Vought, issued a memo to federal managers ordering them to shut down such trainings:

> Executive Branch agencies have spent millions of taxpayer dollars to date "training" government workers to believe divisive, anti-American propaganda.
>
> For example, according to press reports, employees across the Executive Branch have been required to attend trainings

> where they are told that "virtually all White people contribute to racism" or where they are required to say that they "benefit from racism." . . .
>
> The divisive, false, and demeaning propaganda of the critical race theory movement is contrary to all we stand for as Americans and should have no place in the Federal government.

Antiracist training—along with an academic field known as critical race theory—became the subject of a vitriolic, often-uninformed debate, which would soon turn into a big, if hokey, political wedge issue in elections for school boards, governorships, and congressional seats. It would lead to book bans, state laws promoting censorship, and telephone hotlines for parents to call in and report teachers for educating about race in ways parents didn't like.

Among the critics of antiracist training was, naturally, President Trump and his far-right movement. But they were joined by moderate rightists and even some self-described liberals who viewed antiracism as brainwashing, as even being tyrannical in its impulse to dictate the contents of other people's hearts. In a blistering review of Kendi's book in 2019, the blogger Andrew Sullivan wrote,

> Everything in the world, he argues, is either racist or antiracist. . . . The book therefore is not an attempt to persuade anyone. It's a life story interspersed with a litany of pronouncements about what you have to do to be good rather than evil. It has the tone of a Vatican encyclical, or a Fundamentalist sermon.

From Kendi, Sullivan extrapolated what he called "the intersectional left's ultimate endgame":

> The ultimate aim seems to be running the entire country by fiat to purge it of racism (and every other intersectional "-ism" and "phobia," while they're at it). And they demand "disciplinary tools" by unelected bodies to enforce "a radical reorientation of our consciousness." There is a word for this

> kind of politics and this kind of theory when it is fully and completely realized, and it is totalitarian.

That kind of ranting, rather removed from the raw material it criticized, was predictable enough from figures like Sullivan, who became notorious in 1994 for publishing an excerpt of the book *The Bell Curve* as a cover story in *The New Republic*, positing a link between race and IQ. But other lines of criticism were less expected. Some critics worried that the vogue for antiracist training was a dangerous weak sauce—a wooing of white hearts and minds that forestalled real change.

For starters, much of it failed to address material conditions. Mehrsa Baradaran, a law professor who studies racism in the financial system, wrote a series of online posts questioning the sudden popularity of "books teaching white people how not to be racist." "A lot of them (though not all) assume that doing 'the work' of dismantling white supremacy is about 'listening to POC,' 'speaking out' and generally not thinking certain things," Baradaran wrote. "So far so fine," she went on, "but . . . every white person could do all of this stuff and we would still have different credit systems, race-based home values, differences in school funding, employment disparities, etc. None of this stuff needs racism to be perpetuated. . . . [I]t seems to me like we'd get much further toward dismantling white supremacy if we had fewer seminars where we talked about feelings and privilege and more school board meetings and zoning fights and congressional hearings." The antiracist books, Baradaran said, "seem to start and stop at personal comportment and thoughts or at organizational representation and that's not enough."

There was a risk, some of these critics felt, that a certain kind of white liberal saw antiracism as moral acupuncture—an uncomfortable but good-for-you practice you could book for ninety minutes, then resume regular life. As the writer Jia Tolentino told *Interview* magazine,

> I think there's some portion of white people who are going from awkwardly saying "African-American" to awkwardly saying "BIPOC," people who were "taught to treat everyone equally" and are now being taught to verbally negotiate their own whiteness better—but who are still enmeshed in white

> communities, their affective habits altered a little but their enacted priorities still the same.
>
> I'm also suspicious of the way that Not Being Racist is a project that people seem to be approaching like boot camp. To deepen your understanding of race, of this country, should make you feel like the world is opening up, like you're dissolving into the immensity of history and the present rather than being more uncomfortably visible to yourself.

As these arguments continued, I reached out to Ibram Kendi, who had become the lightning rod of American racial retraining, to get his help in processing the events at Transracial Journeys. The difficulty with such trainings, he told me, is that many white people go into them with the expectation that "it's the job of the trainer somehow to challenge them and make them feel good simultaneously," he said. "'If I am feeling uncomfortable right now, if I'm feeling made to think that I may be racist, then therefore what you're doing is actually not effective.' I think that's a false concept that people are going in with: 'If I'm feeling bad, you're alienating me. And if you're alienating me, I'm not going to change.'"

It made Kendi think of the moment years ago when his doctor told him he had stage 4 colon cancer. The doctor wasn't trying to alienate him. He was applying rigorous diagnostic tools. But the news felt to Kendi not just scary but like an attack. "I was like, 'I have no risk factors,'" he said. "Which is precisely what some of these liberal Democrats say on race: 'I have no risk factors. I'm liberal. I have friends that are Black. I'm this, I'm that. My child is a child of color.' It's the same sort of thing. I have no risk factors, so how could you say that I have this serious illness?"

The difference, Kendi said, is that people generally trust the medical system. "Within the context of race and racism," he said, "you have so many racist propagandists who are constantly telling white Americans particularly that when people diagnose you as racist, they're trying to hurt you and attack you. They're constantly being told that. So when they are described in that way by someone, of course they cannot see how someone diagnosing their nation or even them personally as being racist could actually be trying to treat them."

Kendi said he had anticipated this potential resistance when writing *How to Be an Antiracist.* That is why the book leans so heavily on how its author, a Black man, himself once trafficked in anti-Black ideas and narratives. "I suspected that if I led with that, that would indeed open more people to say, 'You know what, let me think about the ways I've been wrong, too. Let me think about the ways I've been racist, too,'" he told me. "I wrote it that way because the heartbeat of racism is just denial, constant denial. And I wanted the book to have a different heartbeat, which was confession, acknowledgment, self-criticism." But somewhere along the way various political actors had seized on the new currents of thinking and had done everything in their power to ensure that people heard the "you're racist" part without hearing "and it's not your fault."

I also found myself wondering what Erica Merritt, the Black trainer in the duo, had made of the events at camp. Late in the summer of 2020, we spoke.

Looking back on the workshop, she asked herself whether she and Adele had pushed too hard, too fast. "I might have walked into that conversation imagining a greater degree of capacity on the part of the parents because of the capacity that I had seen exercised over the past few years," she told me. The problem was that there were first-time attendees who hadn't been on the journey, sitting beside people like Kurt who had been attending for years. "I think a lot of what we saw bubbling up—this was new for them. This camp was new for them. This conversation was new for them. And so we might have missed something in assessing a little bit who was in the space."

But, also, Erica wasn't afraid of scaring people off. She had her own theory of persuasion, which was different from Kurt's: "I actually do want to push people. And I don't expect that everyone—even if people aren't quiet, I never assume everybody is agreeing with every single thing that we have to say. But I do have a hope that they will continue to think about it. The way that something lands today might not be the way it lands on them a week from that time, or a month or even a year. So on the whole idea of persuasion, I think about that as a dial more than a switch. For some people, there is this watershed, lightbulb moment where everything becomes clear and they have some sort of epiphany. But for most people, it is a gradual shift over time where they keep hearing some of the same messages and they start to interrogate their own thinking and their own beliefs."

Erica rejected the veto of hearability, which asked trainers to temper the training until it could be comfortably taken in. She believed hearing what you don't want to can put you on the road to getting it: persuasion as a battle of mental attrition.

In the spaces Erica worked in, one often heard the mantra of "meeting people where they are." But for her it wasn't without its perils. "I think understanding where people are is helpful, but I think that's different from waiting for them," she said. She brought up the work of Paul Gorski, a fellow racial equity trainer, who has criticized what he calls "racial-equity detours":

> The detours vary in scope and nefariousness but share a function: They create an illusion of progress toward equity while cementing, or even exacerbating, inequity. They can be more devastating than explicit racism because they do racism's work while consuming resources ostensibly earmarked for racial equity. They are the anti-anti-racism.

Among the detours Gorski highlights is the "pacing-for-privilege detour," in which "an equity approach coddles the hesitancies of people with the least racial equity investment while punishing people with the most investment."

"It can be a strategy for doing nothing," Erica told me. "If you are just going to wait for white people to be ready to talk about racism en masse, how absurd is it, really, that Black folks and other people of color are the ones experiencing the harm of racism? And our focus is on figuring out whether people who theoretically are in the position of power are comfortable talking about that?"

Erica was less interested in waiting for people to become ready than in creating the conditions for readiness. These were the questions she asked herself: "How do you create some sense of urgency, some desire, some curiosity, not necessarily an immediate shift in belief, but create some fertile grounds for people potentially to think about things differently?"

Though Erica herself conducted these workshops on race, among other consulting activities, she was concerned about the limits of such work. "I worry it is a fad," she said. "If you look at the movement cycle, there's something that happens, and then there's this big uptick, and then there's an equally big dip back down. So we're at this moment and all of these things are happening. How long does it last?" She, too, worried about the hearts-and-minds approach changing things on the surface while leaving the undergirding of American racism intact: "In the grand scheme of all of the things that need to happen, I personally could care less if you call a master bedroom a 'master' bedroom. I want you to stop discriminating against people. Stop institutional and structural racism."

Racism, she said, is reinforced daily by structures. "We could put all the openly racist people on a boat or a plane or wherever we want to put them and make them go away," she said. "And because of the history of our country and because of the way that racism has been institutionalized, it's not going to disappear when those people go away."

3

A MOVEMENT THAT GROWS

Bernie Sanders first ran for office in 1972, campaigning for an open U.S. Senate seat from Vermont—and, separately, for the governorship of the state—as a member of the small Liberty Union Party. When asked the reason for his Senate candidacy, he told a reporter, "The concentration of power makes the average man feel irrelevant. This results in apathy. As for my qualifications, I am not a politician." Sanders reportedly carried around a 1970 report by a U.S. congressional committee that illustrated the hold of financial institutions over American business at large. "Time after time," Sanders later wrote, "I pointed out that such disparity in the distribution of wealth and decision-making power was not just unfair economically, but that without economic democracy it was impossible to achieve genuine political democracy." He was known to quote directly from the report during campaign events. A friend of his named Sylvia Manning later told a reporter, "He ran so he could get air time. Not to win but to educate people. He thought of himself as the educational candidate."

One of Sanders's opponents was a Democratic state representative named Randolph Major. As Sanders recalled in his memoir, Major devised a "brilliant publicity gimmick": skiing around the state to meet voters. Sanders later complained, "Here I was, giving long-winded statements to a bored media about the major problems facing humanity, and the TV cameras were literally focused on Randy's blisters." Sanders, who was thirty-one years old then, brought in 2 percent of the vote, and the blister man got 33 percent, and the vast majority went for the Republican, Robert Stafford, a former U.S. House member who had been temporarily appointed to the Senate seat and now would keep it.

Sanders's loss in 1972, and subsequent losses throughout that decade, did not dissuade him from sticking to that campaign's basic philosophy for the next half century. As he ran and ultimately began to win—first the mayoralty of Burlington, then a U.S. House seat, then a seat in the U.S. Senate, then successive reelections—Sanders continued to be serious and issue focused and to chastise those in the media and elsewhere whom he thought unserious. He trained his focus on a program of structural change while steadfastly avoiding the predominant political grammar of the personal and the sentimental and the emotional, the cultivation of relatability and the desire of the public to have a beer with you. He kept at his long quest to raise consciousness about issues like universal health care and the squeezing of wages and political corruption, showing less interest than many of his colleagues in compromising and cutting deals.

For years, this made Sanders highly influential by the standards of gadflies but middlingly significant by the standards of U.S. senators. That is, until the country began to come around to him and his way several years into the new millennium. In the presidential campaign of 2016, the gadfly surprised everyone by winning nearly two dozen states against the juggernaut of Hillary Clinton, and he transformed into an icon, a rock star, even a meme: white hair akimbo and white glasses framed against a dark backdrop, sold on T-shirts and other paraphernalia that traveling vendors made a living selling out of their vans. Sanders had done something radical in politics: refusing to give in to the prevailing modes of persuasion—the selling of the self, the pursuit of connection—that he saw as inextricable from the structures he railed against. At last, he was recognized for it.

As the breakdown of the American political and economic orders accelerated, as the long organizing against these erosions paid off, the ground became more hospitable to a man who had charged the plutocratic class with stealing the American dream long before it was in vogue and back when it was half as true as it would become. This was now the era of the celebrity economist Thomas Piketty, of a new capitalist-bashing pope, and of surging membership in the Democratic Socialists of America. Both Republicans and Democrats could be heard running against a "rigged system," and one noticed a new contempt for billionaires not because of conduct any one had engaged in but simply because of their membership in that hoarding class, and words like "Aspen" and "Davos" became punch lines. By late 2019, *The New York Times* could, under the headline "For Very Rich, a Rocky Path Paved in Gold," write, "There is probably never a bad time to be a billionaire. But this, at least, is an especially complicated one." Heralding "a public moment uniquely fraught for the three-comma set," the *Times* observed that "across politics, technology and popular culture, the wisdom and purpose of the extremely wealthy is being questioned as never before."

Sanders's 2016 campaign benefited from this long political turning and helped power it. His candidacy mainstreamed the discussion of capitalism and its discontents on cable news and editorial pages and presidential debate stages. He moved the so-called Overton window of the politically discussable on policy issues like single-payer health care and, more generally, on an unabashed politics of class struggle. He inspired young activists who worked for his campaign to run for office, including the organizer who would become Representative Alexandria Ocasio-Cortez.

And as Sanders embarked on his second run for president, in 2019, his success at moving the culture and building a constituency for his ideas had created something of a problem for him. Other progressives and even some centrist Democrats were glomming on to parts of his agenda, at least rhetorically: Medicare for All, massively subsidized college education, a $15 minimum wage, a federal jobs program. "Sanders sounds less 'radical' than he did in 2016 because Democrats have moved his way," *The Washington Post* observed. By the spring of 2019, this had become a refrain in Sanders's own speeches: a "funny thing had happened" since 2016, and Sanders's ideas were suddenly no longer "radical." "Brothers and sisters, we should be enormously proud that we have come a long way in transforming politics in America over the last four years," he declared one sunny April afternoon in Warren, Michigan. Sanders's task became to take credit for the transformation of politics in the Democratic field, while making a pitch to "Accept no imitations." And, among less informed, less ideological voters, there was a risk, which Sanders himself seemed to acknowledge, that people would confuse candidates-come-lately who were only opportunistically seizing on these ideas (and would soon desert them) with a man who had campaigned for them for many decades.

Given that many of his rivals were now offering variants of his policy proposals, it mattered more than it otherwise might have that they tended to be fluent in the lingua franca of American electoral persuasion: biography and appeal to sentiment. With many of his fellow candidates now at least gesturing at the visions of sweeping economic transformation he had long championed, they sweetened the deal with the personal stories and appeals to emotion and sculpting of authenticity he had long eschewed. Up on the debate stage during the Democratic primaries, there was Kamala Harris talking about school desegregation and busing and telling the story of a little girl whose life was changed by it and then saying, "That little girl was me." There was Joe Biden telling his folksy anecdotes about his mom and dad and Scranton, parables for a country that, like them, didn't have it easy but could, he believed, pull through. There was Cory Booker talking about moving to inner-city Newark two decades earlier and being told by a mentor from church, "Boy, if all you see in this neighborhood is problems, that's all there's ever going to be." There was Elizabeth Warren recalling growing up on "the ragged edge of the middle class" and getting pregnant and losing her job and finding the resilience to go to law school and getting divorced and struggling as a young single mom and then making her way into teaching. There was Pete Buttigieg talking about love and coming out a "gay dude in Mike Pence's Indiana."

And then there was Bernie Sanders, standing beside them, doing what he had done in every race since 1972: avoiding the drama, the emotions, the touching stories, being serious and structural. He didn't just believe that America needed a new kind of politics if it was to solve its problems—less centered on blisters, so to speak, more focused on congressional committee reports. He was practicing that kind of politics already, refusing to play the game. He gave the cold shoulder to the corporate media that had always given him the same. He avoided, as much as possible, the small-talk sit-downs with Important Local People as he campaigned. He refused to make it about himself, even when asked to share his story and what drove him. He showed little interest in presenting himself to the public as some warm and fuzzy and inspiring human mascot for his program.

To some admirers, this refusal had now become a real problem because of how far Sanders had come. "Sanders refuses to engage with things that annoy him," Ryan Grim of *The Intercept*, a writer and a publication sympathetic to the cause, wrote in 2019. "But he is no longer a protest candidate and can no longer escape the old adage that you may not be interested in politics, but politics is interested in you. He's running not to make a statement or drag the conversation to the left, but to be the leader of the most powerful country in the history of the world and to rescue it from its collision course with a dystopian future." He was in a new game, playing by the old rules.

Sanders's challenge for 2020 was to persuade the voters most sympathetic to his ideas that he was the one who was really going to deliver the kind of structural change that others were only now taking up and, at the same time, to persuade a greater number of voters who weren't sympathetic to his ideas, at least not at the outset: those who liked capitalism just fine but could, perhaps, be drawn to someone who seemed to be a decent person and to fight for people like them; those who didn't like the attacks on inequality they saw as needlessly negative or the class critiques they saw as us versus them but who could use the free tuition; those who recoiled at Sanders's affect but could, perhaps, be moved by stories about his early hardships and what deeply animated him.

"A movement that wins is a movement that grows, and you've got to find a way to grow," Faiz Shakir, Sanders's campaign manager, told me during my time following the campaign in the spring of 2019. "It's one thing to talk to your 20 to 25 percent who are your core believers, but we've got to work on persuading people into the fold. And that's why I think it takes, I believe, a continual evolution of the message, freshening up the message, and also sharing more about him." Shakir was stating softly what many on the campaign felt but hesitated to say out loud: that Sanders himself would have to change if he wanted to do more than change the conversation. Among the things he would have to do was to tell his story more and win the hearts of more reluctant minds.

The complication was that Sanders, owing as much to his nature as to his convictions, was not especially excited about other people's visions of reinvention for him. "He's the kind of person, to say the least, who doesn't encourage 'Hey, tell me what you think I should be doing and what you think I'm doing wrong,'" David Sirota, a longtime Sanders associate who served as a speechwriter and famously fiery Twitter defender on the 2020 campaign, told me. "He's not that kind of person. There are people like that. I'm like that. I'm like, 'What do I need to do? What am I not doing right? What am I not . . . ?' He is not like that.

"And the funny thing is," Sirota continued, "pushing him to do something could get you both success and punishment at the same time. You could push him to do something. He might ultimately end up doing it if you've made a good case and he comes to a realization. And you could still be made to feel like you shouldn't do that, or be intimidated for doing that or face punishment for doing that."

Those years on the margin, waiting for the country to come to him, had left scars. Here was a man who spent most of four decades "shouting at a cloud," as a staffer on a rival campaign put it to me, half put-down, half compliment. "I mean, can you imagine being a democratic socialist, a populist, a left-wing politician in the years of Ronald Reagan and Bill Clinton?" Waleed Shahid, who volunteered for Sanders's first presidential campaign and later served as communications director for the progressive advocacy group Justice Democrats, said to me. "He was very alone." But the time of isolation was over. "I have cast some lonely votes, fought some lonely fights, mounted some lonely campaigns," Sanders wrote in his memoir. "But I do not feel lonely now." At last, America had come around. It had met him where he was. A question he faced now was how far he would go toward using its reigning grammar of persuasion against the political order that had produced it. Could he find an authentic way to be Bernie and, nevertheless, win?

In the 2020 campaign, one sign of a turning was a novel event format I witnessed in Iowa.

In 2016, Sanders had been famous for his large rallies and exhortations about the political revolution. But in Iowa this time around, the campaign had developed a new event style: intimate, almost confessional town halls. A panel of three or four ordinary citizens would share stories of their hardships, and others in the audience would be invited to share their own tales of difficulty, and Sanders would respond with a mix of awkwardly given sympathy, synthesis of their various situations, and bits from his stump speech.

It wasn't that Sanders had turned away from talking about the rigged system. But a campaign under new leadership seemed to realize a need to connect more humanly with voters about those evergreen themes. The new format highlighted the psychological, even spiritual, ramifications of a rigged system, more than just the rigging. As one staffer explained, Sanders was "assigning an emotion" to the rigged system. He had long practiced the politics of logos, the appeal to reason. He was veering now into the territory of pathos, the appeal to emotion. It was dangerous territory, because all too often it was used to divert away from meaningful change. He was reaching that spring in Iowa for a way of appealing to emotion that led voters toward the structural. He was, in this way and other ways, learning to be personal, but in keeping with his deepest commitments.

"From the very beginning, he was always concerned about policy. Always concerned about making a meaningful difference. He didn't have time for the niceties," Jane Sanders, the senator's wife and his closest political adviser, told me. She added, "He has, over time, really become more—still very issue oriented, but he's placing focus on the people and the impact that those policies have on people."

In Burlington, Iowa, one afternoon that week, in the theater of a local school, there were three panelists, all women, onstage with Sanders. The first, Carrie Duncan, spoke of her trouble getting health insurance: not having coverage when she worked in a school cafeteria in a nonunion job, getting coverage when she landed a union job in an ammunition plant, then losing it again because of rising costs. "The fat cat continues to grow richer by drinking from the big bowls of cream that us little cats get for them," she said. "It's time to make the fat cats meow!" A nurse-practitioner named Teresa Krueger then spoke of living with type 1 diabetes and her work caring for patients with that condition, many of whom could not afford vials of insulin that have surged from $26 a vial in 1996 to $275 today. Hearing this, a man at the back of the auditorium yelled, "Blood money!" then crouched behind the seats. "No one should suffer or die in the United States of America," Krueger thundered, "because they cannot afford the medication they need to live!"

Then came Pati French. "I've been married for twenty-six years and had three great kids," she said. "We have had a good life. We have made lots of memories." One of her kids was Trevor. He was into music and politics, and in 2016 he canvassed for the Sanders campaign. He also had a pill addiction. He struggled and then he got help and got sober and was sober seven months when he got his own job and own apartment and made everyone proud. Then he felt a surge of anxiety, the old demons returning, and went to a clinic and got 140 pills and an instruction to go see a counselor whenever he could get in, but he didn't get in before an accidental overdose killed him. "We have never been the same," French said. Sanders, turning bright red and somber with emotion, reached out and gave her a few comforting pats. (He mostly remained silent through these presentations and spoke afterward.)

Then it was the audience's turn to give its own testimony. A woman named Emily spoke of the dearth of mental health care and how she had seen two friends die by suicide. "I have also seen countless people in small towns suffer getting the help they need from schools and hospitals in the town," she said, "including myself, who I have almost lost many times." Her words hung in the air for a long moment. A man who worked at McDonald's spoke of scraping by on nine bucks an hour; a man from the local steel plant spoke of jobs vanishing to India and the Czech Republic; and a woman who grew up on a family farm spoke of crop prices falling and bankruptcies climbing.

Faced with these testimonies, Sanders didn't generally do what other leaders did: hug people, say he felt their pain, ask follow-ups about the family. What he did with their pain, once it was his turn to speak, was analyze it; contextualize it; connect it to laws and agencies and instances of greed they may not know about; and, having processed it, offer it back to them as steaming, righteous, evidence-based anger. People told him of the bill they couldn't pay that kept them awake, and he told them that the chief executive of the local insurance company made however-many millions of dollars. Throwing facts and figures at them like little darts, he gave them the statistics that could explain their pain, gave them a thesis to connect the dots of their lives. He was teaching them to look at themselves in a new way—systemically.

"There's a lot of individual credit and blame in a capitalist society," Jane Sanders told me. She described Bernie's message in the town halls as this: "You know, this is not an individual failure that you're having trouble meeting your bills, or that your health has suffered because you can't afford health care. He tries to give them a context that says, 'Hey, stop blaming yourself. Start thinking about how you, in a democracy, can help change the system.' "

In the town halls, Bernie had found an approach that, in some sense, gave in to the persuasive method of stories and sentiment, but did it in a way that felt authentic to his larger project: to move attention from the personal up toward the systemic and the structural. He was inviting the testimonies from voters in order to give them the language and information to know that it wasn't their fault. His speeches were like that famous hug in *Good Will Hunting:* "It's not your fault; it's not your fault." The system did this. Big corporations did this. A bought-and-paid-for government did this. He was taking the passive voice out of the grammar of American hardship.

I asked Sanders one day what he was attempting with these new town halls. "I think one of the political crises that we face, in fact one of the reasons that Donald Trump is president, is that we've got millions of people who are in a lot of pain, families are suffering, and they turn on the television and they don't see a reflection of their lives," Sanders told me. "And they don't see politicians talking about their lives. So what we try to do is bring people up. Ordinary working people to talk about what's going on in their lives." His hope, he said, was that others would hear these stories and say to themselves, "Yeah, that's me. I'm glad somebody is talking about that." He added, "I think if we can do that all over this country, people understand that they're not alone."

Sanders and his team had recognized that many of the next 10 or 20 percent of voters they needed would be drawn from the majority of Americans who didn't like the word "socialism," who perceived Sanders as too angry or his ideas as "class warfare." To win them over, they were educating people about the systemic origins of their personal problems, raising consciousness.

The campaign's slogan this time around was "Not me, us." And one meaning of those words was that individual pain and suffering can atomize people, separate them from each other, even if the causes of that pain are held in common. Now, more than before, Sanders had figured out how to speak to that pain in a way that didn't separate, that saw the "me" but pulled it up into an "us."

Not me, us" could be understood in another way, too. While Sanders was more willing now to walk on the emotional terrain on which voters lived, he was reluctant to make himself—his own difficulties early in life, his innermost motivations for his long struggle—part of the campaign. Unlike most people in politics, he tended to treat his personal history as a state secret. He didn't talk in much depth about where he was from. He didn't talk much about his parents or school days or offer suspiciously convenient family aphorisms (*As my grandpa said, "Son, when you get knocked down, redistribute!"*). He felt no need to remind people that Jane is the love of his life. "He just does not trade on his personal story," she told me. "I mean, he could. He could make a lot of connections with that and get a lot of empathy, a lot of support, and that's not where he wants people's attention to be. He wants it to be on the vision that he's outlined and have them be thinking about that, not about him."

David Sirota, the Sanders speechwriter, told me it was a matter of principle and ideology, in addition to Sanders's personal limitations. The system Sanders was fighting was built on the promotion of the sentimental and the self and on the avoidance of the structural. Personal narrative and emotional appeals were how a politics that presented like change but avoided real change was sold to people, so they wouldn't notice how little they were getting. Sanders was resisting that status quo culture.

"Part of the reason he's been resistant to it is you can see a celebrity-driven politics and media become so hyper-obsessed with individual personality and charisma," Sirota told me. "I think that he fundamentally believes that that kind of politics is, at best, distracting and, at worst, undermines the building of the social movements that are necessary to actually change the policies and change the society.

"I always have gotten a sense from him that he feels that touchy-feely human emotions in a politician are inauthentic and Bill Clinton-y," Sirota continued. "I remember when I worked for Bernie twenty years ago, and Bill Clinton did this very eye-rolly 'I'm fighting for the working guy,' and Clinton is out there pushing the China trade deal to sell everyone's jobs out. But he goes on MTV, and it's like, 'I feel your pain.' " What bothered Sanders, according to Sirota, is that politicians "can build up a following based on their charisma, despite and regardless of what they're actually doing on policy."

Given the near universality of this biographical and emotive approach in modern American politics, it was surprising that, late in his life, Sanders's politics of renunciation had succeeded. His rejection had acquired its own persuasive force. If the personal stories and goose-bumps appeals of politicians had proven alluring and persuasive in your lifetime, and none of those politicians turned out to change your life in the ways you had hoped, maybe someone not working that hard to persuade you was your best bet. "Bernie's antipathy to that has actually become almost like a quasi-charisma-charm-brand thing unto itself," Sirota said. But he also felt Sanders had taken the avoidance of feeling too far. "There's a part of him that doesn't want to feel like Bill Clinton, like a fraud. But you can do that without being a fraud."

Finally, I raised the question with Sanders directly. "You know, in politics, a lot of politicians go around talking about all these things, their personal life," he said. "And often that disguises their real views and what they would do when elected. To me, I think it's important for the American people to know what you're going to do. It's not me; it's what impact we have on millions of people. So I don't talk about myself all the time. I get criticized for that. But, you know . . ."

He seemed to be saying two distinct things here. One was that personal story could serve as a mask, concealing agendas. The other was that it could function as a kind of subsidy, keeping the public in thrall to you even if you failed them. Resisting both things was important to his politics.

But 2020 had fostered something of a shift. Sanders seemed convinced by some advisers of the need to offer more of himself as a vessel for his pursuit of systemic change. Sirota put it this way: "I think he's gotten better at basically bringing in his own personal experience as a way to let voters know that his beliefs come from a lived experience. He's not a brain in a jar."

If Sanders was learning to be more personal, it was because it had become clear after the last time around that he needed every vote he could get, given the powerful enemies he had made. There was great integrity in resisting some of the personal dimensions of politics, in withholding the story of his own life, but was it worth squandering the chance to change millions of people's lives?

"I think it's good that Bernie has started to tell that story," Shahid said, "but if he doesn't tell that story in a consistent way, it's a little bit of a disservice to both his supporters and people who could be persuaded. I think when he says, 'Oh, voters aren't interested in stories; they're interested in issues,' it's a little bit of a mask for his deep inability to really go there."

Sanders didn't want it to be about the self. He wanted it to be about the system. And yet broken systems translate into broken hearts and broken backs, and that is often how people experience them. Some people will connect to your quest to fix the broken system because they share your sense that it is broken. But others will connect to it because they connect with you, because they feel that trust that is political gold. Sanders was at risk of running a campaign whose animating thrust went unspoken. In a moment when his challenge was to grow his appeal to people who maybe liked someone else better now but could come around, hiding the human being who cared enough about certain problems to devote his life to changing them could feel foolish.

"If you went around the country and were like, 'Do you know Bernie Sanders?'" Faiz Shakir told me, "the answer was generally, 'No.' If you ever asked, 'What does he stand for?' you would get a very clear, concise, and wonderful answer. I mean, he stands against billionaires and the corruption of the political elites, for Medicare for All." But the same surveys, Shakir said, showed that many voters "don't know him and what drives him. What motivates him? What does he like? What does he not like? In this age of politics, when you're campaigning for president of the United States, I think people have an expectation that they want to really get to know you."

Shakir's goal was to soften up voters beyond the 2016 hard core. He hoped that "even when you disagree, you would ultimately believe, hey, he's doing it for the good of humanity. He's doing it because he really gives a damn. He cares. That's why he does it." And that new approach had its coming-out party on a March day in 2019, when Sanders returned home to Brooklyn and gave a moving speech making his campaign as human as he ever had.

"If I might, as I return here to Brooklyn, let me take a moment to become personal," he said. "As we launch this campaign for president, you deserve to know where I come from—because family history heavily influences the values that we adopt as adults." And he told his story.

For Sirota and Shakir and others who had long pressed for Sanders to move in this direction, it was a breakthrough. "What happened in the Brooklyn speech," Sirota told me, "was a break from a tradition." It would seldom happen again.

But maybe none of this mattered. Maybe it worked in his favor. Maybe there was a kind of principle in it: the persuasiveness of resisting the forms of persuasion responsible for so much stasis.

Gruffness could be its own kind of sincerity. So many of the people who flocked to Sanders were used to being spoken to in slick, kind-seeming language that obscured what was really going down. They were being "rightsized," not fired. Their pension wasn't being cut; it was being shifted to a cash-available model, the smiling HR lady said. There is a way in which people associate apparent kindness with BP ads about being good corporate citizens of the Gulf, and a rumpled remoteness as realness. Someone who didn't care to be nice wasn't lying, couldn't be bought, wasn't going to become a lobbyist later. "There's a way in which his curmudgeonliness and his laser focus on issues that matter to him and the issue of inequality are helpful," Shahid said.

Sanders's was a vision of politics emancipated from the culture of the self, the culture of the capitalism he lambasted. He didn't invite your interest in his self, nor did he take interest in yours. Self and sentiment and symbolism were, in his picture of the world, distractions from genuine change. And, despite some minor concessions this time around, he would mostly hold fast against them. He wouldn't use those methods to turn the system against itself. He would hold true to what he thought politics was about and what, for him, it wasn't.

Shakir recalled with a laugh an episode in Nevada. In the campaign's new way, Sanders ran briefly through his Medicare for All talking points and then invited testimonies from the audience. A veteran named John Weigel held up one of his medical bills, which a staffer ferried to Sanders, who now called on Weigel to share. Unwieldy on his feet and struggling with his words because of Huntington's disease, he spoke of losing his veterans' health insurance because of some administrative confusion and then plunging neck-deep into debt.

"John, I'm looking at a bill that says, 'Account balance: $139,000.' What is that about?" the senator asked.

"It's because somehow, after the fact, they claim that my Tricare, I chose to end it, which I didn't," Weigel said. "They're saying that I didn't re-sign it or something."

"So how are you going to pay off?"

"I can't, I can't," Weigel answered. "I'm going to kill myself."

"Hold it, John," Sanders said firmly. "Stop it. You're not going to kill yourself."

"In that moment, you saw Bernie Sanders be Bernie Sanders," Shakir told me. "That's why I wish people would get access to that Bernie Sanders. He and Jane are at this event and say, 'We want to talk to you after this event.' They go over, hug him, talk to him. And Bernie pledges to him, 'I will fight for you. I will not forget. We're going to go fix this.' I remember him giving me a call right out of the event and saying, 'Let's figure out a way to help this guy.'" And help had eventually come from the offices of Nevada's two senators and from a GoFundMe page launched on Weigel's behalf. His bills had gone away, his health insurance had come back, he now had some money on hand.

Three months later, Sanders was back in Nevada. John Weigel was present at the rally. He stood up once again and this time told the story of how Sanders intervened and addressed his problem. "Thank you for rescuing me," Weigel said. And then, very proudly, he offered him one of his most prized possessions—a leather jacket he had received during his time in the navy, adorned with a patch marking his search-and-rescue work.

Shakir delighted in recounting the next part: "So here's a perfect emblem of who Bernie Sanders is. Here's this guy holding this jacket. He says, 'I want to give it to you. It means so much to me that you fought for me. Please take this.' And Bernie says, 'No way. I'm never taking that jacket. You earned that. You earned that. It's yours.'" (Weigel reportedly then ripped off the flight patch and gave that to Sanders.)

"And I remember the guy giving a quote to the press right after that event saying, 'Well, it really hurt me that he didn't take this jacket.' And I was like, 'Yeah, right there is Bernie Sanders.' He sees your pain reflected in that jacket. And he says, 'That means a hell of a lot more to you than it does to me right now, and you're going to keep it because I know out of it your joy will be far more enhanced. My joy means nothing compared to that.' That is to understand Bernie Sanders. Despite the fact of that guy saying, 'Oh, it would have meant so much to me. I'm a little hurt that he didn't take it.' Bernie's like, 'No, I know that actually you care more about that jacket than I would.'"

"Bill Clinton would have put the jacket on right there," I said.

"We actually got all of our camera guys ready for it because we're like, 'Okay, this will be a moment. He's going to try to put this jacket on. We're going to have something here.' But Sanders—you see it in the video—he holds it up with one hand far away from him, kind of out to the side like the jacket stinks or something. He's holding it far away, and he's waiting for this guy. This guy is telling him the story of this jacket. And he's holding it out far away. I remember I was sitting in the office watching, and me and a colleague were like, 'He ain't going to take the jacket.' He just turns it right back over to him, never got anywhere close to it."

So, for Shakir, the story was about the empathy of the candidate beneath the layers of guardedness—*I can generate a viral moment by accepting your jacket, but you would miss it, and it means so much more to you than me*—but not only that. Sanders was refusing in that moment to engage in the kind of politics that he perhaps held responsible for Weigel losing his care in the first place. The politics of charm and goose bumps that gives elected officials a way of performing compassion while slashing through an already threadbare safety net. The politics of feeling pain while doing the bidding of corporations.

To accept the jacket would have been to close the loop of feeling that began with the story of the veteran and his crisis and his thoughts of suicide. In the way of a Hollywood movie, the inciting incident would have culminated in a satisfying resolution that inspired great emotion. The tidy resolution would have left people feeling that, in the end, the right thing was done: all good. Sanders was the leader of a political movement that was invested in keeping that loop open, because it was fueled by the anger of the shafted and the scorned. What I understood of Sanders told me that taking the jacket might have felt to him like a cheap way of tying things up that doused rage he wanted to keep aflame. But not taking it could seem like political malpractice if you're trying to win an election. This was another manifestation of Sanders's dilemma: How do you meet voters where they are by tapping into emotion and helping people see issues on the human scale of a man and his jacket while refusing the politics of loop closing?

By September 2019, the Sanders campaign was in decent shape but, as the primaries approached, not showing robust enough signs of being Shakir's "movement that grows." A poll found Joe Biden in the lead with 27 percent support, and Sanders behind him with 19 percent, and Elizabeth Warren surging but still just behind Sanders at 17 percent.

In his ongoing quest to get people to know Sanders the man, Faiz Shakir reached out to the Democratic Party's new supernova, Alexandria Ocasio-Cortez, a freshly elected U.S. representative from the Bronx and Queens who had cut her teeth in politics as a Sanders organizer in 2016, then won an upset election to Congress, and quickly became the young face of the progressive movement. Ocasio-Cortez was a Sanders devotee, but the two barely knew each other. "I just said like, 'Hey, people need to know Bernie Sanders,'" Shakir told me. "Guess what? Who else wants to know Bernie Sanders? AOC does, right?" (Ocasio-Cortez, it should be mentioned, had yet to endorse anyone in the presidential contest. There was much speculation about whether she would go with Sanders or Elizabeth Warren.) Late in September 2019, Shakir invited her for an overnight trip to Burlington for the purpose of forging a human bond to gird the ideological alliance.

"I had never really met her in person before," Shakir told me. "But we went up to Burlington, where she flew into the airport to meet with the senator. I was there and picked her up from the airport. We hung out at Bernie's house for a night, and then stayed over one day in Burlington, went to brunch the next day." It was a getting-to-know-you session, and Shakir was even a little surprised at how open his boss was. "He talks openly and candidly with her and shares, 'Here's how I'm thinking about it.' And she is interested and asks, 'What's your path to victory? How are you going to do this? What coalitions do you need to win?' All this kind of conversation is going on."

A few days later, Sanders was at a campaign event when he felt chest pain. It was a heart attack. He was admitted to the hospital, where two stents were inserted to open a blocked artery. To many campaign pundits, it was over. "On the night he fell ill in Las Vegas, Sanders was lagging in both national and early state polling," an article from CNN said. "To the many observers who already doubted his staying power in such a deep field, the consensus hardened: Sanders, surely, was done for."

Shakir recalled being with Sanders in the hospital room on October 1, the day he was admitted. "It's not as if we seriously contemplated fully dropping out," he told me, "but I think there was a moment of 'Why would we keep going at this moment?'" And Sanders had an answer that was as much philosophical as tactical: "He's like, 'Faiz, yeah, I've been fighting for this my entire life. Voters deserve an opportunity to vote on this.'"

Sanders was taking the long view. It was important to document the growing support for ending the neoliberal era and ushering in transformation. "It really was this sense of 'People deserve a chance to at least register where they are on these fundamental issues,' and that's how he thought," Shakir said.

The next day, Sanders was recovering well, but his prognosis remained far from clear. The conventional wisdom of doom hung heavily in the air. A phone call came in from Ocasio-Cortez.

"She says, 'I'm with you,'" Shakir recalled. "Basically, without really a full diagnosis of where he is and how he's doing and if the campaign is going to continue, she makes the call and says, 'Senator, I just want to let you know I'm with you.' And I remember that moment. I remember a fist pump from him sitting in a chair. It just lifted his spirits in this incredible way.

"He's like, 'Wow, incredible,'" Shakir went on. "And in that way, it was this really remarkable act of courage where, honestly, she didn't even really know. It was almost, like, irresponsible of her. Didn't even know what state of health Bernie Sanders was in. But she was like, 'Hey, I just believe so much in this vision that you're offering.' And in some sense she's telling him, 'I want you to keep going.' She's saying, 'Please keep going, and I'm going to be there with you when you get out,' and it was a wonderful thing."

"I called him when he was in the hospital, and I wished him well," Ocasio-Cortez told CNN afterward, "and I said, 'We're going to move forward. Let's do this together.'" Though she had been holding out on any endorsement, the heart attack had been, for her, a "moment of clarity." She told CNN, "He was just really happy. He just said, you know, 'Great, great,' and, 'Let's change the country,' or something to that effect. He really cares. But it was also pretty short, too. You know, he has a very strong economy of words."

Several days later was another debate. Sanders beat expectations lowered by his heart attack. "People were assuming he would just fall down on the stage or something or be too tired to stand, and he just rocks it," Shakir recalled. And, shortly thereafter, the campaign teased a major announcement. On Saturday, October 19, in Queensbridge Park in New York City, there would be a "Bernie's Back" rally, along with a special guest: Representative Alexandria Ocasio-Cortez.

"If you start the clock there, there's a lot of success that this campaign had," Shakir told me. "I think that we were well positioned to have a lot of success. But there is no doubt in my mind that she pushed the gas on a lot of the growth and started the wheels turning." In short order, other leading progressives jumped aboard, and major progressive groups endorsed him. By the spring, after the first three contests, Sanders would have stunned the American political establishment into panic.

4

THE INSIDE-OUTSIDE GAME

On a temperate October day in 2019, on a stage in New York City's Queensbridge Park, Alexandria Ocasio-Cortez came to the microphone.

"What's up, New York Cit-eeeeeeeyyyy?" She wasn't satisfied. "Let me ask you again: What's up, New York Cit-eeeeeeeeeeyyyy?" She was wearing a dark power suit and one of the more fiery lipsticks in her arsenal that she sometimes referred to as war paint and that signaled to the colleagues who knew her best that she had big ambitions for the day. Facing Manhattan, with the borough of Queens, which she represented, at her back, and the Bronx, which she also represented and where she was born, to her right, she stood before a glistening sea of placards. Bernie. Bernie. Bernie.

"Last February," she said, pointing across the East River, "I was working as a waitress in downtown Manhattan—at a taqueria. I worked shoulder to shoulder with undocumented workers, who often worked harder and hardest for the least amount of money. I was on my feet working twelve-hour days, with no structured breaks. I didn't have health care. I wasn't being paid a living wage. And I didn't think that I deserved any of those things."

Upon hearing these words, from out in the sea of placards, a man yelled, "I can relate!"

"Because that is the script that we tell working people here and all over this country," Ocasio-Cortez continued, "that your inherent worth and value as a human being is dependent on an income that another person decided to underpay us. But what we're here to do is to turn around that very basic logic." And then she delivered a sentence that I, having heard many political endorsements, will not soon forget. "It wasn't until I heard of a man by the name of Bernie Sanders," she said, stopping mid-phrase here to take in the crowd and the roars, "that I began to question and assert and recognize my inherent value as a human being."

She went on to catalog the virtues of the senator from Vermont. But it was that line that hung in the air and that helped me to see Sanders's achievement even more clearly. She wasn't saying Bernie had persuaded her into an ideology—at least not at the beginning. She wasn't saying he had enlisted her in the battle for a particular policy. He had persuaded her that she was human, fully human. "I used to, frankly, abuse myself mentally about how I'm nothing," she once said of those days before her political awakening, with those gross men hitting on her at the Flats Fix taqueria and her $200-a-month health insurance that came with an awful $8,000 deductible and no stairway to a better life in sight. "I realized that I need to choose myself," she had said, "because if I don't, I'm just going to waste away. I'm just going to give up." Sanders's 2016 campaign, for which she ended up volunteering, had given her a new way of looking at herself. And now here was the disciple, a few years after she learned his name, standing on that stage as perhaps the most significant new arrival in Congress in American history, rescuing his cause.

In the months that followed, with the wind of Ocasio-Cortez's endorsement at his back, Sanders would come back from the political dead, claiming victory in the first three contests. For the first time in Sanders's pursuit of the presidency, he was the front-runner. And this development intensified the preexisting debates within the campaign: How could Sanders close the deal by going wider, calling in those who remained skeptical of his ideas but might come around?

One line of advice came from the actor John Cusack, a die-hard progressive who sometimes traveled with the campaign. Cusack felt Sanders should begin to sound more unifying, more like a general-election candidate. "His campaign needs to create a unit that is charged with outreach to groups who do NOT identify as progressive, but have strong views that are aligned with his," Cusack wrote in an email to Sanders campaign officials. "EXPAND EXPAND EXPAND."

Another line of advice came to be associated with Ocasio-Cortez. It had less to do with the framing and more to do with how the Sanders movement carried itself. The concern was about the candidate himself to an extent, but also the campaign and its most avid supporters online and in the physical world. Ocasio-Cortez was worried about the movement's posture in the face of skeptics and potential converts (these being to Faiz Shakir's way of thinking the same people). She, having been awakened and transformed by the movement a few years earlier, having felt the righteous anger that animated it, was, at the same time, worried that elements of the movement were potentially off-putting as well. The movement that had helped her discover her humanity was coming off to too many other people who didn't have that same experience as hostile, judgmental, and unwelcoming. Clearly, the things that made some feel seen in their humanity and welcomed, as she had felt in encountering Sanders, could turn other people away. The deploring of injustice, the propulsive force of the movement, did not on its own create a sense of home for some, and at times the stridency could prevent it.

At first, she delivered this message privately, internally. I asked David Sirota—the former Sanders aide and someone very much associated with the strident, pugilistic, at times angry posture that Ocasio-Cortez was questioning—about her critique. "I think she was right that for millions of voters who aren't paying attention to the internecine details of this policy or that policy, there can be, there should be, a more positive, open message and themes from the campaign. That was sound counsel," he told me.

She had other advice, too. Shakir told me she was also adamant about the importance of building Black support for Sanders and the need for Sanders to change some of his ways to do that. "She gave some specific recommendations that we adhered to," Shakir told me. "Her big thing was, how are you going to change your language to reflect that you're hearing many of the newer kind of dynamics and voices of the movement?" Shakir told me Sanders trusted the advice and made an effort. But ultimately, he said, "he's Bernie Sanders, and he knows the things that he knows quite well, and he feels comfortable talking about those things in certain ways at rallies that he feels like more people will access. He's not somebody who plays with the rally speech well."

But it was, as Shakir tells it, the question of posture that Ocasio-Cortez raised most fruitfully and that he took to heart. "She was a little worried about whether some of the Twitter demeanor of the constellation of people around us could be seen as antagonistic or off-putting. She was definitely somebody who worried about the perception that could create about who we are. Are we just angry all the time, or are we the people looking to aspirationally build a better future for people?"

One day, she made her case to Sanders directly, Shakir recalled. "She says to the senator, without naming any names, 'Senator, I think that the way in which we should project this campaign is to give people the opportunity to see what values we're about—a high-minded, aspirational, better society, an advanced society for all. And I don't think that's always reflected in the language of the campaign and you. So I think we should do our best to make everyone understand that this is the message that we want to send.'"

Shakir understood the advice, but it was harder to act on than he might have wished. For one thing, the anger and antagonism that many perceived in the Sanders movement were anger and antagonism justified by the systemic realities of the age and sentiments that were fuel for the working-class movement to change the country's power equations. Take away the anger, and you might take away too much. It was anger rooted in the heart and identity of the candidate, who was not easily changed. It was also late in the game to make adjustments. "You pull one thread, and it can kind of disrupt the entire fabric of the campaign," Shakir told me. And it was complicatedly political within the campaign. "I don't have a mute button," Shakir told me. "I don't control everybody's tweets." He said the campaign's more strident defenders had been brought in for a reason: Sanders, knowing the establishment he was up against, wanted people who could fight.

At some point, Shakir realized that what he could do was be a role model for the welcoming posture that Ocasio-Cortez was talking about. Until then, he had largely been behind the curtain. Late in

2019, he began to do livestreams of campaign updates: "If you go back and track what I was saying in those, one of the most oft-repeated things I would say is that we are a welcoming movement. We need to bring people in. We understand that everyone is on their journey, some people further along on that journey than others. And we need to give space and allow for people to basically be welcomed into it. I would use that phrase all the time: 'a welcoming movement.'"

But there were also potentially real costs to meeting the conditions that would make some people feel welcome in the movement, feel seen in their humanity, and find in the movement a home. These costs posed complicated trade-offs of persuasion: Why should working-class people mad as hell about being shafted for decades graft a fake smile onto their cause? Doesn't coalition building invariably end up meaning compromised positions? Isn't the desire to win over the middle of the road why the middle always wins? Do you build a movement capable of smashing oligarchy by rallying your armies or by reaching out? Is it possible to be at once angry and generous? How do you make the cause exciting and warm and soul stirring without descending into empty sentimentality? How do you construct a movement on the foundation of widespread frustration while offering voters something more inspiring than the sum of a million frustrations?

These were questions swirling around Sanders's campaign when Ocasio-Cortez gave another speech, less noticed but no less significant, a few months after the endorsement—after Sanders's winning streak had come to an end in South Carolina, which went for Joe Biden, but with the contest still up in the air. She had campaigned for Sanders on and off in the preceding months, but had been more absent from the trail than some expected, leading to speculative headlines. But now here she was in Michigan, on the cusp of its primary, and she delivered a somewhat different-sounding message that seemed to reflect the advice she had been giving on the inside, now made public.

"We are here because we have been separated from each other," she said. "As sister Rashida Tlaib here in Michigan says, 'We are not divided; we are disconnected.' That is, at its core, our problem today. And that means that the antithesis of that is to connect, to fight for someone you don't know, to love our neighbor, to bring people into the cause. To listen, to adapt, to open a posture of acceptance. That is what we must do in order to win on Tuesday."

It was brief, subtle, but carefully worded advice. If the movement was determined to combat the disconnection and alienation and brutality of America in the age of capital, it had to embody, to *be,* the opposite of those things. It had not only to argue for a politics of love and solidarity but also to incarnate it with a sense of welcome and home and humanity. And that persuasive approach demanded new behaviors from the movement.

Not long after the speech, I asked Ocasio-Cortez what lurked underneath those words.

"Granted, I don't think the progressive movement overall is like this," she told me, "but I do think that a very loud and small sector of the movement can be like this; as we know, very loud but small populations and communities can have an enormous amount of sway because they are loud." She was referring to a certain type of progressive who came off as uncompromising, who, to paraphrase the journalist Michael Kinsley, was more interested in finding heretics than converts.

"It's not about giving up your principles," she continued, "and it's not about changing your positions, but it is about opening up your posture. Because if we're just about finger wagging and nagging and shaming people into positions—sometimes that needs to be done in our politics. Sometimes—a lot of times—politicians and pundits deserve to be shamed. But it's not the only thing that we can do. And it's not the only tool that we have. And sometimes the most persuasive way that I find to bring people into the fold is what my mentor called 'the golden gate of retreat.' You create a path for someone that perhaps started out a conversation disagreeing with you."

Yet even as Ocasio-Cortez gave this advice, she wasn't teaching what she had mastered so much as voicing what she herself was grappling with at that moment. It was the spring of 2020 when she shared these reflections with me, and there was a special poignancy in her advice to Sanders and the movement, about the open posture and the spirit of grace and the golden gate of retreat and a sense of welcome, because at times she seemed to be speaking to herself, too.

All her life, as far back as she could remember, she had cultivated that spirit of openness and outreach. She was an organizer who knew you had to meet people where they are and pitch the same thing fifteen different ways to eleven different people. And then lightning had struck. In a way no person on this earth could ever plan for, she had landed on the world's stage, and landed in a particular way that bore a real but fractional resemblance to the person she knew herself to be. Suddenly someone who would probably strike you in a first encounter as quiet and shy was, in the public imagination, queen of the strident, duchess of the doctrinaire, countess of the clapback and callout. This picture of her was based on very real things about her; at the same time, it wasn't *her.* But you don't always get to choose where you're standing and what you're wearing when the lightning strikes. And so when Ocasio-Cortez spoke to Sanders and his armies, she was also, and quite consciously, speaking to herself, asking herself and others if it was possible to change big things by summoning in yourself the humility, patience, and openheartedness to move individual human beings.

In 1938, the MetLife corporation bought a 129-acre tract of land in the Bronx that was owned by the Catholic Church and used as the site of an orphanage where more than twenty-five hundred children lived in wait. It was destined to become the largest condominium development on earth, with some twelve thousand units, built on the concept of a "city within a city"—a place, as a local website puts it, "where one can shop, work and live without ever having to step foot outside." The development straddled two different Bronx neighborhoods, Park Versailles and Westchester Heights. Which is how it got the real-estate-branding portmanteau of Parkchester.

The development was open only to white people at first, from 1940 to 1968. The president of MetLife was quoted as saying, "Negroes and whites do not mix. Perhaps they will, in one hundred years, but they do not now." In 1968, the city ordered the development integrated. Coincidence or not, that was the year MetLife decided to sell. It sold the development to a real-estate magnate named Harry Helmsley, who at first continued to run Parkchester as a sea of rentals but later converted the units into condominiums. He and his wife, Leona, were later found to have engaged in financial shenanigans involving their vast business empire. While Harry was ruled unfit to stand trial, Leona did in the summer of 1989. On August 30, she was convicted on 33 charges, including tax-fraud conspiracy, tax evasion, and filing erroneous returns. She received a sentence of sixteen years, which was later reduced to four. She was eventually released after 19 months. (She received help with her appeals from a cunning young lawyer by the name of Alan Dershowitz.) The iconic moment in Helmsley's trial came when a former housekeeper recalled hearing Helmsley say, "We don't pay taxes; only the little people pay taxes."

Two months after Leona's conviction, a young couple living in the Parkchester complex—an architect named Sergio Ocasio and his wife, Blanca Iris Ocasio, who, as it happens, would also work as a taxpaying housekeeper—welcomed a daughter. They named her Alexandria, which, translated from the Greek, means "defender of humankind."

Blanca was an evangelical Christian, born in Puerto Rico, who cleaned houses to help the family's finances. Sergio owned a small practice in architecture, remodeling, and landscaping. He had grown up in the Bronx during the tumultuous 1960s and 1970s, when the borough was said to be burning. As the journalist Joe Flood later wrote, "Seven different census tracts in The Bronx lost more than 97% of their buildings to fire and abandonment between 1970 and 1980; 44 tracts (out of 289 in the borough) lost more than 50%." At the time, the prevailing narrative was that the fires were mostly the result of arson—landlords taking advantage of insurance or tenants taking advantage of welfare. But, as Flood reported in his book *The Fires: How a Computer Formula, Big Ideas, and the Best of Intentions Burned Down New York City—and Determined the Future of Cities,* arson turned out to explain a small fraction of the blazes. The actual problem, Flood argued, was the new vogue for business thinking in public affairs: private-sector technocrats from the Rand Corporation advised the city to close firehouses and curb inspections, all in the name of "efficiency." While many blamed "hoodlums," Flood writes, they gave a pass to the "whiz-kid consultants with plans to save the city through technology." Amid the wreckage of burned-out buildings they left in their wake, Sergio Ocasio "wanted to be one of the people that helped put the buildings back up," Alexandria, or Sandy, as she was known as a child, later said.

Sandy had a younger brother named Gabriel, who one day would nominate her for Congress.

As a congresswoman, Ocasio-Cortez told a moving story about her father. Around age five, she had talked her way into joining him and two of his friends on a road trip to Florida. "Three burly men and a five-year-old in a sedan," she told David Remnick of *The New Yorker*. "One day, his buddies went to get a beer or something, and he took me to the reflecting pool of the Washington Monument. I put my toes in the water, and suddenly the goldfish started to nibble my toes. It was a beautiful day, the sun was out, totally clear. And my dad pointed to all of it—the reflecting pool, the monuments, the Capitol, and he said, 'You know, this is *our* government. All of this belongs to us. It belongs to you.'" Years later, when she returned to the scene as a new congresswoman, she recalled, "I thought about that. I feel like it's *supposed* to belong to us. Not all of it belongs to all of us. Not yet. But that's the whole point of going to Congress, isn't it?"

From the earliest days, Ocasio-Cortez's life was defined by the straddling of worlds, being at once on the inside and on the outside, at once alienated and at home in both positions. And one of those straddlings began around that same age of five, when she and her mother half uprooted from the Bronx for a two-bedroom house in the tranquil suburb of Yorktown Heights, less than an hour's drive to the north of the Bronx, in Westchester County. The Bronx is one of the poorest counties in the country. Westchester County is among the richest. But it wasn't a dramatic change of fortune that propelled the move. Rather, Ocasio-Cortez's parents were concerned about the quality of education their daughter could receive in the Bronx, and so they called in resources from across the family, hitting up aunts, grandparents, and other relatives, to scrape together a down payment on a home in a place with good public schools.

Sergio stayed behind in the Bronx, where his renovation and remodeling work was rooted. Blanca and Sandy spent the weekdays in the suburbs, the daughter going to school and becoming by her own account a nerd consumed by science, her bedroom decorated in a jungle theme with a monkey adorning the wall. Her mother polished their neighbors' kitchen counters and scrubbed their toilets to get by. Often, they would return to the Bronx on the weekends, where

Sandy would melt back into the mix of cousins and friends who didn't have the escape hatch to mobility she did. Before she became a famed critic of inequity at a national scale, she encountered inequity between cousins—a "gaping maw," as she has put it, in which she had the upper lip. Her cousins' lives had the constant, whirring stress of insecurity. In later years, Ocasio-Cortez would anchor the story of her convictions in her time as a bartender, understanding, as she did better than most, the necessity of narrative simplification. But those convictions were shaped equally by those seasons of her life when she was on top relative to others and experienced the survivor's guilt of opportunity.

"This very regular drive between Westchester County, this small town Yorktown, and the Bronx, to where my cousins were, where we were being essentially raised as siblings, was really formative, because I would always see the difference between my school and their school, my air and their air," she later reflected in a public conversation with the writer Ta-Nehisi Coates. "And I recognize that the only thing, the only difference, between their outcomes and my outcomes was a forty-minute drive. Because we were born in the same place. It was just this one decision that my parents were able to make at a very young age that changed such a wide scope of the trajectory of our lives."

If she would end up with advanced powers of speaking to those at the bottom about what goes on at the top, and of speaking to those at the top about the plight of those at the bottom, and speaking without apology or fear in either circumstance, it was perhaps because she grew up toggling between social orders herself, being brown and relatively poor in a white and affluent world one day, the lucky suburban *prima* the next.

Some remember Ocasio-Cortez as being precociously political. Her mother told a reporter, "There was nobody who could shut her up. I saw the political tendencies since she was very, very young." There is a story of how she was so aghast at the dirty, dead, frogless pond outside her middle school that she showed up at a town board meeting to petition for an aerator machine. "It was the first time that I realized that there's a world outside of school that I could change," she later told a reporter. (For the record, aerator: denied.) Her family, she has said, wasn't overtly political—"they weren't in the streets, they weren't activists"—but their relatives were always in and out for coffee, talking about the world. And her parents were generous in the way that people who themselves rely on generosity can be. "I always kind of called them informal or unrecognized community organizers," she told Coates, "because they would always find the people in need in our community. They would always have them over for dinner, but they were never politically active in the way that we think of people being politically active."

In later years, she would speak of a leftist politics that grew out of experience more than theory. "It's not like I grew up reading Noam Chomsky," she told a reporter. "I grew up scrubbing toilets with my mother."

If she was relatively fortunate among her cousins on weekends, on weekdays she was an outsider of an altogether different kind, a "brown girl" in a white town who "didn't have crimped hair like the rest of the '90s kids," as her brother, Gabriel, put it once, a girl from the Bronx, no longer in the Bronx, whose house "wasn't ever going to be the sleep-over house," he said.

One summer day, I spoke to Ocasio-Cortez about those early years in Yorktown. She told me she had only as an adult begun to understand the dualities and toggling that defined that time.

"The world inside of our home, when I opened the door and got home from school, was completely different from the world of my classroom and the world of just the broader town and culture that I grew up in," she told me. "And so I wasn't conscious of the fact that I was learning to navigate all of these wildly different worlds." Her mom was working much of the time, and her father "was struggling the majority of time that I was growing up, and so the person who took care of me growing up was my grandmother." Her grandmother's father had been a medicine man back in Puerto Rico, which left a family "penchant," as Ocasio-Cortez put it, for gardening—herbs, cures, veggies. "I would go home, and she would set down all of these green peas for me to unpack."

Ocasio-Cortez spoke mostly Spanish at home in those days and then English out in the world. She had actually spoken no English until entering school. "We moved to this white neighborhood, and then my parents were like, 'All right, she's going to learn in preschool.' And so I literally showed up to preschool not speaking a word of English, and that was my introduction to this dual world."

I half joked that that abruptness sounded similar to her early days in Congress in 2019.

"Yeah, it pretty much feels very similar, culturally and all of that," she said. "First of all, when you're in that experience as a young child and you literally don't speak the language, you become hyper-attuned to people's disposition, to try to glean meaning from how they're feeling, where they are, without words. That was actually a skill that I really developed, to a wild degree, when I was waitressing. Because waitresses and bartenders, their job—our job—is to look across the room and read people's faces and figure out who's feeling what, who's having a good time, who's not having a good time, who looks like they need help. And so 90 percent of this work isn't even verbal.

"I struggled so much as a child to be heard and to be recognized," she continued. "They tried to hold me back in the second grade and get me to repeat the second grade, because these little things started adding up: I was left-handed; English was my second language." Her parents fought for her not to be held back. She was put in remedial classes. It wasn't until she took her first state test a few grades later that she scored in the ninety-ninth percentile "across the board in every single category," she recalled. The calls to hold her back went silent.

"I had to really learn how to advocate for myself," she said. "It took me a really, really, really long time to realize that these basic challenges to be heard and to be believed were not challenges that my parents had." The parents at home didn't see the cowed girl at school whom no one listened to. The kids and teachers at school didn't see the confident, opinionated child whom Blanca saw. No one saw Ocasio-Cortez in her complicated fullness, across these walls. "For more affluent kids or white kids, it's a much more seamless transition between home, get on a school bus, school, and come back," she told me. "And for me, it was like all of these different worlds. And trying to be myself in all of these different worlds required me to learn those kinds of communication skills."

Had she felt like the same self in each of those spaces, or like a different person in each one, a character playing a role?

"I don't know if I necessarily was conscious of being different in different worlds, but I remember feeling kind of misunderstood," she said. "I remember having this feeling of like, 'They don't get it in school.' " Everyone in the books they read was white. Most characters on the TV shows she watched were white. "Everyone else's experiences were reflected, uplifted, affirmed in the books they read, in the curriculum that we had, in the examples that were used in texts, in the things that we spell—all of it, it's so pervasive." She couldn't shake a feeling that "people just didn't understand experiences like mine."

This was one difference with her hero Bernie Sanders. He was less concerned than she was about being understood. He was interested in the content of the case he was making against the system, and less so in how that case was reaching people, drawing them in or turning them away. It was why he had done less than he could have to heed her advice to make sure that people were receiving the transmissions of his movement of love, rather than being content that he was transmitting it. But that self-confidence in not worrying about being misunderstood was not a luxury Ocasio-Cortez had felt. She wanted to be understood. His was the persuasive approach of *If you say it and say it again and again, they will come.* Hers was that of the brown girl in the white town who wanted to be seen and recognized and was willing to try this way and that way and the other way to reach you until she was, though without compromising her stance.

In high school, her life goal was to be an obstetrician-gynecologist. Excelling in science, she achieved second place in the Intel International Science and Engineering Fair. One of her teachers, Michael Blueglass, later told a reporter this story about the presentation of her research on how antioxidants can slow aging in roundworms: "One of the administrators wasn't there at the beginning and came in after she started, and he said to the superintendent, 'What company is she from?' The superintendent said, 'She's a 17-year-old senior in our high school.' She presented herself, verbally, visually, everything, as if she was a 30-year-old professional presenter businesswoman even though she was 17 years old." In honor of her success in the Intel fair, a team of scientists that controlled naming rights to asteroids it had discovered named one after Ocasio-Cortez. "Somewhere between Mars and Jupiter floats 23238 Ocasio-Cortez," *Vanity Fair* reported. Because of the enmity and apocalyptic fantasies the eventual congresswoman would come to inspire, the magazine felt compelled to add, "According to the experts who named it, there's 'zero chance' it will destroy us." Fresh out of high school, Ocasio-Cortez phone banked for a political candidate to whose rhetorical talents hers would one day be compared, who shared with her a shape-shifting youth and a hunger to be holistically understood in one's teeming variety, and whose consensus style of politics she would seek to challenge: Barack Obama.

Cobbling together some scholarships and loans, Ocasio-Cortez entered Boston University in 2007. She got on to the premed track, with a plan to major in biochemistry. In the fall of her sophomore year, her father, Sergio, was diagnosed with terminal lung cancer. Sandy visited him in the hospital as he lay dying. "Make me proud," he told her. He died days later, leaving no will and leaving behind a country tumbling into a financial crisis of generational proportions. "My mother was done," she told a reporter years later. "My brother was lost. I took it hard, too, but I channeled it into my studies. That's how I dealt with it. I was home for a week and went right back to school." His words "Make me proud" stuck with her: "I took it very literally. My G.P.A. skyrocketed."

But it was a giant loss of someone who had taught her to dream big. "I don't think there's any way to overstate how close I was with my dad," she has said. "That sense of ambition to try things when the odds seem so unfavorable, that very, very much comes from my father." She has said that, over and above losing him, she felt as though "I also lost myself."

For her mother, back in the Bronx, it was grueling in its own way. The prospect of foreclosure descended. "We were really working on the classic American dream," Ocasio-Cortez later told an interviewer, "and overnight it was all taken away. My mom was back to cleaning homes and driving school buses, to keep a roof over our heads."

Back in college, friends noticed that Ocasio-Cortez had a laser-like new focus. She was no longer going to college just to cultivate her mind and widen her opportunities. She was now on a mission to save her family. And she was more determined than before to have immediate impact.

She drifted away from premed and into majoring in economics and international relations. She didn't think her father's passing changed who she was, she told Ta-Nehisi Coates, "but I think it really clarified a lot of things. Because having my father pass away at such a young age forced a lot of questions of mortality. What am I here for? He passed when he was forty-eight years old. And so it really forced me to grapple with questions of legacy and what is important, and what do I want to do with my life at eighteen? And so I really started to feel when I was kind of on this pre-medical route that it was going to take another twelve years for me to actually kind of serve as a doctor after your residency, after medical school, after undergrad. And even then it would be treating patients on a case-by-case basis. And I wanted to examine issues on a more macro scale."

Her new interests were reflected in a discussion series where she became a fixture. Most Friday afternoons, students would gather on campus for "Coffee & Conversations" to discuss such topics as the merits of the Affordable Care Act. Among the regulars at these sessions was a student named Riley Roberts, who enjoyed playing devil's advocate. He and Ocasio-Cortez forged a bond, and they remain a couple today. She also got her first real taste of Congress, volunteering for Senator Edward M. Kennedy. She helped field inquiries from people with immigration problems. And she spent a semester of her junior year abroad, in Niger, working in a maternity clinic.

College complete, Ocasio-Cortez knew where she wanted to go. She could have gone many places, but she returned to the Bronx. She would come to call the next period of her life "the crucible."

Make me proud," her father had said. And for a time after his death, the obvious fulfillment of Sergio's wish was for Alexandria to succeed in college. But with college behind her, the crisis that had resulted from Sergio's death rose to the fore. Blanca was sinking in debt. Her daughter returned to the Bronx to help even as she got on her own feet.

In the abridged and oft-repeated narrative of Ocasio-Cortez's life, what happened next is some waitressing followed by the parlaying of waitressing into a seat in Congress. What this narrative skips over is Ocasio-Cortez's early career in the Bronx, a period in which she encountered and trained herself in some of the ideas and methods that would gird her subsequent life in politics.

Straight out of college, she took a job with an organization called the National Hispanic Institute, run by a charismatic founder named

Ernesto Nieto who would leave a profound imprint on her. She had first become connected to the organization in high school, attending a conference that drew students from across the country. "That's when I was like, 'Holy shit. I'm Latina. Like, Oh, wow, there's actual other people like me,'" she told me. "It wasn't until I met other people from across the country that were like me and I was like, 'Oh, there are other people like me.' That changed my narrative in my life." She kept coming back to the organization, volunteering with the NHI during college at its high schoolers' conventions, then taking a full-time job with the NHI after Boston University.

The NHI was animated by a particular philosophy that Nieto has called the "third reality," a path between what he saw as the road of protesting the white establishment and the road of seeking to engage with it at the risk of assimilation. "Should we surrender to the omnipresence of mainstream culture and merely attempt to fit in, whatever the costs to our identity as community and culture? Should we continue the fight for social justice and reform? Or is there a third choice, a third reality?" Nieto writes in his book titled *Third Reality*. That third reality, in Nieto's view, broke both from the cultural erasure of the melting pot and from the endless waiting of fighting the Anglo power establishment. Instead, it focused on helping the community see itself in new ways. "A third reality was needed, one that would lead our young to shape a different Latino community. They no longer needed to spend time reacting to issues outside their control. Efforts had to concentrate on reshaping and recreating a different self-identity and belief, one that enthused youth about their future in the Latino community." But Nieto wasn't interested in identity for its own sake. Rather, he spoke of how the development and sharing of self-knowledge could aid the pursuit of system change—how, as Sanders would later grapple with, the personal could aid the structural.

In keeping with Nieto's vision, Ocasio-Cortez was given a grant by the NHI to develop projects in the Bronx, focused on helping Latinos tell new stories about themselves and cultivate a new self-image. An early project was starting a small publishing company called Brook Avenue Press, which had a goal of making children's books that reflected the demographics and issues of the surrounding community and helped change the dominant perception of the Bronx. Another project involved creating a new curriculum to teach young Latinos in school.

Suddenly she was a teacher of sixth, seventh, and eighth graders in the Bronx. "Bronx middle schoolers? Trump would cry," she told me. "I think middle-school teachers in general probably have some of the hardest jobs in the country. Kids are hormonal; they're distracted by changes in their bodies, by emotional developments, by these ideas of manhood and adulthood and what have you. They're learning so much socially that trying to teach them a damn thing in those years of prepubescence is extremely difficult."

She taught the kids about storytelling, and community storytelling in particular. She had them build out characters and make stories about them. The sixth graders wrote stories for the third graders, which Ocasio-Cortez then parsed with them to tease out their worldview. "I tried to use that as a tool to say, 'Now, what values do you think are important? And how are you going to tell a story the same way that you were told stories to share these values with your younger brother, younger sister, et cetera?' "

It was trying work. "I had no idea what I was doing. There were days where I had zero control of the classroom," she said. On certain days, the children were into it. On other days, Beyoncé had just delivered her first child or some other conversation fodder was dominant.

She was in the schools one or two times a week. Much of the rest of the time she spent in a co-working space called the Sunshine Bronx Business Incubator. The New York *Daily News* described it as having been founded to redress "the lack of future Facebooks and Googles in the struggling borough." Dozens of start-ups paid a few hundred dollars a month each for space in the eleven-thousand-square-foot incubator, including, the *Daily News* reported, a composting company, a marketing outfit, and Ocasio-Cortez's publishing house. At age twenty-two, not quite yet the democratic socialist firebrand, Ocasio-Cortez was quoted in the newspaper playing booster: "You see a huge return on your investment here. People pay $500 an hour for consulting that we get for free by the water cooler."

Working in the incubator, Ocasio-Cortez, like many in her precariously employed generation, developed a side hustle. She had always been a strong writer in college and had even nursed the idea of becoming a professional writer one day, and now she began to sell her ghostwriting services. One day a corporate CEO who also worked in the incubator came to her in a panic. He was delivering a commencement address the next day. The only catch was he had failed to write his speech. His dyslexia was a further complication.

"What do I do?" he asked Ocasio-Cortez.

She tried to calm him down: "Okay, just sit down and tell me about yourself." She began to interview him, pull out the things he wanted to say but had been too cowed to write, and she drafted a speech. Afterward, he told her he had gotten a standing ovation.

Ocasio-Cortez began to do more of it, interrogating people to find out what they had to say and then doing the part they struggled to do as well as she did: framing it for others to hear. Many clients were entrepreneurs in the Bronx who were struggling to relay a narrative that changed perceptions of the borough in order to get support. "I started really just working with all of these other entrepreneurs and telling their story in a way that was compelling to attract attention, or investment, or what have you," Ocasio-Cortez told me.

It was this early phase of her career that made Ocasio-Cortez's future turn less of a lark than it might have seemed, and left her with lessons about how to change minds in pursuit of greater changes. As she worked on projects for the National Hispanic Institute, she continued to enjoy a close friendship and mentoring relationship with Ernesto Nieto. What he taught her sheds light on what she would become and the worlds she would straddle, no longer as an uprooted kid hoping to fit in, but as a leader specially gifted at combining the sharing of a raw and real self with an unblinking focus on the bigger picture.

If we live in a time that has seemed to many to force a choice between a politics of accommodation and a politics of confrontation, Ernesto Nieto was determined to break that trade-off, or prove that it wasn't one.

Before I spoke to Nieto myself, Ocasio-Cortez told me about him, and it was interesting to hear how she processed the lessons of his long career astride the worlds of activism, public service, and civil society.

"He was a radical in the '60s," she told me. "He graduated during the LBJ Great Society programs. He was hired by the Johnson administration, part of this corps of young people, to desegregate the South. His job was to go into the belly of the beast, into KKK territory, into white supremacist territory, as this six-foot-tall, brown-skinned, dark Mexican Chicano man, and tell them that they have to integrate. He ran the gamut in his life. He started off chaining himself to bridges to not allow segregationist vehicles and such to pass forward. But then he also was at this very bizarre point in the administration where he was literally winning these very hateful guys over. He operated in so many different spaces."

His work had been to strike the same forbidding balance that she later would attempt—between being intransigent about what is right, where things must go, what progress is, and, on the other hand, calling people gently in to your visions: to give no quarter while assuming enough of the humanity of those you want to win over that you're willing to try to change them.

I asked Ocasio-Cortez what had most struck her about Nieto's approach. "He spoke directly to people's humanity. It starts with actual mutual respect. I think that that lack of respect is usually the first place where things fall apart," she said. "That's one thing that Ernesto did. He never belittled anybody; he never made anyone feel stupid, even if you were just so off base. He was very Socratic in his approach, and he never, ever, ever expected one conversation to change someone's mind.

"But what he did," Ocasio-Cortez went on, "was that every conversation left you with a powerful experience that made you want to have an experience with him again. If a given interaction can make you think, can make you feel good, can make you feel heard or seen, even if you are at polar opposite ends of things, it encourages the person listening to you to come back and have another interaction with you. If that is a person that you are trying to persuade, that's a very important tableau to set."

When I reached out to Nieto, he was eager to share his stories about the institute's most famous alumna. He remembered sitting on the sidelines of an NHI conference one day, where high school students were debating and college students, of whom Ocasio-Cortez was one, were supervising. At the time, Nieto was working on a new book called

Third Reality Revealed. "All of a sudden," he told me, "this voice comes from behind and says, 'What do you have there?' "

He told Ocasio-Cortez about the book in progress. On the spot, she offered to edit it. "She said it with such assurance that it caused me to laugh, because she was a college freshman," Nieto said. "Long story short, she ended up being the editor."

That editing project immersed Ocasio-Cortez in Nieto's philosophy, the "third reality" between protest and assimilation. In Nieto's view, those who wanted to change systems too often went straight to challenging them, skipping over the work of self-discovery, self-interrogation, and self-assertion. They didn't dwell long enough in their own assumptions and experiences to work effectively to change others' minds. They didn't understand the constraints they placed on themselves even before the world constrained them. They didn't dig in to how their beliefs were a product of their upbringing, which left them ill-equipped to make sense of the people they would eventually try to persuade as themselves products of their upbringings. So a great deal of Nieto's focus was on getting young Hispanics on a path of investigating themselves and what they believed for the ultimate goal of making them more gifted persuaders.

The Nieto school of thought was that the self shouldn't be an afterthought in the pursuit of system change. You had to know yourself to change others. You had to be interested in their inner lives. You had to cultivate warmth even with those you disagree with, without letting that warmth lull you into milquetoast compromise.

In Ocasio-Cortez, Nieto had a sponge of a student. What began with book editing blossomed into a years-long mentoring relationship that included phone calls and long drives and trips to Texas, where Nieto remembers Ocasio-Cortez getting bitten by the ferocious local ants and ending up in the emergency room. As Nieto shared his memories of these travels and talks, it was striking that what he remembered Ocasio-Cortez for cut against what has become the dominant portrait of her as the embodiment of a more confrontational, provocative politics. That perception didn't ring true to Nieto. "She doesn't condemn and judge; she understands," he said. "She's open to inclusion. Alex does not eliminate people."

Among the lessons of Nieto's that Ocasio-Cortez has publicly brought up is one he calls the golden gate of retreat—that notion of giving people who might change their mind a face-saving way out. All too often now, a latecomer to an idea is dismissed for their tardiness rather than celebrated for coming around, which was the whole object of trying to persuade them. Nieto told me he had gotten the idea from one of his own mentors, Ben McDonald, a former mayor of Corpus Christi, Texas, who later ran the Texas Department of Community Affairs, where Nieto served as his assistant. McDonald would go from city to city, having difficult confrontations with citizens. One day he told Nieto, "Whenever you confront somebody and you win, don't walk away from the table. Always give them the golden gate of retreat."

The point was not that you let the other side advance. The word "retreat" was key. That was the intransigent part. You needed your vision of progress to prevail over theirs. What was up for grabs was how it would go down. Retreat itself was not negotiable, but there could be ways of their retreating that bred resentment and made the conflict live on forever and other ways of retreating that made those who had lost or had changed their mind feel considered and seen, feel that they still had their dignity intact, which allowed them to let go of having to be right and having to win.

"That, to me, is at the core of change," Nieto told me. "If you push people up against a wall where they're defending whatever they defend, then you've lost the battle to begin with. They just shut you out and you shut them out and you move on." Many years later, when his mentee, then Congresswoman Ocasio-Cortez, noticed a Republican senator, Mitt Romney, declare that "Black Lives Matter," she broke from many on her own side who pounced on him for offering too little, too late. "Not long ago, 'Black Lives Matter' was *also* a rallying cry for justice that politicians worried polled too poorly, was too 'divisive' & required 'too much explanation,'" she tweeted. "Now Mitt Romney is saying it. Progress is a process. It's normal to work through discomfort along the way." She was giving him the golden gate of retreat.

On the night Ocasio-Cortez won her primary in 2018, and thus all but secured the congressional seat, she phoned Nieto in the middle of the night. She told him the news and began to cry.

"How can I tell you how proud I am of what you've done and what you've accomplished?" he said to her.

"I want you to know that all these lessons, all this time we spent together, was behind it all," Ocasio-Cortez said. "I want you and NHI to feel that you won, too."

It was around this time of working on the NHI projects and ghost-writing on the side that the story of Ocasio-Cortez's early career intersected with the better-known narrative. With her mother still underwater in the wake of the financial crisis of 2008, she was now on the verge of losing their home. "So I walked into a restaurant in downtown Manhattan and I was just like, 'You guys have any openings?' That's the story."

She worked endless shifts at Flats Fix, making cocktails and enduring the boorishness (and worse) of men who feel that ordering a drink buys fractional ownership of a waitress. "People touch you, they tell you things," she told a reporter of her time at the restaurant. Sometimes she made $200 a day or so; sometimes, a third of that. She thickened her skin through it all, and serving in the trenches with co-workers was a radicalizing experience politically. Long before she railed against politicians who sounded the right notes but failed to act against historic, growing inequity, she and her colleagues were living it, cramped by low pay, precarity, and debt. America was in the late years of Barack Obama's presidency. The Affordable Care Act was the signature domestic achievement of the administration. It was making health care available for millions who hadn't had access before. Or so the dominant story line went. Ocasio-Cortez once told a journalist about asking several of her co-workers at Flats Fix whether any of them had health insurance. "Not a single person that I worked with was covered," she said. She did have coverage, but with that high deductible that accustomed her to taking a fistful of tips to the doctor's office to pay the bill in cash, according to *Vanity Fair*.

It was around then that the public narrative of AOC was born. Early in the 2016 Democratic primary, Ocasio-Cortez was said to have been torn between Hillary Clinton and Bernie Sanders. But as the campaign went on, something in her clicked for Sanders. She began to connect what Sanders was saying, had forever been saying, to the facts of her own life—the debt she still hadn't paid off, those fistfuls of cash at the doctor's, the long days on her feet, the sense she sometimes had of letting her late father down. That was when she went to work as an organizer on his behalf. It was her first real foray into electoral organizing. She helped find the campaign a physical base in the Bronx. She rubbed shoulders with activists from various groups in the Sanders coalition.

Sanders, of course, lost that 2016 primary. And the Democratic Party he had tried in vain to change lost that election to a faux populist. And in the aftermath of that cataclysmic defeat, party officials and activists and organizers began a period of reflection and autopsy, and a thousand PowerPoint decks were born. Why did the Democrats lose? What was the answer to rising populism? How do you win over white working-class voters, Black voters, suburban women? Is the answer to Trumpism to resist populism or to embrace it?

One of the more insightful of these PowerPoints was titled "Race, Class, and Why We Can't Have Nice Things," developed by Waleed Shahid and other progressive activists. It laid out, in a hundred picture-studded slides, a strategy of persuasion. What the left needed to do to win, in its telling, was to merge the rival persuasive approaches of two of the party's most effective recent movements: Bernie Sanders's and Barack Obama's—to combine, as Shahid put it to me, "Bernie's message of 'them' with Obama's message of 'us,'" the Sanders campaign's critique of an unjust system with the Obama campaign's rousing call for unity and hope.

In the PowerPoint's telling, each of these approaches was powerful but, on its own, inadequate. Obama's approach had won two presidential elections on behalf of a Black man whose middle name was Hussein. "My parents have been citizens since the early '90s," Shahid told me, "and the first person they ever voted for was Barack Obama, in part because he told a story of multiracial America that they felt included in." The weakness of the Obama approach, though, was that it shied away from a structural critique of the powerful forces stoking the divisions that Obama wanted Americans to transcend. Obama's politics, in Shahid's view, risked blaming Americans for their own divisions rather than the media owners and funders of gerrymandering and shadowy right-wing Astroturfers who were really responsible.

"Someone is causing these divisions," Shahid said. "Someone is causing these problems, and that is the billionaire class." The politics of an expansive "us" was powerful and beautiful and resonant, but without a politics of "them" added to its analysis, it risked advocating for what Shahid likes to call a "rainbow oligarchy," an America that looks more inclusive, that celebrates diversity, but is fundamentally still controlled and exploited by the few.

That was where Sanders came in. "Bernie made a structural critique naming clear enemies in American politics and clear adversaries who were holding the country back from its whole potential," Shahid told me. In the PowerPoint, this politics of "them" is defined by a generative calling out: calling out the Democratic Party leadership for being too cozy with Wall Street and neglecting working people, and calling out the divide-and-conquer politics that define the modern Republican Party. If Obama had tried to bring Americans together around a common humanity and a new pluralist patriotism—"There is not a Black America and a white America and Latino America and Asian America. There's the United States of America"—Sanders had rallied voters around a common enemy, the powerful billionaire and corporate class preying on their dignity. But Sanders had his own limitations. Unlike Obama, he hadn't won. And he hadn't assembled a sufficiently broad coalition, with a particular weakness among Black voters and older voters.

Was there a way to put these political projects together? the PowerPoint's authors wondered. To combine Barack's call in with Bernie's callout? To rally voters around what they share with others, tapping into those warm and fuzzy sentiments that put Obama in the White House, while rallying those voters to "punch up" at the ruling class? Could you combine we-are-all-in-this-together inspiration with righteous anger? The authors of the slide deck believed you could. And they described this hybrid approach they were advocating as "inclusionary populism." This approach would punch up "by pointing at the economic power at the very top," while lacerating the corporate-friendly party establishment from within the tent, while at the same time articulating "a We the People that includes *all of us,* regardless of race, ethnicity, sexual orientation, country of origin." The slides' authors envisioned a new generation of Democrats who could be mad as hell and inspiring as hell, who could whip up your anger at that powerful "them" while making you feel part of the ennobling project of building a more capacious "us." It could add to Obama's uplifting politics a structural calling out of the powerful, and it could add to Sanders's principled politics the missing elements of personal story, the painting of the future one seeks, and the tailoring of messages to particular groups rather than merely universalizing.

After the stinging defeat of 2016, the people behind this PowerPoint not only theorized this possibility but worked to bring their vision to life. Some of them helped create an organization called Brand New Congress, which set as its mission to "elect a new type of Democratic majority." With their talk of inclusionary populism, these strategists weren't merely suggesting a new message. They wanted new messengers. As they began to recruit potential candidates, they stayed away from anyone who had held elective office before. They favored candidates who not only championed the working class but actually belonged to it. They were looking for younger activist voices who could combine the arts of calling in and calling out, of punching up and summoning a vast and colorful all, who were human enough to relate to voters and move individual minds but who never lost sight of using that connection to challenge structures, who could make you feel what Obama had made you feel about doing what Sanders wanted to do.

Late in 2016, Brand New Congress put out a casting call for potential congressional candidates. They received twelve thousand applications. One of them was from someone named Gabriel Ocasio-Cortez, who nominated his sister, Alexandria.

Around that time, she had been invited by a political organizer she knew to drive out west and participate in protests against the Dakota Access Pipeline, not far from the Standing Rock reservation of the Sioux tribe, which straddles North and South Dakota. She and a friend took a road trip in an aging Subaru, passing through Flint, Michigan, on the way, one focal point of activist anger in recent years because of the lead in its water system. The cigarette lighter in the car was past its prime, so Ocasio-Cortez and her friend had to pull over at rest areas along the way to recharge their phones. They had conversations with locals that caused Ocasio-Cortez to see more commonalities with her own life than she might have assumed. As they crossed red states that had voted for Trump and blue states that had gone for Hillary Clinton, Ocasio-Cortez felt a strong sense that the country "wasn't understanding itself," as she put it to a Kansas-based journalist named Sarah Smarsh. "We didn't understand each other, and we didn't understand ourselves as a collective nation." The "us" that Brand New Congress wanted to marshal against the all-powerful "them" didn't feel very much like an "us." But could it?

At Standing Rock, living in camps with fellow activists, both out-of-towners and members of the local indigenous community, Ocasio-Cortez had what she calls a "profoundly spiritual experience." She told an interviewer Standing Rock became a "tipping point" in her career, causing her to realize that you didn't have to have money or connections to make a political dent. Those things helped. But here, she reflected later, were people "putting their whole lives and everything that they had on the line for the protection of their community." Could she do the same?

Just as she was leaving Standing Rock, her phone rang. It was the Brand New Congress people. They had noticed her file in a haystack of twelve thousand. They wanted to know if she was interested in exploring a run for New York's Fourteenth Congressional District, covering parts of Queens and the Bronx. The timing was good. She was interested. That call led to a few more calls and in-person meetings. Brand New Congress was trying to figure out if she fit their bill of the calling-out, calling-in progressive insurgent. Later, Saikat Chakrabarti, one of the leaders of the organization, summed up his impression of her after these encounters: "Holy cow."

Until not long ago, the polite custom among Democrats was to avoid primary challenges to seated incumbents. By all means, lobby them to be better, but to primary them was too much. This politeness kept incumbents in office for decades, even when they failed to deliver for their voters but were rewarded by the special interests they served.

Brand New Congress's theory of change jettisoned politeness. In the 2018 election cycle, it would put forward Ocasio-Cortez and dozens of other primary challengers to encrusted incumbents who it felt no longer, or never had, represented constituents and the working class in particular. Its strategy was dismantling the entrenched system. Each of its candidates was running to take down a supposed colleague of the same party who wasn't doing what they should have been doing.

Ocasio-Cortez's target was a powerful fifty-six-year-old political machine boss named Joe Crowley. He was a white man representing a district that is more than two-thirds voters of color, and by all accounts he didn't even live in his own district. But over two decades in Washington, he had amassed the all-important capital of seniority to become the fourth-ranking Democrat in the House of Representatives. He was a kingmaker in New York City politics, too. In other words, he was a terrible guy to primary. "Anybody who knew anything about politics in New York City told me not to do this," Ocasio-Cortez later put it, summarizing their advice: "(a) You're wasting your time; (b) it's pointless; and (c) you'll never have a career in New York City politics ever again if you do this."

But Ocasio-Cortez did it anyway. And her opening salvo was a video ad that went viral and reflected the persuasive methodology of that PowerPoint presentation. "This race is about people versus money," she said in the spot. "We've got people; they've got money." There it was, Bernie's "them" and Barack's "us" forged together. She told a story about a city that was rigged against working people and an out-of-touch lawmaker who had slept on the job. She derided Crowley as an outsider, saying that a congressman who "doesn't send his kids to our schools, doesn't drink our water or breathe our air cannot possibly represent us." But to her structural critique was added human outreach of the kind Sanders might have been loath to attempt. Here she is taking off her flats on a subway platform and switching to heels. Here she is talking about waiting tables. Here she is doing her makeup in a humble apartment. She was offering both relatability (I'm like you) and authenticity (I'm me, as is). There was something of Nieto's mentorship in this approach: system change from the self out. After watching the spot, you might have been the type of person who wanted to go where Ocasio-Cortez was headed because of her plan for a jobs guarantee and tuition-free public college. But you might instead have been the kind of person who chafed at those ideas and would still be cheering for her because of how she made you feel.

From the beginning, Ocasio-Cortez engaged in this multimodal form of persuasion that brought together traits lesser talents might have struggled to blend: being provocative and capable of seizing attention while meeting people where they are and offering vulnerability and humanity.

It was a scrappy campaign that had people knocking on doors and taking no voter in the district for granted, focusing less on conversion than on activation—getting people who had not voted before, or had voted rarely, to do so. "My act of persuasion, my persuasion mission, was not 'Vote for me instead of voting for Crowley,'" Ocasio-Cortez told me. "My mission of persuasion was, 'You should vote in a primary election for the first time in your life, and here's why.' My whole message was tailored to persuade people to show up, that this one could actually matter.

"My strategy and my opening argument," she continued, "was, 'You matter, and we have taught ourselves, and we have accepted, in so many ways, conscious and subconscious, that we don't matter, our lives don't matter, our input doesn't matter, our opinion doesn't matter, and so we're just going to try to survive.' My argument was, 'We can't live like this anymore, we deserve better, and you matter. And because you matter, you not turning out decides this election, and you turning out also decides this election in a different direction, but you're making a choice. I want you to know that you matter to me.'"

Ocasio-Cortez's argument for the agency of her potential constituents wasn't necessarily intuitive in one of the poorest districts in America; it wasn't the message life sent; and in spite of that and because of that, the pitch resonated.

Even as her prominence began to grow, she shared of herself, of her own human struggles to know that she mattered, as if to tell others that they did. She spoke of her own fears and doubts about running and what made her persist in spite of them. "I'm glad I didn't listen to myself when things got really difficult and no one was paying attention and I was like, 'Why am I doing this?'" she told a reporter during the campaign. "I just hope that more people will ignore the fatalism of the argument that we are beyond repair. We are not beyond repair. We are never beyond repair."

The press marveled at the biographies of the next-generation operatives who ran her campaign—a "campaign manager who moonlights as an energy healer," a "photographer who sings in a heavy metal band," a "Muslim progressive activist who runs a cooking blog," a former actor "who signs emails with his preferred pronouns ('he/him')," a press secretary "who operated a pair of food trucks in Tennessee, processing his own steers, until he heard the gospel of Bernie." But at the heart of the operation was Ocasio-Cortez herself, who combined the humble, bottom-up approach of chasing every vote and out-knocking the competition with a once-in-a-generation talent for pushing the boundaries of conversation, raising the profile of marginalized subjects, and forcing a response to the provocation of her ideas.

Part of the provocation was what she proposed, and part of it was how she proposed it. She championed a fearlessly left agenda, with a robust and largely unprecedented role for the state in American life, and what amounted to a transformation of the basic structure of the society. She didn't just want to reform Immigration and Customs Enforcement like most of her Democratic colleagues; she wanted to abolish it. She didn't just want college to be affordable; she wanted it to be free. She didn't just want to expand renewable energy; she wanted the entire country to be running on it before she turned fifty. She didn't just want the government to nurture well-paying jobs; she wanted it to guarantee a job for all. She didn't want to give people tax credits to afford health insurance more easily; she wanted health insurance obsolete. Setting aside the rightness of any particular policy, these ideas reflected a political understanding, which many of Ocasio-Cortez's colleagues lacked, of the importance of simplicity in policy communication and, in the age of social media and of a culture of confrontation, the power of the maximalist stance.

From the beginning, she deployed this method of first staking out a provocative position, a fearless goal, the raw, undiluted version of a thing. This separated her from those more sober-minded politicians who negotiated against themselves in their own minds and began with the half measure. But then Ocasio-Cortez also distinguished herself from those of a more activist bent by her willingness to follow the provocation with a meet-them-where-they-are approach of dealing with people's skepticism, explaining the sensibleness (not the radicalness) of the idea in question, bringing them along. She understood, more than most in politics, the importance of that punch of a first sentence. But she always had the second sentence ready, and the third and fourth and fifth.

You can watch her engage in this persuasive work in this interview with the NPR *Morning Edition* host Steve Inskeep:

INSKEEP: So one of the things that you called for is something that some Democrats have called for—abolishing ICE, Immigration and Customs Enforcement. Now, I understand ICE has been fiercely criticized for its role in separating parents and children in recent days, but what do you mean by abolishing customs enforcement and immigration?

OCASIO-CORTEZ: Yeah, no, it's an excellent question. One of the things that we talk about in that call is essentially that ICE was just established in 2003 in the same suite of legislation as the Patriot Act, the AUMF [Authorization for Use of Military Force], the Iraq War. And so what we're basically saying is that the structure of ICE, in the similar manner as the structure of the Patriot Act, is kind of built on the scaffolding of questionable civil liberties infringement and abuse. And so what we're really talking about is reimagining immigration to be humane and in a way that is transparent and accountable.

INSKEEP: Although, I mean, you're still going to have immigration officers, right? You're still going to have customs officers, if you got your way. I mean, there's going to be border enforcement. It'd just be under a different name.

OCASIO-CORTEZ: Well, I think it's a different name and a different approach, you know? Before ICE, we had Immigration and Naturalization Services, but it wasn't until about 1999 that we chose to criminalize immigration at all. And then once ICE was established, we really kind of militarized that enforcement to a degree that was previously unseen in the United States.

So she started with her position of abolition, and then met the journalist where he was, explaining that ICE was built on a bad foundation, that she really wanted immigration to be reimagined, that, yes, there would be immigration authorities, just with a different name and approach. And she also seemed here to show a long-game patience that was hard for some activists. The Immigration and Naturalization Service's ways had probably not been especially to her liking, either. And she had broader critiques of the criminalized approach to social problems in general. But she had the strategy and the discipline not to attempt it all in a day. You could tell the NPR journalist that, yes, ICE needs to be abolished and that's only the beginning, because we need to abolish the carceral system in general, and so on. And she believed in many of those ideas. But she picked off a smaller target in that moment: take the idea of abolishing ICE and explain it to the mainstream as rebuilding from the ground up an institution set on the wrong foundation. People with a range of views might be convinced of the idea that orienting an entire immigration system toward preventing terrorism was outdated and wrong. Ocasio-Cortez's was a politics of critique, but often, to rather powerful effect, of patient critique.

In addition to this method of provocation followed by gentle teaching, Ocasio-Cortez showed a talent for recognizing and shaping and making the most of politically opportune moments. She understood that provocation, commanding attention, didn't just come from putting ideas out there; it often required those ideas to be attached to a moment that people were trying to make meaning out of. Sometimes you sought to imbue a preexisting moment with the ideas you sought to advance. And sometimes you had to manufacture that moment yourself in order to have a vessel for your ideas. So, for example, in addition to calling for the abolition of ICE, Ocasio-Cortez spent the last weekend of her campaign—traditionally a time a candidate might want to stay close to constituents and local media—flying to Texas to confront ICE agents at a migrant internment camp. Sanders, her hero, might have staked out the policy position, but he might have seen the trip as a stunt. Ocasio-Cortez, with an intuitive grasp of where people's minds are and what it takes to make them focus, had no such qualms.

What she seemed to understand natively was that small moments could be made into big moments, but that this was not a natural, automatic process. The meaning of a political moment was not necessarily self-evident. There might be a vacuum at first, and this she could fill.

She could offer interpretation of the moment, help people see it a certain way, provide the frame, gin up the outrage, and then a moment could gain its own momentum. Days before the primary, Representative Crowley ducked a debate with Ocasio-Cortez, which was bad enough. To make things worse, he sent a former member of the New York City Council, Annabel Palma, to debate on his behalf. Palma is a Latina, and Crowley's cynicism (surely masked as a gesture of respect) was not hard to miss. And some in politics, trained in an earlier generation's norms, might have left the issue to make its own case, to speak for itself. Not Ocasio-Cortez, with her feel for what would pull people in and make them focus on a campaign that was desperate to be seen, noticed, and covered.

"In a bizarre twist, Rep. Crowley sent a woman with slight resemblance to me as his official surrogate to last night's debate," Ocasio-Cortez wrote on Twitter. Boom. That would do it. By interpreting the event in that trenchant way, she gave news outlets permission to report the idea of a racial stand-in in a way they otherwise might have tiptoed around, which in turn fueled social media outrage and dunking, which bought precious attentional currency to market what Ocasio-Cortez really wanted to sell: those plans to remake the society.

This way of reaching people and changing minds required Ocasio-Cortez to be many selves and to juggle a wide array of approaches. Her multimodal method owed a debt to Nieto and his lessons of confronting white racists, wooing them, and helping them save face, all at once. In some moments, Ocasio-Cortez would be provoking with an attention-seizing idea. Then she would be walking a skeptic through the utter prudence of that idea. Then she would be cutting a social media video sharing her own fears and process. Then she would be in living rooms having coffee parties and humbly listening to constituents, to show and not simply tell them that they mattered. Then she would be in the car, typing out a hopefully viral sideswipe of a guy for his earlier sideswipe of her. Then she would give a speech trying to inspire young nonvoters and invite them into the political process despite their sense of it being too negative and vitriolic. At one moment, she was calling in; the next, she was starting shit and calling out. She pushed. Then she pulled others in.

Early on, when she remained invisible to much of the press, *The*

Nation commented on her ability to straddle these modes of being in a way that felt different from the progressives they were used to, from Howard Dean to Ralph Nader to Bernie Sanders: "full of righteous fury and matching political conviction, yet clear and controlled and unafraid of the camera. There was no 'Dean scream,' Naderite arrogance, or Bernie-style gruffness, and none of the coltish uncertainty you'd expect from a 28-year-old newcomer, either." Ocasio-Cortez could combine the stridency of the activist with the media skills of an insider; she could do anger without seeming angry; she could advocate radical ideas without seeming out of her mind. She had, of course, grown up straddling worlds—the Bronx and Yorktown, Spanish and English, being among her people and sticking out as the brown girl whose house would never be the sleepover house. In her political style, she was comfortable with not needing to be one thing for all occasions. She operated, or so it seemed, with a faith that with her multimodal approach her elongated NPR explications wouldn't undermine her pithy sloganeering and that her sloganeering wouldn't undermine her NPR explications. There was a time and place and medium for everything. You could be many yous. You could shift shapes and thus be more, not less, authentic. It was a distinctly modern approach.

On June 26, 2018, it carried Ocasio-Cortez to victory. "Representative Joseph Crowley of New York, once seen as a possible successor to Nancy Pelosi as Democratic leader of the House, suffered a shocking primary defeat on Tuesday, the most significant loss for a Democratic incumbent in more than a decade, and one that will reverberate across the party and the country," Shane Goldmacher and Jonathan Martin wrote in *The New York Times,* reflecting the magnitude with which Ocasio-Cortez's rise would thenceforth be treated by media. Because the Fourteenth District was safe Democratic territory, the primary victory was pretty much as good as a general-election one, and Ocasio-Cortez was now on track to be the youngest woman ever elected to Congress.

While campaigning for the primary, Ocasio-Cortez had struck that delicate balance between being human and relatable and accessible, meeting people where they are, and, at the same time, tossing the occasional bottle rocket into the national political conversation. Now, as she headed toward her seat in Congress, she faced the next incarnation of this balance: being a righteous and radical thorn in the side of her new colleagues and someone capable of doing things with them.

How hard this balancing act would be became evident in the first days of her newfound celebrity as a Democratic dragon slayer. When the House Speaker, Nancy Pelosi, was asked about her soon-to-be colleague, she minimized Ocasio-Cortez's win as a quirky local story: "It should not be viewed as something that stands for everything else." Ocasio-Cortez was unafraid to return the favor, refusing to endorse Pelosi's reelection as Speaker.

"Should other House leaders go, in your opinion—particularly the Democratic leader, Nancy Pelosi?" she was asked by a radio interviewer.

"I think it all depends on a case-by-case basis. I think that the party itself—I look forward to us having new leadership just in general."

"Well," the host persisted, "let's do the case of Nancy Pelosi specifically, then."

"Well, I think that it depends on our options, you know?" Ocasio-Cortez said. "I'm open to looking at who are other candidates for leadership." In another postprimary interview, she said that "the issues we even have today may have to do with some of the calcified structures and relationships."

This was not the customary so-honored-to-be-here curtsying that the encrusted congressional leadership expected. And as several establishment Democrats, including powerful women like Senator Claire McCaskill, tried to cut her down to size on television, Ocasio-Cortez was not shy about hinting that she, and insurgents like her, were coming for them. "Primaries are healthy for our democracy," she said in a television interview. "I think there's plenty of incumbents who are doing an amazing, amazing job. But just because you're in a seat doesn't mean that you're entitled to keep it." And she meant it. The very night of her victory party, she was touting the names of other progressive challengers in other states, including Cori Bush, running for the House in Missouri. With her own primary victory secured, she reportedly seconded volunteers from her campaign to the campaigns of Cynthia Nixon, Julia Salazar, and Zephyr Teachout, who were running state-level primary campaigns in New York against more moderate figures, with the election that September.

Congress is a strange workplace, where you need your colleagues to get things done but you work for and report to not them but the hundreds of thousands of people you represent back home—and/or, in many cases, the lobbyists and donors you may choose to put before everyone else. Even so, it was a fraught way to show up, warning your new co-workers and teammates that you are coming to take them down.

Still, shortly after her victory, Ocasio-Cortez and Pelosi had a courteous phone call. "She said that she loved working with Joe, but that she's actually always wanted younger women in Congress," Ocasio-Cortez told a reporter later. "Men tend to run at younger ages and women tend to run at older ages. She's actually very happy to see, you know, some new blood."

In the months after her primary, Ocasio-Cortez took to the road and took to the airwaves and almost instantaneously transformed into a figure of international renown. She made campaign stops in Kansas, Missouri, Hawaii, Michigan, and California on behalf of local progressive candidates—a road show *The New York Times* described as "a critical test for whether she and her Bronx-born brand of Democratic socialism resonate in the heartland—and whether she is overplaying her hand." She gave interviews. Her movements and utterances began to make headlines around the world. She had still merely won a primary in an election for a House seat. Nevertheless, she very quickly had become an icon and a target.

The journalist Raina Lipsitz captured the swirl of Ocasio-Cortez's new life vividly:

> On June 26, few people outside New York's 14th Congressional District knew who Alexandria Ocasio-Cortez was. But by the next day, when news spread that she'd toppled her opponent, 10-term Representative Joseph Crowley, in the Democratic congressional primary, she was a national celebrity. She appeared on CNN, *Meet the Press,* PBS's *Firing Line, The Late Show With Stephen Colbert, The Daily Show,* and MSNBC as the fresh face of a revived American left. Her

> lip color of choice—Stila Stay All Day Liquid Lipstick in Beso—sold out in several stores.
>
> When she appeared a few weeks later at a rally near Wall Street's *Charging Bull* statue in Lower Manhattan to endorse Zephyr Teachout, who was seeking the Democratic nomination to become New York's next attorney general, a large crowd cheered—many of them clearly there to catch a glimpse of Ocasio-Cortez, not the candidate she was supporting.
>
> Photographers—paparazzi?—shouted out, "Alex! Alexandria! Over here!" An "I Love NYC" tour bus pulled up alongside the statue. "Hey, I know her! That's her!" yelled a guy in a baseball cap, standing and pointing from the bus's top deck. Dozens of tourists began frantically snapping photos of the young woman whose face, if not name, they recognized—or assumed they did.

Her communicative talents were now being compared to those of legends of American speech making. Her Twitter account, which had mushroomed toward one million followers, had come to be seen as a political nuke—something you wanted working on your side, something you never wanted launched against you. Her endorsements became an incredibly coveted prize in politics because of their sheer power to send money, volunteers, and social media followers in your direction. She would begin to use her social channels to let you hang out with her while she was cooking, or sometimes she would go live to explain a particular point of policy, or she would manage to do both things at the same time.

"It was just a completely alien change. I was extremely stressed out because it felt like everything I said had so much more weight overnight," she later told *The Intercept.* "Even though I didn't feel like a different person, I felt this immense responsibility of all of these people's hopes and dreams for our future. It is something that I grapple with a lot because I know it's not me. It's like this avatar of me."

What felt especially strange was watching—almost as if standing outside herself, looking in—as the world grabbed hold of a part of her and sought to turn it into the whole her. She had the ideologue in her, she had the meet-them-where-they-are organizer in her, but there was room for only one story. "It felt like my brain was literally splitting apart," she told me. Right after she won her primary, she was driving from Kansas, where she had done a rally with Sanders, to Missouri, where she would do one with Cori Bush. As the car sped from Kansas City to St. Louis, she remembers taking in the media coverage that was coming at her from all sides and realizing the strange process under way: a complicated, many-sided person was being turned into a made-for-TV ideological warrior. "What was starting out as a Fox News headline and a Fox News caricature was being adopted as a mainstream narrative," she told me. "I saw the trajectory and how all of this was being built up. And it's an ego death, in a way, which is what I was experiencing in that car ride. I had to let go of trying to control this, of trying to say 'No, you have it wrong.' That car ride was the time I was like, 'There's AOC, and then there's me.' "

What she labeled the "AOC" caricature, the not-her, was, she hastened to add, not *not* her. There was enough truth in this portrayal of her to give it purchase and power. She imagined a Venn diagram "where there's a whole bunch of stuff that's said that's completely not who you are; then there's who you are, but there is that overlap of what is projected and what is true. Am I staunch in my convictions? Yes. Do I believe that late-stage capitalism has largely failed millions of people? Also yes. Do I believe health care is a right? Yes. Do I believe that huge parts of our governmental and electoral systems have been corrupted? Yeah. And I did protest in the Speaker of the House's office. I did do that. I am the person who did that. So it's not that it's completely false."

Still, the pigeonholing bothered her. She tried to cope by thinking of it as a tool: "It was like, okay, this just is what it is. And so how do I try to look at this objectively and use it?" In the coming years, she would often lean in to this image of the strident partisan, the bomb thrower, and in other moments she would defy it. But she seemed to make an early peace with the idea that the public would never know the real her. "I don't think anyone who has written about me has ever accurately captured who I am as a person," she told me, encouragingly.

Framed in the media as the warrior princess, Ocasio-Cortez became subject, brutally and instantaneously, to the kind of criticism that stalks so many women of great ambition. A reporter photographed her wearing a black jacket and posted it to social media, along with a suggestion that it was "too nice for a girl who struggles." She began to be framed as an extremist by the right-wing media echo chamber. She wasn't, in their telling, just wrongheaded. She was dangerous. (The Trump strategist Steve Bannon later told me Ocasio-Cortez was the only Democrat he truly feared, because he thought that she, unlike others, understood how to shift the terms of the conversation and rally the society toward transformational policies.) Meghan McCain, on *The View,* derided Ocasio-Cortez's ideas as "petrifying" and worried about their being "normalized," as though free health care and free college were akin to fascism. The conservative *National Review* ran a hit piece on Ocasio-Cortez under the headline "The Unserious Face of an Unserious Movement," drawing the bizarre parallel that her "approach tracks closely with the peculiar insistence of the modern Republican primary voter that if an outlandish candidate is widely reviled, that must mean he's onto something good." When Ocasio-Cortez confessed publicly that she was stressed about having to rent an apartment in Washington before her congressional paychecks started rolling in while having to continue paying rent back home in New York, she was chastised for being financially irresponsible, when in fact she simply happened not to be affluent like most people in Congress. She did a photo shoot for *Interview* magazine, wore designer clothes they lent to her for it, as is the custom in media shoots, and then spent days battling stories that she, a democratic socialist, couldn't be serious about her ideas if that was a Gabriela Hearst blazer. She became subject to the tedious but unavoidable entreaties of the Debate-Me Guys, such as when the right-wing commentator Ben Shapiro offered $10,000 to her campaign or a charity if she agreed to duel on his show. At first, she ignored him. Then, facing questions about why she wouldn't debate a Debate-Me Guy, she tweeted, "Just like catcalling, I don't owe a response to unsolicited requests from men with bad intentions. And also like catcalling, for some reason they feel entitled to one."

Even as she was succeeding with her approach of seizing and holding attention, diverting that attention up to the larger causes she favored, using the eyeballs to teach, her critics were trying to blunt the edge of these skills by dismissing her command of notice as inherently unserious. They were trying to cast her as a provocateur.

Later that summer and into the fall, when several of the insurgent candidates Ocasio-Cortez had backed came up short—having in many cases been long shots—many in the press and in politics treated it as proof that she had been overhyped and overestimated. "Down Goes Socialism," read the headline in *Politico*. "The Ocasio-Cortez wing of the Democratic Party thinks its policies are the path to victory in red states. Tuesday night's results suggest otherwise." In New York, Governor Andrew Cuomo, a fellow Democrat of the kind Ocasio-Cortez had put on notice, including by embracing a primary challenger to him in Cynthia Nixon, tried to get even, dismissing any supposed Ocasio-Cortez "wave." It was, he said, "not even a ripple." Later in the year, Senator McCaskill would call Ocasio-Cortez a "shiny new object" and declaim that "rhetoric is cheap." (Unlike Ocasio-Cortez, McCaskill didn't win her race that year and left the Senate to become a television commentator offering advice on how other politicians could win their races.)

That fall, for a profile in *Vogue*, Ocasio-Cortez sat down with a reporter and some of her aides and spoke of the personal toll of being at the center of a hurricane:

> "It's just not a normal human experience I'm going through. There's so many cameras on me out of nowhere. Like, I'm not media-trained—"
>
> "We can't say that anymore," says [her adviser Corbin] Trent, who's media-training her. "It's not helpful."
>
> "OK, sorry, sorry," Ocasio-Cortez says. "I'm just overwhelmed. I'm a normal person, and people treat me now like I'm this two-dimensional caricature that they project narratives onto. It can be emotionally taxing. Like, what do you do with young brown women who are intelligent and whose faces are symmetrical? You paint them as a narrative."

Provocation wasn't who she was. It was something she used. It was a tool she owned that was being turned by some into her biography.

To play with narrative as effectively as she did put you at risk of being manufactured into a narrative, too.

It was a *Financial Times* headline that would perhaps best capture the blaze of the new congresswoman's arrival: "Idealist. Infuriator. Influencer: The Year of Alexandria Ocasio-Cortez."

What may now be called the AOC style—the provocation, the meet-you-where-you-are second sentence, the recognizing and crafting of moments and meaning making around them, the long-game teaching, the offering of the self in service of forcing a conversation about systems—this methodology wasn't a given; it needed to be invented and developed. And in November 2018, shortly after the formality of beating her Republican opponent, Ocasio-Cortez went a ways toward defining that style on a visit to her new workplace.

It was freshman orientation for new members of Congress, a time to meet your heroes, see your new environs, learn some of the tricks of the trade. But for Ocasio-Cortez, the isthmus of the inside-outside game was inescapable. One moment, she was taking a selfie with a group of three other progressive women of her unapologetic ilk—Ilhan Omar, Ayanna Pressley, and Rashida Tlaib—and, via Instagram, they turned themselves into "the Squad." More of the we're-coming-for-you vibe. The next moment, she was worrying about whether the congressional leadership would give her decent committee assignments or would try to shaft her. "Mind you, this is in the middle of lobbying for your committees," Ocasio-Cortez told me. "This is the work that you are going to do. It's where you're going to spend the most amount of your time as a legislator, is in committee, if you're doing your job and actually going to hearings. This was a time when leadership was determining committee seats. The entire time, even the moment I was elected, people were calling, saying, 'What committee do you want to be on? What committee do you want to be on?' And so you could very well get put on what I call the dog-catching committee. You could make all these requests, have all your requests denied, get put in a very small committee that doesn't really matter much or that is not of interest to you or is not powerful."

Speaker Pelosi had great leverage over Ocasio-Cortez right then. So when Ocasio-Cortez, that very week, received an invitation to join a protest occupying Pelosi's office, her first thought, she said, was, "I'm just going to get totally screwed by this, probably." She told me, "Ninety-nine point nine-nine-nine percent of me did not want to do that."

The organization that had reached out to her was the Sunrise Movement, a decentralized network of young climate activists known for their fearless methods. They were pressing Pelosi because they wanted her to empower a House select committee on climate change to draft a Green New Deal. Pelosi had given the committee a more nebulous mandate, denied it subpoena power, refused the suggestion to exclude members who took contributions from polluters, and placed it in the hands of a chair, Kathy Castor, who said the Green New Deal had "some fabulous proposals" but stopped shy of endorsing it. Sunrise was, in other words, protesting the kneecapping of Ocasio-Cortez's big idea. But at first, the activists didn't ask her to protest with them. They just invited her to meet them the day before their planned action, at a church in Washington.

"These kids were sleeping in a church like twenty minutes away from the Capitol," Ocasio-Cortez told me. "I'm like, 'Man. Okay, I'll meet them.' And then Rashida Tlaib came with me. This was the first time that Rashida and I really did anything together.

"We show up," she went on, "and all these kids see us walk in, and they start crying." They were in the midst of a training on getting arrested and how to engage in civil disobedience.

"I'm talking to these kids, and, first of all, I'm closer to their age than I am to most of my colleagues," she said. "I relate very much to their sense of urgency, and I know what it's like to be them. I don't yet know what it's like to be a fifty-something-year-old legislator. I'm watching, and they're just telling their stories. I know these kids. Like, they're applying to college. Getting an arrest on your record at that time—they're putting their whole future on the line. They're putting college acceptances on the line. I recognize the very real-life sacrifices that these sixteen- and seventeen-year-olds are making.

"At that point, Rashida and I stood up on a table," Ocasio-Cortez continued. "There's some photos of it. We had literally gone straight from orientation, so we took our blazers off. I'm up there on some folding table with a pencil skirt. We're just standing there talking to these kids. I went home that night, and I'm like, okay, this is going to happen no matter what.

"I wanted to throw up. Because, for me, I wrestle with decisions, morally, a lot. And when I wrestle with something, I really try to distill it down to an essential question that is most important to me. And that was the essential question that it had boiled down to: these kids are either going to get arrested for nothing, or they're going to get arrested for something, and I'm the difference. I felt I would have been the difference. And so I was like, 'All right, I guess that answers that for me.' "

The next day, in footage beamed around the world, the youth of Sunrise piled into Pelosi's office for their protest, and Congresswoman-elect Alexandria Ocasio-Cortez visited them. In her mind, she had been mild. "I didn't sit down myself. I didn't refuse to leave. I didn't obstruct. I didn't get arrested. But I visited them," she told me.

Did she understand in that moment that she would be seen as entering Congress by in effect declaring war on Congress and her own party leader?

"I didn't feel that way," Ocasio-Cortez said, "but I also knew that it would be interpreted that way. Which is why if you actually pull up the CNN clip from that day, I worded my response very, very carefully. Because I didn't want this to be about me and her, because then it would all be for nothing if this got distilled into some petty beef, an AOC-versus-Pelosi type of thing, which is what the media so desperately wanted, because conflict between individuals is easier to characterize than what's actually happening.

"So my response was like, 'This is about all of us against this issue.' And I know that she is a strong champion for this, and I know that she is hearing these young people. And I'm looking forward to translating their demands and representing them, as a party."

This was why, from the moment she arrived in Congress, people routinely said they didn't know what to do with Ocasio-Cortez. Here she was occupying the office of the Speaker of the House of her party—basically, unprecedented in and of itself—and she was doing it while under tremendous pressure to please the Speaker, for the sake of avoiding the dog-catching committee. Ocasio-Cortez was creating a moment and using her stardom to frame a window of decency around her policy ideas. To act on the Green New Deal, given the impending crisis, was decent; failing to act was indecent. But then, having established that uncompromising frame, having occupied Pelosi's office and stood with the youth of Sunrise, she did the meeting people where they are. She made that comment to CNN about how Pelosi was really on their side, how she was surely hearing them, and how Ocasio-Cortez was looking forward to acting on these ideas—not just her, her whole party, which apparently she was now speaking for, even as she occupied its leader's office. Here she was both being gentler toward Pelosi than she had to be and, at the same time, boxing Pelosi in. Having framed her way as the right way, she was advocating for a future she wanted that was not inevitable by portraying it as inevitable, at once summoning Pelosi to rise to the occasion and making it harder for her to say she was opposed. She was giving Pelosi a golden gate of retreat with her remarks. At the same time, she was telling Pelosi, "My way or the wrong side of history."

I suggested to Ocasio-Cortez that this moment was the perfect example of the outsider-insider approach that had become her political signature.

"Yeah, exactly," she said. "I spoke to Speaker Pelosi that day, and I told her personally, 'Please don't take this personally. I just really believe in what these kids are doing. And I do this with utmost respect for you as a person. This is just an issue that we need to have a lot of urgency and attention around.' "

Did Pelosi buy it?

"I mean, she did it via a text," Ocasio-Cortez said. "She was like, 'Okay'—I don't think it was a scary, like, 'Okay period,' when you're like, 'I'm in trouble.' "

In retrospect, Ocasio-Cortez told me, she had more sway in that moment than she felt at the time: "Because she was in the midst of trying to lock down her bid as Speaker and get reelected, and it was not necessarily certain. I think there was leverage on both ends." And, finally, to the chagrin of many of her hardest-core supporters, Ocasio-Cortez gave in—not the last time she would hear that charge—by ultimately voting for Pelosi's speakership. She didn't frame the decision as a result of rapture. "At the time," she told me, "there wasn't a more progressive candidate."

A moment later, she wanted to clarify something about her dealings with Pelosi. There was, she said, an insincere approach to politics that resembled her provocation and human smoothing over but, she said, was fundamentally different. "Something I'm very sensitive to is that there's a huge difference between doing that versus there being a wink and a nudge, like, 'Don't worry, this doesn't mean anything.' That's a very different kind of tack, which people do. And it's important not to conflate those two things, where it's like, I'm doing this publicly, but I'm doing something different privately."

She wasn't annulling what she had done, I offered.

"Right, and I wasn't apologizing for it. I was just saying, 'This isn't personal. It's politics.' "

A few weeks later, Ocasio-Cortez was at Harvard for an orientation the university organizes for new members of Congress. Many Americans had probably never heard of this peculiar ritual of new members going to a private university to learn how to do their jobs—until that year, that is.

What changed that year was the arrival of Ocasio-Cortez, who showed up for orientation and was incapable of overlooking what so many new members before her had abided. "Was this a multi-decade, pro-corporate lobbyist project the entire time?" she tweeted in the middle of the orientation, sharing glimpses of what was being presented to the members and who was presenting it. She criticized the organizers for bringing in bankers and lobbyists to make presentations while leaving out representatives of labor. She criticized hearing about how great the recent Trump tax cuts were and how bad a $15 minimum wage would be. And, again, she couldn't have been the first person to chafe at some of this. But she was pretty much the first person to call it out in the way she did, not taking her hosts aside, not suggesting some changes for next year, but blasting to hundreds of thousands of people that her own institution, her very own teammates, had been corrupted.

I asked Ocasio-Cortez how she had thought about—to use her word—her "posture" in these early moments. How strategic or spontaneous was the political style that was gelling?

"I think part of it was I was so tied to why my constituents sent me here," she told me. "At that point, I wasn't a member of Congress. I was, like, a waitress." And, working in the restaurant, she remembered all the conversations she had with customers and co-workers speculating about what they would do if any of them ever got into the rooms where things happened, if they ever came up close with the powers that be. The Harvard orientation, she told me, "was like one of these insane situations that people talk about at the bar all the time: 'I wish I was in that room. I wonder what it's like. What are these people thinking when they see these things?'

"All of a sudden, in a matter of three months, I went from behind the bar to walking straight into this room with all of these people—like, 'Holy shit, this hypothetical situation is real.'" And the bar banter came back to her, even haunted her: "All these people talking shit at the bar, like, 'What would you do, man? Would you say something? Would you just kind of duck out?' People are like, 'No, man, I would say something. I would say—.'" And a fellow banterer would inevitably hit back, skeptical: "Oh, yeah, would you?" Out of all the people at that bar on those nights, she had somehow been chosen and teleported into the hypothetical. And the question could no longer be theoretical: If faced with bullshit, would you say something? Would you?

So there she was at Harvard. The CEO of Goldman Sachs was over here. Samantha Power was over there. "I just looked down at this binder, and it's like, 'The congressional orientation, brought to you by AEI.'" The American Enterprise Institute is a conservative think tank that, just five months earlier, had run a blog post titled "The Uninformed Economic Views of Alexandria Ocasio-Cortez, in 2 Charts." "I'm like, 'What the fuck?' I'm sitting here, and I'm like, 'How is this bipartisan?'"

There was a big dinner one night. Huge room, circular tables. "The waitresses are winking at me, and I relate more to them than any fucking person I'm sitting down with," Ocasio-Cortez said. "Everyone stands up, and each person, one by one, says, 'Hey, I'm so-and-so, I represent this district.' One sentence. Most people, because it was pitched and marketed as a bipartisan thing—there were Republican members there, there were Democratic members there—everyone's like, 'I can't wait to work across the aisle and get things done.' There's like sixty people in the freshman class.

"Almost everyone said a variation of that: 'We're looking forward to working with you guys and getting things done.' How wonderful bipartisanship is and the virtue of bipartisanship. I'm sitting here, and I'm just like, 'Fuck. No one's talking about health care, no one's talking about wages, no one's talking about any actual substantive issue. They're just talking about how amazing bipartisanship is.'"

She was seeing up close how it happens, how the machinery grinds ideals to dust. "It's brainwashing. It's like a cult," she told me. "I'm sitting here, and I'm like, 'Oh my God.'" So the introductions go around and around, leaping from one table to another. And guess who happened to be last? ("This was not planned or anything," Ocasio-Cortez insists.) An incoming member who had already revealed her special talent for creating moments somehow wound up as the closer.

Ocasio-Cortez was sitting next to Naureen Akhter, a Muslim woman who had been an organizer for the campaign. "She's this hijabi woman, and she has to listen to all these Republicans being like, 'Love everybody.' It's like, 'Go fuck yourself.'" So Ocasio-Cortez stood up. Across the room, everyone turned to look at a woman many of them had yet to meet in person but all of them seemed to know.

"I'm looking forward to working with everybody," she remembered saying, "but I'm less a believer in bipartisanship, and I'm more a believer in common ground. And so I'm hoping to find common ground in expanding people's health care and their wages, et cetera, because bipartisanship got us war. It has gotten us tax cuts for the rich."

She remembers silence. She noticed the servers suppressing laughter. Dinner ended a few minutes later. There was a group photo on risers with all the members. As soon as it ended, the servers swarmed Ocasio-Cortez to take their own photo with her.

She told this story by way of explaining why she had chosen to call out the orientation by tweet instead of engaging from within. She did it during one of the panel discussions. The more she did things like that, the more people would begin to ask her—young women especially, she said—"Where do you get the confidence?" "I'm like, 'Confidence?' I'm like, 'You tell me.'" She added, "I don't know if people really understand it, but I'm scared shitless half the time I'm doing any given thing. I'm always scared. I'm in a perpetual state of fear." Still, unlike most new members, she sent the tweet, made the callout, stayed true to her bantering promises to the guys at the bar. "What would you do, man? Would you say something? Would you just kind of duck out? No, man, I would say something. Oh, yeah, would you?" Yeah, she would say something.

On January 3, 2019, Ocasio-Cortez was sworn in to her seat in Congress, officially becoming the youngest woman in American history to serve in those chambers. And, with the bar banterers still seemingly on her mind, she pursued a persuasive approach of provocation laced with personal warmth topped with head-down diligence that, for a moment in time, turned the nation's capital into her town. She became the lightning rod next door.

That very week, in an interview on *60 Minutes*, she casually suggested taxing the superrich who make more than $10 million a year at a top marginal rate of 70 percent:

> You look at our tax rates back in the '60s and when you have a progressive tax rate system, your tax rate, you know, let's say, from zero to $75,000 may be 10 percent or 15 percent. But once you get to, like, the tippy-tops—on your 10 millionth dollar sometimes you see tax rates as high as 60 or 70 percent. That doesn't mean all $10 million are taxed at an extremely high rate, but it means that as you climb up this ladder, you should be contributing more.

That was it. Not even a specific proposal, really. It was not clear that she had planned to unveil anything. But the idea of a 70 percent marginal tax rate on income above $10 million became an AOC proposal in the public mind, and she ran with it. Soon the Nobel-winning economist Paul Krugman was weighing in, lending his clout to the idea. Other writers were helping to flesh out what the "plan" could pay for. Centrists in the Democratic Party were forced to go on record accepting or rejecting her "plan." *The Guardian* observed, "She has realized what Republicans have known for a long time: if people are talking about your agenda, even if they're talking about how bad and silly it is, you are making that agenda more plausible." Her fellow progressives were giddy about her knack for forcing an issue. "She absolutely does have the ability to put issues on the map," Congresswoman Pramila Jayapal, head of the Congressional Progressive Caucus, told a reporter. "It's not that there haven't been champions of these issues before. But when you've got 2.1 million Twitter followers and a press that will cover anything you say, it's a huge opportunity for us."

Ocasio-Cortez was, to use a term she was helping to popularize at that moment, "moving the Overton window." She was changing the boundaries of discussion, rendering the undiscussable discussable and the outlandish plausible. You never got the sense that she wasn't sincere about the underlying ideas. But you also got the sense that, in a way many of her colleagues had been incapable of, she understood proposing things to provoke conversation, break taboos, force side taking, and, perhaps, make far-reaching and unlikely ideas more probable—ideas that powerful oligarchic forces were working to make unpersuasive and scary seeming.

And with the offhand tax proposal that wasn't really a proposal now in the bloodstream of the nation, there was polling on it a month afterward. An idea straight out of left field now had three-quarters of Democrats persuaded, nearly half of independents, and more than one-third of Republicans. For as long as anyone could remember, the persuasive approach of mainstream Democrats had been outreach through dilution. Reach across to moderates and Republicans by tempering your ideas as much as possible. Here was a different, and effective, method at work: force the unthinkable to be thinkable, get everyone talking about it, rile up your diehards to become your conversational army, and actually change some minds.

In the same *60 Minutes* interview, Ocasio-Cortez generated another days-long story. When asked if President Trump was racist, she didn't do the hedging that had been common even among his detractors. "Yes. Yes. No question," she said.

That same week, an old video surfaced of Ocasio-Cortez dancing on a rooftop with college peers. It was far from embarrassing. But for a young woman trying to establish herself as credible in a citadel of patriarchal power, it wasn't the most convenient timing. Her critics were trying to discredit her seriousness by portraying her as human and normal. And rather than try to convince them on their terms that, no, she was serious and sober, she sought to change the terms of worthiness with her response. Her staff recorded a fresh video of her dancing to Edwin Starr's "War (What Is It Good For?)" outside her new office and then ducking in with a smile.

One moment she was calling out her new colleagues for not paying their interns. The next she was livestreaming herself fixing dinner on Instagram, explaining some of the finer points of policy and, at times, wrestling aloud with her own decisions. Within weeks of taking office, she released her blueprint for a Green New Deal. It was criticized in many quarters as extreme, and a clerical error resulted in the premature release of a draft that led to exaggerated stories about Ocasio-Cortez wanting to abolish beef and air travel. "The green dream or whatever they call it—nobody knows what it is, but they're for it, right?" Pelosi said to a reporter. As Pelosi seemed to fear, the most radical plan on offer also became the plan that every top-tier contender for the Democratic presidential nomination in 2020 signed on to. Ocasio-Cortez had become famous over the previous few months. "Today," the NPR journalist Steve Inskeep intoned when she launched the Green New Deal, "she tries to leverage her fame."

She took a risk in opposing Amazon's bid to locate a new headquarters in New York, in the shadow of her district. A risk because the Amazon site would supposedly have generated many jobs. But she saw the giant tax breaks local officials had offered the company and came out swinging. She told me at the time, for an essay in *The New Yorker*, that the deal was "dressed-up trickle-down economics." "What we're seeing here is a complete public cost for a private corporate benefit," she said. "When you give a three-billion-dollar tax break to the richest company in the world, that means that you're giving up our schools. You're giving up our infrastructure. You're giving up our community development." Eventually, Amazon withdrew from the deal. It was later reported to have dramatically expanded its workforce in New York, without any tax breaks needed.

Ocasio-Cortez also began to make waves in legislative hearings, in particular with a rotisserie grilling of Michael Cohen, Trump's former lawyer, in late February. Thereafter, several of her committee-hearing moments went viral, revealing, once again, her talent for accommodating disparate qualities: she was the diligent student who had done all of her homework, and she was the performer who knew how to create a moment millions would watch. "A lot of people expected a show pony. But it turns out she's a workhorse," Caroline Fredrickson, a longtime legal operative in official Washington, told *The Guardian.*

In parallel, she proceeded with her bear poking. On a visit to the South by Southwest conference in Austin, she called capitalism "unsustainable" and "irredeemable" and did not mince words about the more incrementalist approach associated with many of her own Democratic colleagues. "This idea of like 10 percent better than garbage shouldn't be something we settle for," she said. When challenged about her use of the label "democratic socialist," Ocasio-Cortez did not back down or try to soften her views. "When millennials talk about concepts like democratic socialism, we're not talking about these kinds of 'Red Scare' boogeyman," she told *Business Insider.* "We're talking about countries and systems that already exist that have already been proven to be successful in the modern world." She called Trump a "fascist" before many members of Congress would, and referred to the border camps where his administration had directed the separation of families as "concentration camps." Once again, an increasingly familiar loop would play out. She would go online to defend her provocation. Outrage would swell among her critics. And then some serious people would weigh in, having her back. In this case, the Holocaust Memorial Museum in Washington, D.C., put out a statement condemning her use of "concentration camps." Soon afterward, though, hundreds of scholars organized to sign a letter taking her side of the argument. In this case, it was hard to accuse her of taking the provocative stance for demagogic purposes, because just 25 percent of Americans agreed with her use of the term, according to a poll. But that didn't seem to matter. For good measure, around that time Ocasio-Cortez also suggested that the Department of Homeland Security be abolished.

She showed a prodigious talent for insults and clapbacks, hitting back at people in a way that stoked her fans' ardor but was, for many, out of keeping with the way a member of Congress operated. When Ron DeSantis, then a Florida congressman, called her "this girl, Ocasio-Cortez, or whatever she is," she fired back: "Rep DeSantis, it seems you're confused as to 'whatever I am.' I am a Puerto Rican woman. It's strange you don't know what that is, given that ~75,000

Puerto Ricans have relocated to Florida in the 10 mos since María. But I'm sure these new FL voters appreciate your comments!" An affirmation of ethnic identity, a statement of female strength, and an electoral threat, all in one! Another day, she pushed back against Fox News: "1. @FoxNews, why can't any of your anchors say my name correctly? It's been 5 months. 2. It is bizarre to see 1%-salaried anchors laugh at the US housing crisis."

Ocasio-Cortez explained the ferocity of her style to one interviewer as "a Bronx thing," part of a "call-and-response culture, which is very much in the wheelhouse of people of color. There is a certain amount of street cred that comes with being able to cleverly defend yourself." Even in the moment, pundits of long standing felt they were seeing something novel. "It's kind of amazing that one of the most naturally talented politicians to emerge in some time also happens to be a highly effective, aggressive, and rather merciless combatant in social media messaging," the journalist Glenn Greenwald had said even before her primary victory. "What I think is fascinating about AOC is how differently she views the upside and downside risk of public presence," the MSNBC host Chris Hayes said. "Most politicians don't actually want a lot of attention because it brings scrutiny. AOC takes a very different approach, and one I think we'll see more politicians take as time goes on."

In her conversation with Ta-Nehisi Coates in the January of her swearing in, she addressed the matter of the clapbacks and combat. How, he asked her, did she decide when to engage?

"I had some of our organizers ask me this, and I told the joke that basically it's like, whoever's coming at me in my mentions with a blue check when I haven't eaten in three hours," she said with a laugh. Then, more seriously: "When a really good example comes up, that's when I do that, because when I clap back, it's not just reflexive, self-defense. I'm trying to dismantle some of the frames of misogyny, classism, racism that we've just allowed to go on. And I wish I didn't have to do this, to be frank." For her generation, civility and comity had helped to uphold systems of injustice and hadn't delivered much besides forever wars, fragile employment, and foreclosures. "Sometimes I just feel like people aren't being held accountable," she told Coates, "and until we all start pitching in and holding people accountable, I'm just gonna let them have it."

Her straddling of these multiple, even at times contradictory persuasive approaches boggled the mind: provoking, patiently teaching, constructing moments, shifting norms, clapping back, baring herself as a lure for her policy ideas, calling out her own side, summoning and boxing in at the same time. All of this reflected, it would seem, an acute and unusually adept understanding of attention in the new era and how it could be marshaled for persuasion.

"They used to talk about the Oprah effect," the progressive economist Stephanie Kelton told a reporter. "I think it's the Ocasio effect at this point." The German newspaper *Die Welt* summed up her powers thus: "The Walking Provocation; Alexandria Ocasio-Cortez is many things: for the Democrats a star, for the Republicans a spectre of terror, for everyone else the face of a modern campaign." And all of this attention, it should be said, came with terrifying and awful side effects. Suddenly there were fake nude selfies of Ocasio-Cortez online, being amplified by big publications. Suddenly a Coast Guard lieutenant and avowed white nationalist was arrested in Maryland for threatening to kill Ocasio-Cortez, Pelosi, and the then Senator Kamala Harris. Suddenly Ocasio-Cortez was among the chief targets of the right-wing media machine.

In one of our conversations, I asked her about the development of her talent for seizing attention and using it politically. Her hero Sanders, I suggested, pursued a persuasive strategy built on consistency and purity—saying the same thing the same way a thousand times and refusing the media games and sound bites and crafting of viral moments. She, ideologically aligned with him but of another generation and another temperamental mold, had been more willing to play those games, to employ a wider array of tactics in service of the same fundamental strategy.

"For me, where I've landed so far, at least at this moment," she said, "is that I don't compromise on my values, but I'm willing to compromise in how we get there, how we talk about them, if it doesn't undermine the ultimate value and the ultimate goal. I think that's very different than saying it's my way or the highway."

She made a revealing distinction between Sanders and her on this score. He was an older white man whose aloofness the society tolerated, even if it didn't quite love it. He could refuse the corporate media game, the attention game, the sound-bite culture, the self-revelation (though he was doing more of the latter). But, Ocasio-Cortez told me, "especially for people of color, in order to survive and thrive, you have to find open pockets to exploit and subvert in systems that weren't intended for your success."

She gave the example of corporate-owned media as a system that Sanders had generally deplored and avoided and that she, while sharing his attitude toward it, had decided instead to seek to commandeer for her ideas' benefit. "Media, for the most part, is a for-profit engine and relies on profits in making editorial decisions. That's why, for example, climate change never got covered in a serious way. Because it wasn't profitable. They couldn't figure out a way to tell this story that would drive ratings they could sell ad revenue on.

"It's not the fault of journalists," she went on. "It's just the business structure. You could take a conspiratorial approach to it and say, 'The media isn't really doing this.' Or you can just understand it. I'm like, okay, this is the state of things." The media is ratings obsessed. It needs drama. That is what it is. You can turn away as a result, in the way that Sanders tended to. Or, in the way Ocasio-Cortez was now practicing, you could harness everything that was wrong with the media to hijack it to advance your broader goals.

"What I kind of figured was like, 'Listen, that is a battle, but that's not the central fight. We aren't organizing an entire movement for the purpose of dismantling CNN,'" she said.

I suggested that, contrary to a figure like Sanders, she saw the media game she deplored as a game she could also win.

"I see it as a game I can play," she said. "Climate change, historically, is not an issue that has been addressed, because it had low ratings. Given the fact that I knew at the time that I had been turned into this firebrand and this lightning rod, I made the conscious decision—because, yes, climate change is the existential threat of our time—that if I could use that intensity of attention, for better or worse, and direct it toward climate change, it will force a conversation."

That idea helped crystallize one difference between Ocasio-Cortez's persuasive methodology and Sanders's. She, too, was animated by principle and strident and full of ambition. But where Sanders had reaped real credibility by refusing to descend into the morass of the political culture around him, had built a movement through renunciation, she wanted to use the media against itself, play the pop culture games in order to make the boring interesting and the ignored unignorable. She knew the system was broken, as he did. But she identified as a woman of color who couldn't afford to yell, over and over, that the system was broken. Instead, she would find the cracks and work inside them. She couldn't afford to wait for people to come to her because of her truth. She was willing to come to them. She understood them to be bored, stuck in routines, full of apathy, fatalistic about things changing, not dialed in to politics 24/7. And she was willing to assume the burden of making them pay heed. Sanders often seemed to feel that any capitulation to the reality of how political persuasion happens in a democracy—broadening his approach to include self-disclosure, emotional appeal, courting of the press, updated terms on race—was a betrayal of his integrity. Ocasio-Cortez, building on his legacy, was trying something different: playing the game to overturn it; being human and personal for the sake of dismantling structures; meeting voters where they are and challenging them at the same time.

Ocasio-Cortez was perhaps reaching for a new model of leadership for the social media age. On this model, the leader didn't merely operate within the realm of politics, trying to implement what people wanted. She doubled as a cultural worker, seeking directly to shape the conversation that in turn shaped what people wanted and what, therefore, could be implemented. To be sure, there have always been leaders with the power to galvanize the public around ideas. But in earlier eras, they went through gatekeepers who ran their ideas on op-ed pages and Sunday television shows. They didn't have a many-times-a-day portal into millions of minds. The new technological realities of office had created a new way of operating that helped to explain Ocasio-Cortez's juggling of approaches and tones. You provoked to make people think and talk. You wooed to get colleagues to sign on to your plans. You proposed to give the people what they wanted, but you also challenged the people to want things they didn't yet want.

In her conversation with Coates, Ocasio-Cortez elaborated on this philosophy. "Part of the responsibility—if we're doing the job right—is to translate public will into the actual law of the land," she said. "But who shapes and directs and moves that public will is writers, journalists, activists, and artists. They shape the public will and bring it to a point where we can take it and translate it into policy. Without that public will existing first, it's very difficult to move the nation forward. People think of elected office as being a leadership position, but I don't think it is. I think it's a position of following, because oftentimes it's only when things are made politically expedient, or politically inconvenient to disagree with, that you actually start seeing this movement happen."

But she was underselling herself. This idea of leaders being hemmed in by public opinion might have applied to others. But Ocasio-Cortez was really trying to do both things at once—to be the influencer and the influenced at the same time, the activist and the acted upon, the bomb thrower and the legislator trying to eke out progress. In an interview on NPR about the Green New Deal, she said, "If I had to decide, would I rather have the resolution passed or would I have rather preferred we start a national conversation about the urgency of the climate crisis, I would have chosen the latter every single time." It was a vision of persuasion oriented toward the long game, at peace with not even being around when your triumph finally comes, and grounded in the notion that whoever sets the terms and boundaries of what people are talking about will carry the era.

"My job is to bring up things that everyone's trying to talk about which powerful people are trying to quell," Ocasio-Cortez told me. "It's also a different understanding of what my job is from others'. The reason I have the freedom to do this is because I have given up attachment to this idea of a future in politics, which has been very liberating. I literally came in, and I said, 'You know what, if it's one term, it's one term. Let's roll.' "

After Ocasio-Cortez's splashy debut on the international stage, the question that hounded her tenure was whether someone pursuing this approach could survive and be granted the space and mercy to navigate it. The isthmus she was walking was narrow: to the establishment on her right, she was at constant risk of being an outcast; to the avid base on her left, she was at constant risk of being a sellout. She was treading carefully. It was grueling and full of risk.

The society rewarded the establishmentarians who stuck to the inside game and clung to their civility and never changed much but leavened stasis with a smile—lavishing them with money and power and office. In a different way, it rewarded the purists, the callers out, the activists who never backed down, with respect, with devoted fan bases, and, more and more, with audiences who would crowdfund their Patreon and give them an independent living. Ocasio-Cortez's rise was a test of whether the society could reward someone who was unwilling to let the duty of outreach compromise all that she wanted to change, but who was also more interested than many of her activist ilk in winning people over to her visions and translating them into collective reality.

It was a question that went back to the Bronx and Yorktown: Could you, *could she,* be both?

In those opening months of her tenure, the political establishment tried to make sense of her, and she, of them. After all the drama with Pelosi, Ocasio-Cortez was eventually granted a seat on the high-profile House Financial Services Committee, which oversees the moneyed industries that were a focus for her anger. It was a sign that the establishment types valued (feared?) her powers of calling out and ability to generate viral moments and were perhaps even willing to risk ire from industry. At the same time, colleagues were reportedly seething—unlike her, anonymously, as ever—about how she had sought a seat on the House Ways and Means Committee, the all-powerful body that writes tax laws, and how her army of online fans had swarmed to lobby Pelosi to give her the seat—her failure, in other words, to work the inside route, to ask humbly. "It totally pissed off everyone," a Democratic House member told a reporter. "You don't get picked for committees by who your grass-roots [supporters] are." You don't, the member was saying, play the outside game.

Ocasio-Cortez was hard for many of her colleagues to read. Was she here to help them or hurt them? One day she was the lone Democrat to vote against reopening the government, because the giant bill contained funding for Immigration and Customs Enforcement, which she wanted to abolish. "Our community felt strongly about not funding that," she said by way of explanation, refusing the kind of accommodation to reality that was customary in those chambers. Another day, she happened to discover that, in her new environs, lobbyists pay people to stand in line outside committee rooms so they can reserve a spot in hearings. As with the Harvard orientation, many members before her had become aware of this practice, and many of them probably didn't love it. But she took it upon herself to take a picture of the line and tweet about it, calling out her own workplace. She made a splashy public endorsement of an all-women list of progressive candidates, including a Senate candidate who was running against the preferred candidate of the party bosses. But then, at the same moment, she was offering her colleagues complimentary Twitter classes to teach the AOC way. The seminar highlighted "the importance of digital media storytelling," according to an invitation sent to members, and promised instruction on how to use the platform "as an effective and authentic messaging tool."

What she was teaching was what she had mastered herself—the building of a direct and loyal and constantly watered connection to one's followers, so as to create a power base that no one could take away. To achieve this was a mark of independence in this time, not only in politics, but also in media, where social followings and solo newsletters became the order of the day, and among young creators, who built multimillion-dollar businesses out of "hype houses" where they made TikTok videos about living in hype houses making TikTok videos. The soloist approach to persuasion relied heavily on the star's ability to marshal public opinion. But in the realm of politics, it left many insiders feeling bypassed and dissed, because their power was being threatened.

In April 2019, three months into her first term, *Politico* ran a revealing article titled "How Alexandria Ocasio-Cortez Broke All the Rules of New York Politics." Filled with the petty grievances of local pols, it is a reminder of how unusual Ocasio-Cortez's inside/outside-game approach was:

> Power in New York has not traditionally been achieved through social media stardom; it has been achieved through the slow and painful courting of various constituency groups. It is achieved block association by block association, com-

> munity board by community board, labor union by labor union. Now that she is a star, city insiders wonder, is AOC willing to labor in those trenches? Does she even need to? What happens if she doesn't?

Part of the anxiety was simple jealousy. "I send a tweet when I see something I think is cool, and it gets, like, six likes," one state senator was quoted as saying. "AOC sneezes and it gets a half-million retweets!" Part of it was the fear of getting in the crosshairs of someone who had not merely the power to draft a bill or call a hearing but also the more immediate and visceral power to drag you online. The article quoted a slightly irked Al Sharpton about his disappointment that Ocasio-Cortez had skipped his annual Martin Luther King Day party in Harlem, where insiders of every variety come to play the inside game by courting the reverend, in favor of that public event with Ta-Nehisi Coates, where she was instead taking her case directly to the public, via a video stream. The fear that threaded through many of the comments in the *Politico* article, often anonymous, was that Ocasio-Cortez's reliance on, and facility with, the outside game would free her from the necessity of making relationships with movers and shakers in power—free her from the need for them. "I say this not to dismiss her," one political type was quoted as saying, the caveat somewhat unconvincing, "because I think she is really smart and capable, but it is like if Kim Kardashian were a member of Congress. Do you think she would be going to community boards? Why do the scut work of local politics if you can get glossy magazine covers?"

The other rap on Ocasio-Cortez's approach in those first months was that this ascendant influencer politicking was fundamentally anti-coalitional when it came to relationships with other legislators. Calling out and staking out window-moving positions were useful for building and revving up a following. But there was a risk of writing off people with valid reasons for hesitancy as corporate stooges or cowardly. "The demand to deny committee seats to anyone who takes money from people in the fossil fuel industry, while useful for brandishing moral superiority, further weakens the prospects for coalition-building," *Politico,* ever the mouthpiece for the Beltway establishment, had written in another critical report earlier that year, this one on Ocasio-Cortez's climate proposals. The article suggested Ocasio-Cortez was "more focused on building an audience than building cases for her positions among her congressional peers." There was that tension once again: the audience was what gave her power, and it was what had made all those presidential candidates embrace her Green New Deal. But what it took to provoke and use attention risked turning a lawmaker into a flattened character of their own authorship, more strident and less forgiving than they actually were, and less effective at translating their own recipes into sausage.

By her first summer in office, the message of some of these criticisms seemed to break through and chasten Ocasio-Cortez. "Alexandria Ocasio-Cortez learns to play the insider's game," the ever-anxious *Politico* now declared. She had tried working with Speaker Pelosi to alter legislation funding enforcement on the Mexican border. Ultimately, it didn't go Ocasio-Cortez's way, and she voted against the bill she had sought to change. But, *Politico* noted approvingly, contrary to expectations on the Hill, "Ocasio-Cortez held no impromptu news conference on the Capitol lawn. She refrained from a tweetstorm. In fact, she didn't write a single post about one of the biggest immigration debates so far under the Democratic majority."

So maybe, in the eyes of the Beltway establishment, she was finding her footing on the isthmus. And then, in the middle of the summer of 2019, before more such articles could be written, there was another Pelosi flare-up.

Speaking to Maureen Dowd of *The New York Times,* Pelosi dismissed Ocasio-Cortez and her fellow members of the Squad. "All these people have their public whatever and their Twitter world," Pelosi said. "But they didn't have any following. They're four people and that's how many votes they got." She was not just minimizing the achievements of several dynamic new women of color in Congress. She was railing against the theory of change that Ocasio-Cortez had articulated in the conversation with Coates—the inside-outside, influencer-legislator approach of a new era.

Ocasio-Cortez was angry. She tweeted, "That public 'whatever' is called public sentiment. And wielding the power to shift it is how we actually achieve meaningful change in this country." It was an instructive collision of worldviews, the inside-inside and the inside-outside games in battle.

Was she a renegade, or had she made peace with the system? Reporters couldn't decide. That fall, Catie Edmondson of *The New York Times* concluded that Ocasio-Cortez had "learned to play by Washington's rules," declaring that she had "tempered her brash, institution-be-damned style with something different: a careful political calculus that adheres more closely to the unwritten rules of Washington she once disdained." The article itemized some concessions on her part—standing down from supporting primary challenges to some senior Democratic Party leaders; inviting her social networks to send money to centrist Democrats in tough fights in red places. But the report was also instructive about institutional Washington's assumptions about what an effective legislator is. "When she first arrived on Capitol Hill, Ms. Ocasio-Cortez and her team made it clear they planned to use their perch inside Congress as a platform for their divisive, outsider brand of politics," Edmondson wrote. The way "divisive" and "outsider" were stacked one on top of the other was revealing. "The approach that she and her cohorts champion—pulling the institution to the left in part by threatening the careers of any Democrats who fail to embrace their ideas—quickly alienated many of her colleagues, and has made it difficult for her to get anything done," the article said. But Waleed Shahid, the Justice Democrats communications maven who had helped her first campaign, had a more nuanced view. Contrary to the pundits and reporters determined to understand whether she was done with the outside game and ready to come indoors, he reminded people that Ocasio-Cortez remained simultaneously committed to both. "Navigating her role as a legislator and a movement builder is basically what her career is about," he told the *Times*. "We'll continue to have that theory of change with one foot in D.C. and one foot in the movement. It's really hard to do that."

Later, when I asked Ocasio-Cortez what lessons she had drawn from the year of her arrival, she said, "In terms of my learning style, I'm very much an observer. I kind of hang back and I watch a lot of dynamics play forward before necessarily inserting myself, which is very different, actually, from my outside game. My outside game, I'm willing to just throw a bomb and say, 'Okay, let's see how this goes.' Because I think that that's what's necessary in shifting public conversation. Behind closed doors, I try to chart out—and this is also the way organizers do—there's a tactic that organizers use called power mapping. And you essentially start mapping out relationships and nodes of power, almost like this web or this network in your mind. Some people do it physically on paper.

"And that's a lot of the work, the inside work that I think I tried to do, is figure out the power map, figure out unusual alliances. Try to find areas of vulnerability that can be leveraged to create pressure on leadership." She added, "There are a lot more people that are cajoleable than many would think at first blush. And many people shift on issues because there's some people that just go with the tide and they just run with the wind. Sometimes that's a really bad quality, but sometimes it's a quality that you can harness in your favor, if you determine where the wind blows."

She thought of herself as power mapping on the inside but not for the inside's sake, in the way of the old boys' club. She was mapping the inside for those on the outside.

She was walking the isthmus. But in mid-October 2019, when at last she made her choice in the presidential primary, pressing her celebrity and legions of followers into the service of the Sanders campaign, she was also planting her flag. She might pull her punches from time to time, she might hold her fire, but she was bent not merely on reform but on a "political revolution."

Ocasio-Cortez's allies on the left, some of whom had begun to chafe at the stories of her capitulation to the capital's ways, cheered. *Jacobin,* the socialist magazine, wrote, "Placating party leaders will do little to help Ocasio-Cortez achieve the kind of transformative changes she wants. She seems to understand this." *Politico,* unpacking the differences between Senator Elizabeth Warren's vision of saving capitalism from itself and Sanders's vision of democratic socialism, wrote of Ocasio-Cortez's endorsement that she "has chosen to remind everyone of which side she's on."

And yet she and Sanders continued to have their own approaches. She cultivated her own image and connection with voters in a way Sanders never cared to. And some of the anxiety that she caused among her own leftist supporters—an anxiety that was quiet at first and then grew louder—involved what she was willing to barter away for the sake of that wooing of the broader public. A question that hovered over her tenure and over the left more generally was whether her own allies would trust her to fight their fight in whatever ways she saw fit or whether, every time she tried to broaden the appeal of the ideas she fought for, they would seek to brand her a phony.

In that season of her arrival, Ocasio-Cortez was most visible for her punching right at centrist Democrats and Republicans and her moving of the Overton window. But throughout, with less fanfare, she was also making a case to allies on the left to trust that what might at times seem like capitulating to the game was actually a bid to win the game—to win, as Faiz Shakir put it, by growing. Yet it was a complicated case to make because those who really did capitulate often said the same thing.

Ocasio-Cortez found herself having to make this case when Senator John McCain died and she decided to put out an anodyne, almost form-lettery tweet: "John McCain's legacy represents an unparalleled example of human decency and American service." Immediately she came under attack on the left for memorializing a war hawk. And she fired back at her leftist critics: "We need to look at: Have the commitments changed? And I don't think my commitments on any of these issues have changed at all. It's one tweet, after a multi-decade public servant passed away—does that mean I'm no longer an anti-war candidate? That's a ridiculous assumption to make." And yet the word "unparalleled" did, perhaps, sound unlike the Ocasio-Cortez her allies had fallen in love with. To some ears, it had the quality of a coded message in a hostage video, signaling her capture by the institution. Ocasio-Cortez wanted those critics to know that you could try to meet, in this case, an institution where it is and still be a true believer. She told a reporter at the time, "I welcome the criticism. But we need to look outward, too. We need to bring people in." She was setting up an opposition between this intramural criticism and an expansionary pursuit of support. Though she was beloved in her district and by her ideological base, she had high negative ratings among more moderate and conservative voters. A statement like the one she had made was the kind of gesture that might make some of those people think she was okay, a little provocative, but fundamentally okay, heart-in-the-right-place kind of thing, and that was helpful if you were trying to sell the country on an agenda of upending the society. Ocasio-Cortez wanted her followers to trust her on when to play by the system's rules and when to break them. But how was one to know when playing by those rules simply overtook a lawmaker, as it had so many? And did the kind of outreach the tweet might have attempted even work? Was it worth the risk of making some in her base cringe to speak to a broader constituency?

There had been a similar kerfuffle when Ocasio-Cortez attended an evening at the residence of Audrey Gelman, the entrepreneur who founded the Wing, an exclusive members-only work space for women. Ocasio-Cortez came in for criticism, and she asked her supposed allies on the left to be more like people on the right who "support their candidates no matter what." She clarified that what she longed for was the faith people on the right have in their leaders, but coupled with a real accountability the right lacks. She understood the anger of those who "rolled their eyes at what they saw as a blatant co-opting of the insurgent left's popularity by capitalist entrepreneurs," as Raina Lipsitz put it in *The Nation.* And it was important to be vigilant to avoid becoming compromised. But, she told Lipsitz, that hankering for accountability on the left risked destroying any maneuvering room Ocasio-Cortez had to expand the appeal of her ideas. As Lipsitz wrote,

> Organizing, she notes, is about persuasion, and bringing people—all kinds—closer to supporting your goals. "Being an organizer is very core to my identity," she says. "And I think it's a word that gets thrown around, and people don't really understand what [the] tenets of organizing are."
>
> "How are we going to achieve the things that we want to achieve if your [average] young, upwardly mobile professional woman doesn't realize that she's part of a class struggle, too?" she continues. It's crucial for the movement "to build power everywhere."

> "Does it mean that The Wing is going to deliver the revolution?" Ocasio-Cortez adds with a smile. "No. But it also means that we can't constantly be rolling our eyes at every person that goes to Starbucks."

She wanted to be accountable to her base, to cultivate some of the ardor she herself had felt for Sanders, an ardor born of his purity and the indubitability of that purity. But she wanted, moreover, the trust of her base to map the equations of power and reach out without being called out for capitulating. She wanted, as ever, to be both. "She'll always be uncompromising on the vision," her friend Jean-Bertrand Uwilingiyimana told a journalist. "The tactics which get the party to that vision, she's pragmatic on."

It was this philosophy, and her own grappling with it, that seemed to lurk behind her advice to Sanders fans in the spring of 2020—"to listen, to adapt, to open a posture of acceptance." To win by growing, to use the system against itself, and—here was the important part—to trust one another.

When Sanders lost that campaign, and Joe Biden, the kind of Democrat Ocasio-Cortez had launched her political career to challenge, won, it ushered in another test of her approach. The challenge was no longer to broaden the appeal of a set of (for America) radical political possibilities. It was to push a historically moderate and cautious and bipartisanship-loving candidate to be bolder than history or instinct told him to.

Thus in the late spring and summer of 2020, Ocasio-Cortez pursued the kind of multitrack politicking that might have been hard for people less prone to world straddling to understand. In interviews, she was cool to Biden, jettisoning the usual Washington custom of coming around to enthusiastic support of the nominee, whoever the nominee is. But when Sanders and Biden formed unity task forces to synthesize positions amenable both to the moderate faction that had won the election and to the progressive faction that had much of the party's grassroots energy, Ocasio-Cortez was invited to join one—as the co-chair, alongside the former secretary of state John Kerry, of the climate task force. She was criticized by some on her left flank for capitulating to Team Biden. But she joined anyway, and a spokeswoman, Lauren

Hitt, told reporters that Ocasio-Cortez would be "fully accountable" to climate activists and "believes the movement will only be successful if we continue to apply pressure both inside and outside the system." One of her fellow task force members was Varshini Prakash, whom she had joined that day in the occupation of Pelosi's office. Facing the same risks of friendly fire as Ocasio-Cortez, Prakash said publicly, "As I step onto this task force, I'm taking each and every member of our movement with me. I will fight as hard as I can for a platform that will do the most good for the most people." And, by all accounts, this time, on this score, their gamble proved correct. Biden's climate plan moved significantly. Noam Chomsky, a hero to many leftists, pronounced Biden's new-and-improved climate plan to me as being "farther to the left than any Democratic candidate in memory" and "far better than anything that preceded it," and "not because Biden had a personal conversion or the DNC had some great insight, but because they're being hammered on by activists coming out of the Sanders movement and others." Chomsky described Biden's new plan as "largely written by the Sunrise Movement."

In one of our conversations, I asked Ocasio-Cortez about the criticisms she received from the inside types about her activism and from the outside types about her capitulating to the game.

"No matter where you are on the political spectrum, the moral of coalition building is this idea that we need each other, especially when it comes to organizing around social change," she told me. "Some people are of the belief that electoralism is the only vehicle that we have to enact change at any sort of broad level. Other people are of the belief that electoralism is broken beyond repair and it is a dead end when you look at the profound influence of dark money and X, Y, Z ways that American democracy is fragile, imperiled, or broken. The thing I keep coming back to is that it really isn't one or the other. It's that we need each other.

"There are certain things that can be accomplished electorally that simply cannot be done with grassroots organizing," she continued. "There are some things that can be done with collective mass movement that will never be accomplished through electoral means. And, in fact, going beyond that binary, both of these types of work and organizing are necessary for the success of the other. Yet you still have hard-liners in both categories."

She was bothered by the monomania that could creep into the discussion of these approaches. She respected the activists who pushed from outside, who reminded her of her; she respected those who, like her, had chosen to go inside. But the loudest voices in politics belonged to those who believed that the only valid approach to change was the one they just so happened to be invested in. She likened her work in politics to her father's work remodeling homes. It took many tools, and there was a time and place for each tool, and different people might use different tools. But in politics some of the metaphorical carpenters "think that if you're painting the house, you're a bad person or being counterproductive."

"Their job is to give us the blueprint," she said of the activists. "And my job is to try to build the damn thing. Sometimes you do the inspection and a beam doesn't have structural integrity. Our job is to actually get the sand and dust in our face, trying to bring all of these crafts together. It's not easy, because while a lot of folks do understand the collaborative and distinct efforts that are necessary, there are some folks who think building a house is just a matter of hammering the wood together and that you don't need anything else.

"Whether we like it or not, these decision-making bodies are full of human beings," Ocasio-Cortez went on, "and not everyone who makes decisions makes them the way that we make them. Sometimes there are some folks who make their decisions based on political conditions. Sometimes they make it out of ego. Some people really do pick a side based on who's nicer to them. We don't like to operate as if that is the reality because we don't think it should be the reality. But just because we don't agree with it doesn't make it less true. There are some people who just need to feel welcome, who need to have the carpet rolled out for them. And some people on the outside may be resentful of that. The way that I feel is, 'Listen, if rolling out a carpet for someone brings them to our side, then I'm okay with that.' I don't expect everyone else to be okay with that. My role is to do some of those things that activists and other folks wouldn't and, frankly, shouldn't."

But Ocasio-Cortez did fear for a progressive movement in which those on the outside and those on the inside didn't have enough faith in each other to let each other take those different tacks toward the greater goal. "Any healthy relationship comes down to trust, and where there isn't trust, you have a very fragile, brittle relationship. And if you have a very fragile, brittle relationship with the people who are most on your side, that proves the point as to why our movement needs to grow and trust, instead of try to gate keep and distrust."

She was making a case for what the scholar Michael Dawson has called "pragmatic utopianism." But she wondered aloud as we spoke whether she, as a woman of color, and one who had landed in the limelight in the way she had, would ever command the goodwill to pursue that dualistic, this-and-that approach. "There is an enormous subtext of racism, classism, and misogyny, and it can be a frustration of mine that white male colleagues, or even just white colleagues or male colleagues, who have the same position and stances that I do, who came in with the same coalition and grassroots people power that I did, are not held to the same standard," she told me. "I don't have the built-in generosity and I don't have the built-in trust that someone like Bernie does," she said. She acknowledged that he, of course, had built that trust over decades. Still, sometimes, like her, Sanders played the inside game and put faith in the process, and he was seldom called a sellout the way she was. Contrarily, Ocasio-Cortez said, "I'm seen as much more divisive than someone like Bernie, even though we have virtually the same platform." The isthmus was especially slender for her.

When it came to the Biden candidacy and, later, presidency, Ocasio-Cortez would continue to juggle the inside and outside ways. The way she voiced the role she wanted to play with Biden was this: "It will be a privilege to lobby him." She told me that with Biden in office "it's really important that we push, because I don't think we can just trust that things are going to move in a progressive direction because the clock is ticking. We have to fight for it. And fighting for things often means that you get labeled as radical and a firebrand and difficult and inconvenient and not a team player. Because team players buckle up and saddle in and they stay quiet and they don't make people uncomfortable. You know, there's something to be said for that, but that's never been who I am."

But that spring and summer, she really was both: the team player on the climate task force, taking advantage of the privilege to lobby Biden, and then a speaker at the Democratic National Convention late in the summer, where her approach spoke of her difficult balancing act. On the one hand, she was lending her voice to the broader party she often criticized. On the other, her choice of words reflected an overriding desire to stay true to her base and her most ardent admirers, and less of an interest in using the moment to win over millions of more moderate and even conservative Americans, many of whom would be hearing her at length for the first time.

Her formal assignment had been to place Sanders's name in nomination, a ritual recognizing the runner-up in the primary contest. In doing that, she began,

> In fidelity and gratitude to a mass people's movement working to establish twenty-first-century social, economic, and human rights, including guaranteed health care, higher education, living wages, and labor rights for all people in the United States; a movement striving to recognize and repair the wounds of racial injustice, colonization, misogyny, and homophobia, and to propose and build reimagined systems of immigration and foreign policy that turn away from the violence and xenophobia of our past; a movement that realizes the unsustainable brutality of an economy that rewards explosive inequalities of wealth for the few at the expense of long-term stability for the many, and who organized an historic, grassroots campaign to reclaim our democracy.
>
> In a time when millions of people in the United States are looking for deep systemic solutions to our crises of mass evictions, unemployment, and lack of health care, and *espíritu del pueblo* and out of a love for all people, I hereby second the nomination of Senator Bernard Sanders of Vermont for president of the United States of America.

I was struck by the intelligence and moral commitment of the speech and by the political choice it seemed to represent. Here Ocasio-Cortez seemed to decide to do the opposite of what she had done with the tweet about McCain's death. Here she was not trying to expand, asking her hard-core supporters to trust that outreach was not capitulation. Here, instead, she was using one of the biggest platforms she would ever have to bring the language of outside activists inside. She was sticking to clear and demanding language that often gets leeched from politics as the price of broadening the tent. She could have told her moving story about being a waitress, sick and tired, and regaining a sense of humanity when she learned about Sanders's campaign, or any of a number of other stories. She could have given the *West Wing* version of the speech, generalizing, sentimentalizing, and softening the language of political struggle: instead of homophobia, saying love whomever you love; instead of colonization, saying people everywhere should decide their own destinies; instead of racial injustice, saying every American deserves a chance to realize their potential. To move in the direction of these other phrases would have been to move away from a galvanizing framing and toward a more broadly appealing rhetoric. But on this occasion, Ocasio-Cortez resolutely stuck to an undiluted, fierce critique of the system. Up to this point, she had, in a way Sanders had resisted, used herself to draw attention to those greater forces. But now, in the spotlight she had won, she did the reverse. She went full structural, worrying less about being appealing to everyone than about being unclear. These were her movement's demands.

It seemed she worried about not only an excess of purity but also an excess of outreach. Reach out too far across the chasm, and you fall in.

The following January was a strange time. Ocasio-Cortez was sworn in for her second term, having cruised to victory in the November elections that tossed Trump out of office. There was an insurrection on the Capitol that attempted to overturn that election and traumatized Ocasio-Cortez to her core, and prompted her to speak publicly and movingly about trauma and being a past victim of sexual assault. There was, later in the month and in spite of that attempt, a new president in office who in many ways epitomized the kind of moderation she had set out to thwart. Yet there were signs when Biden took office that he wasn't entirely the man he had been before, and the persuasive labors of Ocasio-Cortez and her progressive allies were among the many reasons why. In his address to Congress in April 2021, Biden went after the core gospel of the Reagan revolution forty years earlier—that government is the problem, not the solution. "It's time to remember that 'We the People' are the government. You and I," Biden said. "Not some force in a distant capital. Not some powerful force that we have no control over. It's us."

It was an unlikely turn for a Democrat who historically had run on personal decency more than he had pushed for structural decency. Back at the dawn of the neoliberal era, in 1981, when Reagan got to work slashing both government and taxes, he had a perhaps ambivalent ally in the young senator from Delaware. Biden voted for the package of tax cuts and austerity measures that is now viewed as the seedbed of the Reagan age. But now President Biden seemed as if he were embracing the idea of ending Reagan's long postpresidential reign, more than Clinton or Obama had, and backing it up with staffing choices and spending proposals.

When I asked one of his longtime advisers, Mike Donilon, about Biden's change of heart, he said, "This really is the place where we can change the paradigm of how government has operated since Reagan." Then, being the loyal staffer he was, he sought to frame the change in his boss as a continuation: "One thing he has always believed is government can be a force for good in people's lives."

But it wasn't really continuity. Biden had changed, was saying new things, pushing for bolder policy, proposing three separate spending bills, each costing more than $1 trillion, in his first year, touting the idea of a historic repair of a broken safety net. Why? I asked Donilon.

"The pandemic has fundamentally changed a lot about the country," Donilon told me in that spring of 2021. "I don't think you can go through an experience where 500,000-plus people lose their lives and everybody has their life turned upside down and you reach unemployment levels approaching Depression-era levels and come out of that the same." Because the pandemic exacerbated so many other, longer-running trends, Donilon said, the president "believes the country is in a place where it wants to do big things and wants to do transformative things." It was interesting to hear how Donilon put this: it was the country, not Biden himself, that was the protagonist of the story.

Some of these things Biden would go on to achieve; many he wouldn't. On some issues he would fight; on others, such as a minimum-wage increase and his plans to upgrade the safety net and fight climate change, he would give in too easily, in his critics' eyes. But during the campaign and then in those first months of his presidency, what stood out to many political observers was this president, of all presidents, driving a turn away from a center-right consensus of which he had been a card-carrying member.

Many factors had made the new consensus possible. Among them was Representative Alexandria Ocasio-Cortez. And now she had the peculiar experience of watching a legacy she and Sanders and others had helped shape bloom in the hands of improbable others. Her Plan A had been to help Sanders win and, if he had, to be at his side in one way or another. This was Plan B: a moderate president taking aim at the ideas that had guided his own career, because she, alongside others, had helped to discredit them. This, too, was persuasive success, if of a quieter kind. (But also of a less reliable kind: in the end, Biden would fail to get his sweeping Build Back Better bill through in his first year, and talk of progressive influence on him faded.)

It was a complicated line to walk for Ocasio-Cortez. One wanted to be able to recognize the kind of win that can come in losing. But there was also the fear that if you did count your influence on Biden before it hatched, you would end up being a political cheap date, offering him credit for little and letting up the pressure, giving him space to regress. So it was a confounding moment for Ocasio-Cortez, at once frustrating and validating. Yet around that very time when she, along with others in the progressive movement, deserved credit for, at a minimum, changing the course of the conversation, she, of all people, was under fire for allegedly being a sellout to power.

The attack on her as a sellout was propagated by a wing of progressives who wanted her and others to make greater use of leverage in pursuit of her goals. A loud voice in this faction was a progressive comedian, a provocateur named Jimmy Dore, who, through his YouTube show, went after Ocasio-Cortez as a craven insider who had abandoned her outsider integrity. Dore had specifically wanted Ocasio-Cortez and other progressive members to withhold a vote to reelect Pelosi as Speaker until Pelosi brought Medicare for All to a vote. This came to be known as the plea "Force the Vote."

"She is standing between you and health care," he told his fans.

Ocasio-Cortez, like many of her colleagues, declined this outside advice from Dore and from his legions of online fans, who piled on to the idea. The advice also ran contrary to what many other progressive groups thought the shrewdest strategy to be. But the nuance of the position taken by Ocasio-Cortez and these groups—balancing the provocation and primary threatening of establishmentarians like Pelosi with meeting them where they are and seeking to win by growing the coalition—was easy to cast as weakness by a figure like Dore. In calling out Ocasio-Cortez, he built his subscriber base, and he tried to do what damage he could to the political brand of one of the most progressive legislators ever to serve in the U.S. Congress.

"You liar. You coward. You gaslighter," Dore barked at Ocasio-Cortez.

Writing in *New York* magazine, Eric Levitz offered a different view:

> Ignoring the structural obstacles to single-payer's passage, the fragility of public support for the policy, and the simple fact that people can share political values while earnestly disagreeing about the best way to advance them—all for the sake of declaring Alexandria Ocasio-Cortez an enemy of America's uninsured—is a sound strategy for ginning up interest in your rant-based YouTube show. But it is also a recipe for converting your politically naïve viewers into anti-political cynics and making the U.S. left as self-deluded and internally divided as corporate America wishes for it to be.

I asked Ocasio-Cortez about the toll of these attacks. "One of the things that I confide when I talk to other people in movement spaces is that we're not used to winning," she said. "We're used to losing for almost all of American history. Or when we get some sort of toehold, we're used to being crushed. So when we do actually have power, we don't know what to do with power. Because we have spent almost our entire lives critiquing power." She added, "If your whole identity is based on how marginal you are, and if your whole affirmation and sense of self-worth is based on how much you get or see something that other people don't get or see, you will always be losing. Some people, I think, have associated a moral purity with losing. It's as if, if they're winning, there's something wrong, or that you have compromised your morality in some way." She likened the behavior of such activists to that of the music fan who burns a record she has long loved once she discovers that others listen to it, too.

And yet she understood where they were coming from, because very often her colleagues in the Democratic establishment would disappoint her, too, and she wouldn't hesitate to call them out. Late in the fall of 2021, after Democrats suffered a stinging election loss in the governor's race in Virginia, and amid seemingly endless (and ultimately doomed) negotiations to secure Biden's social policy and climate bill, known as Build Back Better, Ocasio-Cortez delivered a stern warning to party leaders in the pages of *The New York Times*. "We always try to tell people why they need to settle for less, instead of being able to harness the energy of our grass roots and take political risks in service of them, the same way that we take political risks in service of swing voters," she said. She spoke of the Congressional Progressive Caucus's insistence, throughout the negotiations, only to vote for Biden's bipartisan physical infrastructure bill if the more progressive social policy legislation was assured. "We're like, listen, we're not going to take these empty promises anymore," she said. In the end, much of that caucus capitulated and voted for infrastructure with a promise, not a guarantee, of the social policy bill. Ocasio-Cortez voted no on infrastructure, however, and immediately she was attacked for seeking to deprive her constituents of help. But she was vindicated when the supposed "deal" to pass both pieces of legislation crumbled. Build Back Better was shelved as soon as the progressives' votes on infrastructure were secured.

Her early tenure revealed the complications and perils of the inside-outside game. She had altered the terms of discussion as much as any new member of Congress in American history, but for a slice of her own ideological base she would never do enough. She was also never going to be trusted by the establishment. The desire for expansion could cost her the trust of her diehards, and perhaps that desire could even risk actual capitulation. Keeping her foot in the movement kept her at a certain distance from the center of power and from the skeptics whose support she needed if she were to achieve major change. What couldn't be taken away was her legions of supporters, who came to her for solace and faith and hope.

The question that hovered over Ocasio-Cortez during that year of her arrival and beyond it was whether, in this moment in the cultural life of a country boiling over, she would be given the space and freedom to go this way—to be all the things.

On a summer afternoon many months later, as we sat on benches in the grass, I asked Ocasio-Cortez what it felt like to watch certain of her ideas and themes take hold in the country even as her own movement struggled to win the victories to show for it. That question took her mind back to the beginning of her foray into politics and to the question of her political future.

It took her back because when she was deciding whether to run, she remembers asking herself, what would make this time, effort, energy, sacrifice worth it to me? she said. "Because there's a way where you win and it's not worth it, and there's a way where you lose and it is worth it—or you lose and it wasn't worth it at all."

The answer she had given herself back then was that if her community was "more invested, educated, and organized at the end of this process than it was at the beginning, then it will have been worth it," she said. She felt good about that when the primary victory came. When she won the general election and headed to Washington, she asked herself the question again, now on a bigger stage. "Something that was really important to me was telling the truth and bringing transparency and making people feel like they actually have power and a say in their government," she said. Because she set herself that goal, she went on, "I was willing to do things that would probably put a very hard ceiling in terms of what would be politically possible for me positionally in the future. It's not that I set out to be edgy and be whatever, but I wasn't going to allow any sort of dangling of positional opportunity to prevent me from telling the truth and engaging people, even if it was uncomfortable within our own party."

She seemed at times to tell herself that she didn't have a political future in order to wring from herself the most honest version of herself.

And now, even as her own fans spoke of a President Ocasio-Cortez, or at least a Senator Ocasio-Cortez, maybe a Governor Ocasio-Cortez, she was asking herself questions more commonly heard among those much older than her. "How do you know when you're done?" she mused as we spoke that day. "How do you know when you've accomplished what you can accomplish? I don't know. I ask myself that pretty often, and it's a tightrope between what's possible now and what could be possible for our country in the future.

"I really struggle with feeling some days like there is no path forward for me in terms of a material possibility, but I'm okay with that because I've decided what's important to me," she said.

I had heard her say this before, and it always caught me off guard. Here was one of the more promising talents in modern American politics, and she often sounded as fatalistic about her own prospects as anyone in the arena. I said I perceived her as being more attracted to being done with politics than to rising higher within it.

"There are some days when I do feel that way," she said. "For me, from day one, practicing nonattachment to this has been very important, because that's what allows me to do what I do. If I was attached to my seat, if I was attached to future political possibility, I would not be able to say the things that I say, and I would not be able to hold our own party accountable.

"The thing that has given me the greatest sense of power is not letting people have power over me," she said. "The way that they try to exercise power over me is, 'You're never going to get anywhere in this party. You're never going to be able to run for anything again.' When you actively don't care about that, it's the political equivalent of having fuck-you money. You can't fire me. You can't bankrupt me. I don't value the things you think I value. That precisely is the source of power. The thing that they fear the most is what they don't control."

5

THE ART OF MESSAGING

It was August 23, 2020. Protests against police shootings of unarmed Black people, and against white supremacy more generally, were spreading around the world. In the lakefront town of Kenosha, Wisconsin, police answering a domestic-violence call tasered and fired seven shots into the back of a twenty-nine-year-old Black man named Jacob Blake as he entered an SUV with his children inside, paralyzing Blake from the waist down. With anger already in the air, protests coalesced in Kenosha.

In the next days, there were peaceful demonstrations at the site of the shooting and episodes of violence: police cruisers attacked; an officer knocked out; buildings set aflame. The chaos intensified as out-of-towners descended on Kenosha: members of the press and citizen journalists, giving the world their perspective on events; activists who were sympathetic to the protests against police but had agendas and methods of protest that departed from those organizing locally; and paramilitaries—mostly white men with guns, radicalized by looping videos in right-wing media—who used a pretext of unrest and imperiled police officers to flock to Kenosha as aspiring vigilantes. Kyle Rittenhouse, all of seventeen and armed with an AR-15-style semiautomatic rifle, shot three men, killing two of them with what would turn out to be impunity. The events in Kenosha seemed to augur, as Charles Homans of *The New York Times* later put it, a "new era of political violence."

That week, a group calling itself Black Lives Activists of Kenosha, or BLAK, came together. Its stated goal was "to end systemic injustice, white supremacy and injustice in Kenosha." Its method was nonviolent protest, and it was determined to take back the narrative of what was happening in Kenosha from all the outsiders with their own agendas. "We felt the need to make a public voice for Kenosha," the group posted on Facebook, "instead of having people that do not live here speak on our behalf."

BLAK's first major public statement was a call for accountability. On August 27, it published a list of demands, developed along with other organizations and community members. It sought the immediate arrest and charging of the four officers at the scene of Blake's shooting; the release of all footage of the incident; the firing of the local police chief and sheriff; the creation of a new civilian review board, a body of everyday community members who would be granted subpoena power to investigate police conduct and hold officers accountable; the hiring of more Black police officers; and a defunding of the police and diversion of resources to jobs programs, health care, a childhood education center, and more.

On Saturday, August 29, BLAK, in concert with Blake's family and other groups, convened a march for justice. At the departure point, volunteers, highly organized with their neon vests and bullhorns, made sure the media was standing over there, security was over here, the family was up front, the marchers were behind them. The first row of marchers, which included Blake's family members, held up a banner that read JUSTICE FOR JACOB, adorned with a black, red, and green fist.

Justin Blake, Jason's uncle, kicked off the march with a rousing speech.

"If you're here, you're positive, and you're ready to change the world, say, 'Hey!'"

"Heyyyyy!"

"Please understand that we're in a time of change," he said. "And when you do that, you have to develop leaders, and you have to be ready to take leadership roles.

"We've been hung," he went on. "We've been murdered. We've been shot in the back several times and noosed on our necks. So when we get in power, we can't turn around and do that. We gotta have power and take control of power to have success in all our communities, so everybody can live in peace." Then he led a chant of "No justice, no peace!" which the marchers would continue as they coursed through the town by the hundreds.

Kenosha had suddenly become a national story. For activists, it was a moment to shape a narrative of what had happened in order truly to change things, not let them go on. But there were risks to this new visibility as well. Some hostile cable channel or website based far away could seize on one image or video of violence and distort it and turn it into the Story of Kenosha. Aware of the complications of all the attention they were getting, BLAK and its partners planned a second event for the following Tuesday, September 1. As it happened, Donald Trump would come to town that day. BLAK and its allies would convene a counter-gathering with its own, very different spirit.

Billed as the "Justice for Jacob Community Celebration," held near the site of the shooting, the event, according to an invitation posted on social media, would include music, free haircuts, food, celebrity guests, and community cleanup between the hours of 11:00 a.m. and 4:00 p.m. That Tuesday, a block party spread along Twenty-Eighth Avenue between Washington Road and Forty-Fifth Street in Kenosha, effortlessly combining the protest of systemic racism with an uplifting demonstration of what the activists were *for*—joy, peace of mind, community, freedom, flourishing. Two men squirted water on a grill and flipped ribs. Smokers smoked. Volunteers handed out brown bags of free food. The Reverend Jesse Jackson huddled with community members. Kids jumped on a bouncy castle. Masks and COVID tests and haircuts were given. Activists made speeches about their demands for justice. People registered others to vote. A crowd of several dozen sidestepped, kicked, and twirled to the "Cupid Shuffle."

"Although most of us have been out protesting and chanting all week, sometimes you just need to sit down and relax and actually enjoy your community," a young woman named Alana Carmickle told an interviewer during the festivities. "Love and peace, that's exactly what we need. But we're also still fighting for justice, so mixing them in is the perfect balance."

Images of the cookout and dance party for justice exploded on the internet. A two-minute video tweeted by a Milwaukee-based photographer named Joseph Brusky drew more than two million views and more than ninety thousand likes. The world was seeing another side of Kenosha from just the images of burning buildings and paramilitaries.

Watching from far away in Oakland, California, Anat Shenker-Osorio was blown away. Shenker-Osorio is a leading consultant on political messaging for the movement left. She had been working extensively that year in Wisconsin, where she partly grew up, a hundred miles from Kenosha. In partnership with an organization called All in Wisconsin, Shenker-Osorio had been developing messaging guides, digital ads, and strategy for local activist groups and those working in the electoral realm, through a project called Race Class Narrative Action. The effort aimed to help political actors crack one of the hardest problems in modern political persuasion: how to frame the quest to dismantle white supremacy and seek racial justice using messages that both unapologetically called out oppressive structures that needed calling out *and* grew political support for those ideas, even among moderate white people. The Race Class Narrative Action project sought an approach to keeping the demands for change ambitious but presenting them in ways that expanded.

When Shenker-Osorio saw the protests and then the celebration in Kenosha online, her spirits were lifted by how Black activists and organizers on the ground exemplified what she had found hard to explain to so many establishment groups she worked with: how to challenge systems of oppression without fear, how to make demands, and how to combine that with a vivid, inviting, liberating, positive vision of the future one seeks.

"This is a pro-us rally; that's part of the thinking. Say what you're for," Shenker-Osorio said of how the Kenosha organizers seemed to conceive of their celebration. "Show that we are united, show that we are this incredible community where we stand up for each other, show Black leadership, show who we are and the world that we want, instead of talking about how horrible everything is. Right?" Shenker-Osorio often speaks in messaging mantras; one of them is "Paint the beautiful tomorrow." Don't merely criticize the status quo; don't merely theorize about the world you're fighting for. Help people *see* it. The BLAK activists in Kenosha had helped people see it. In their pursuit of racial justice, they had practiced a way of being at once unbending about their goals and expansionary in pursuit of support for those goals by showing their vision of the world they were seeking.

Shenker-Osorio was still feeling inspired by their work when she came across a television advertisement that brought her down fast. A reporter tweeted a new one-minute spot from Joe Biden's presidential campaign. Her first thought was that the opening seconds of the ad were among the worst she had seen working in politics.

It opened with a shot of Biden standing in front of an array of American flags. "I want to make it absolutely clear," he begins. "Rioting is not protesting. Looting is not protesting. It's lawlessness, plain and simple. And those who do it should be prosecuted." Of all the things one might say about protests in Kenosha and elsewhere, this was the chosen start. Biden was visually present only for the first second or two of these scolding lines. The next shot was a Ken Burns–style zoom in on a still photograph of a cluster of burned-out cars encircled by "POLICE LINE DO NOT CROSS" tape. Then came a shot of a worn-out, bone-tired white firefighter hauling some hose from a charred building, in front of which plastic beverage bottles littered the street. Then a bank building was shown partially burned out, still smoking, with a mysterious figure in a backward baseball cap, clutching a skateboard, strolling casually past. Then police were seen firing tear gas into a crowd.

Now Biden pivoted rhetorically. "Fires are burning, and we have a president who fans the flames," he said. "He can't stop the violence, because for years he's fomented it." Footage of tiki torches in Charlottesville now appeared. After seeming to lecture places like Kenosha on keeping calm, Biden blamed Trump for the overall climate of violence in the country. That, Shenker-Osorio thought, was better. But then Biden reprised his original theme: "Violence will not bring change; it'll only bring destruction. It's wrong in every way." We return to scenes of protesters scuffling with heavily armed police. Before signing off with his approval of the message and a quotation from Pope John Paul II, Biden reiterated his point: all of this violence is deplorable, as violence always is, but it's happening not only because of these violent actors but because Trump "is determined to instill fear in America" and he "adds fuel to every fire."

Given how protest continued to be viewed by a large cross section of voters, and in particular how Black people protesting was viewed, the ad might not have seemed problematic to many. But for Shenker-Osorio, who spends her days poring over data about what voters hear when they encounter a message like this, the ad was an unmitigated disaster—especially when seen side by side with the way those activists in Kenosha had spoken to the world. She was disappointed and angry and worn down. Here, as she put it, was "*War of the Worlds* Kenosha"—or any of the number of places the ad could have been trying to depict. Portraying them that way wasn't doing Biden the favors his campaign seemed to think.

"It's hard for me to even—," Shenker-Osorio said, struggling to find words, which was rare for her. "I'm so upset about it and so angry." She didn't know who the writers were, but if she did, she said, she would send them the Reverend Dr. Martin Luther King Jr.'s "Letter from a Birmingham Jail." "This was exactly what he was talking about," she told me. "It is both-sidesing. It is equating destruction of property with destruction of human life." In fact, the ad made zero mention of the police killings that had originally fueled the protests whose lapses into violence Biden condemned.

A day later, Biden would fly to Kenosha and meet with Jacob Blake's family, and he would condemn the shooting. But he would once again slip into the stentorian lecture so many politicians who court and fear the white voter give at some point or other. "Protesting is protesting, my buddy John Lewis used to say," Biden said. "But none of it justifies looting, burning, or anything else. So regardless of how angry you are, if you loot or you burn, you should be held accountable as someone who does anything else, period."

Shenker-Osorio was offended by the ad's both-sidesing on moral grounds, but she was just as upset by the political stupidity the spot represented. "Let's forget the morality," she told me. "Pretend you don't care. Just strategically, cold, hard campaigning, it's such a classically unpersuasive maneuver to essentially adopt and echo your opposition's message." It was one thing for Democrats to run an ad like this a decade or two ago. But there was reason to know better now, or so she thought. She and allied experts on what moves and persuades voters, though still outliers in the party, had been telling every Democratic politician and progressive organization and activist leader who would listen that so many of their habits of courting support—especially when race was involved—were counterproductive, that they often failed, that there were better ways. Often, the message didn't resonate, drowned out by the more traditional establishment advice to court the white voter at any price. But at times, it actually felt to Shenker-Osorio that the new thinking was breaking through. Then you saw an ad like this one.

A day later, Shenker-Osorio was still angry as she rattled off the errors manifest in the ad. It was as if someone had designed a spot for Shenker-Osorio to use as a 101-course teaching tool.

First of all, by choosing to broadcast that chargrilled, *War of the Worlds* picture of urban chaos, the day before flying to Kenosha, Biden was playing into the hands of the right, which was expert at ginning up white fear and perceptions of danger and violence and exploiting them to sell authoritarian rescue. "The biggest reason is fear," Shenker-Osorio told me. "When you are terrified, you cling to what you know. You cling to what's familiar." At the same time, this kind of violent imagery "demotivates and demobilizes" voters of color, Shenker-Osorio said. It is a two-birds-with-one-stone act of self-harm for Democrats. The campaign might have countered that what Biden was saying in the ad made it more nuanced: he was pinning the blame for this mayhem on Trump. But Shenker-Osorio was suggesting that the ad wouldn't read to many voters like a critique of Trump. On levels beneath the verbal, it was telegraphing to them what the world was like—a violent and dangerous place. It could have shown them many different pictures of the world. It chose this one. Later testing proved her point: in a randomized controlled trial, the ad from the Biden campaign increased persuadable voters' affinity for Trump.

Shenker-Osorio did understand what Biden was trying to do, and why. Like so many Democratic politicians before him, he had been reared on a fear of the fickle white working-class voter, who might be with you if times are good and the paycheck is solid and things are tranquil around their virtually all-white suburb and who might succumb to the right's appeals to fear and resentment if they feel economically or culturally dislocated or vulnerable to crime and unrest or if their berth in the caste hierarchy feels at risk. Biden might have feared that the occasional bouts of violence accompanying the mostly peaceful protests would dominate the headlines and push voters toward Trump. So he wanted to disavow that violence. To make clear to those white voters that he, Joe Biden, was pro–law and order, too.

This mentality led him to violate another of Shenker-Osorio's principles, which is to have the conversation *you* want to be having, not the conversation your opponent prefers. Law and order wasn't Biden's lodestar or theme or allure. It was the Republicans' conversation, their promise, their mantra. "If you're responding to law and order—*rioting is not protesting, looting is not protesting*—if that's what you're talking about, that's what's coming to people's mind. You're reinforcing what they're saying." You are never going to win on someone else's conversational terrain. Once you're talking about law and order, playing catch-up, really, on law and order, you will inevitably be an also-ran on the subject. "They're not going to want the B-minus version," Shenker-Osorio said.

For the Democratic Party, this reflexive lurch to court white working-class voters in this way carried a cost that campaigns that should know better seemed to ignore. The most passionate and ardent supporters of the party didn't merely tune out when a figure like Biden spoke about riots being bad and law and order being good. They felt unrepresented and disengaged. And this was a problem, because, according to another of Shenker-Osorio's core precepts, it was that base you needed to champion your visions, loudly and often, to woo the undecided.

Instead, what had happened? Biden had cut an ad all but encouraging on-the-fence white people to think things were unsafe; had predisposed them, in the deep recesses of their brains, to seek safety in the right's authoritarian offering; had equated resistance to oppression with the oppression itself; had potentially demoralized his most passionate voters, the Black community; and had used precious airtime to elevate a law-and-order topic he was never going to dominate. Above all, the ad had shown, in vivid detail, what Biden was against, when, right there in Kenosha, shortly beforehand, there had been a vivid, moving celebration of what Biden might have claimed to be for: an America of justice and dignity for all, freedom from fear, joy in solidarity, and safe communities.

"I don't know what to do anymore," Shenker-Osorio told me, "because it's going to air and it's just going to devastate all of our organizers. And it's going to devastate Jacob's family. I'm just really sad."

I asked Shenker-Osorio to give me an alternative script for a Biden ad given the uprisings in Kenosha and beyond. Without skipping a beat, she launched into an incarnation of a theme she had been testing in five battleground states recently. She imagined the voice-over atop images of the dancing and barbecuing and voter registering and bouncy-castle jumping in Kenosha that week:

> No matter what we look like or where we're from, we want our families to be safe, our voices to be heard, and rights to be respected. But Trump is trying to divide and scare us into silence by sending federal forces into our communities, stopping people from protesting and provoking aggression. With the election coming up, he hopes to distract us from his corruption and failure to ensure we have the care, services, and support we need during this pandemic. By joining together—Black, white, and brown—to demand liberty and justice today, and to vote in record numbers in this election, we can swear in a government of, by, and for the people.

The more I talked to Shenker-Osorio, the more time I spent around her words and carefully crafted messages, the more I began to recognize the patterns at work in a message like that one and to understand her larger project.

Language, the power of words, communication across barriers, what people say, and what people hear—these themes recur in Shenker-Osorio's life.

She is an American born in Israel to parents born in Poland, and she is married to a man born in Honduras. Her parents' first language was Polish; hers was Hebrew; her husband's was Spanish; her two sons speak English at school but are required to speak Spanish at home. When her husband and her father met for the first time, on her wedding day, a translator accompanied them. In her experience, comprehension is not a default state, to be taken for granted. It is something to be achieved through effort.

Both of Shenker-Osorio's parents were born in Poland, in 1949. They were Jews standing in the immediate shadow of the Holocaust, from which their own parents had harrowing tales of survival. Shenker-Osorio's father and mother immigrated to Israel as teenagers, the latter moving when Poland began another round of anti-Jewish purges. They got together at university, settled outside Tel Aviv, began a family. Then Shenker-Osorio's father, an academic physician, uprooted the family to America, first to Ann Arbor, Michigan, then to Madison, Wisconsin, where Shenker-Osorio attended middle and high school.

The language of her household growing up was a complex mélange that Shenker-Osorio, later in life, having studied these things, would say configured her brain and her particular way of seeing the world. The parents mostly spoke Polish to each other—even though, because of the history of Jewish persecution in that country, they had, Shenker-Osorio said, "this very complicated relationship to Poland and to the notion of their Polishness." When a new American acquaintance would learn their origins—"So you're Polish!"—Shenker-Osorio's mother's reflexive retort was, "Just because you're born in a stable, doesn't make you a horse." But you can feel conflicted about where you come from and still long to be understood as a person from that place. Which is why it had been important to her mother to marry someone from Poland. She wanted a husband with whom she could speak without an accent. But their children spoke Hebrew at first, and then, more and more, English, as their American roots deepened. Eventually, like so many third-culture families, they had forged their own language. Shenker-Osorio remembers her little brother opening the door to let the dog back in and announcing, "She zrooped," an Anglicization of the Polish verb *idź siusiu,* "to go pee." Her mother worked as a medical interpreter, Polish to English. Shenker-Osorio would later do the same, in medical and legal settings, but Spanish to English.

"I am obsessed with language," Shenker-Osorio told me. "I am obsessed with the act of translation and interpretation, and with how deeply powerful language is, but also how deeply inadequate and flawed, imperfect and imprecise. And how we try and try always to get to a place of greater clarity, of greater precision, of a greater match between stimulus and response—the thing that you want people to understand sometimes being not at all the thing, the words, that you should actually use."

Shenker-Osorio left home to study political science and Spanish at Columbia, in New York. She also dipped her toes into linguistics, reading the books of a professor named George Lakoff, who had applied his academic work to the realm of politics. She started to be exposed to a more formal understanding of how a polyglot childhood like hers wires the brain. Monolingual children learn that that thing is a chair, and a chair is that thing. Subjects come before objects. And so on. But a child exposed, as she had been, to multiple languages early learns that that thing is a chair, and it is a *krzesło,* and it is a כִּסֵּא, and it is a *silla.* Subjects come before objects, but subjects also come after objects. Adjectives are gendered, or not gendered. "You learn that lots of different things are possible," Shenker-Osorio told me. "And the way I think about language now is through the lens of a greater amount of possibility than is perhaps apparent in dominant status quo discourse. I am willing to be more experimental with different ways of trying to say things."

Even as she thrived academically in college, her real passion was performing. Yet the immigrants' daughter was too pragmatic to let herself attempt a career onstage. So she dabbled in stand-up comedy on the side. It was a street education in linguistics, the slightest tweak in language one made in setup or premise or punch line or mix having a wildly disproportionate effect on laughs. Years before she was lecturing her clients on "message ordering," she was practicing it herself, inviting people in with a relatable observation of the world and then, and only then, twisting it for laughs. At open-mic nights, Shenker-Osorio tested her material, saw what worked and what didn't, moved things around, this word to the end of the sentence, this joke to the top of the routine, observed the audience observing her, and then adjusted some more.

Drew Westen, a political psychologist who does work similar to Shenker-Osorio's, has a line she loves about empiricism being the cure for ego. "I think that stand-up is a nonscientific form of empiricism," Shenker-Osorio told me. "When lots and lots and lots of people don't think what you just said is funny, it doesn't matter if you do. It's not funny." Whether you are a comic who knows you're funnier than that audience member who isn't laughing, or a message guru who knows you know more than that focus group participant who doesn't like your killer line, subjecting yourself to humbling and edification by the crowd takes discipline and a faith in the rewards.

"That has been incredibly useful to me," Shenker-Osorio said, "because the number of times that I have watched focus group participants be like, 'Who wrote this message? This is bullshit. This is stupid.' Well, I wrote it, and I'm behind the mirror watching, and I'm eating M&M's." A moment later, she added, "A lot of people who do messaging never actually watch people respond to what they say. They don't look at it. Because they don't look at it, they're able to retain their ideas or assumptions of what 'works,' because it feels like it works to them."

Another thing performing taught her, she said, was the art of surprise and, relatedly, of making use of "persuasion windows." That is a term Shenker-Osorio learned from Maya Bourdeau, an expert in psychological marketing. From time to time, something happens in the culture that radically opens people's receptivity to certain ideas and messages. For example, as soon as the pandemic began burning through the world, ads for expanding health care tested way better than they had weeks earlier. When the Supreme Court inched toward gutting *Roe v. Wade,* Shenker-Osorio said she would expect ads about abortion rights to surge in effectiveness. School shootings create persuasion windows. Murders by police do, too. And these persuasion windows open, Shenker-Osorio said, because a new story has jarred people into surprise. "People are primed to hear a new thing about that topic because it's in the ether, it's in the media, and they're ready to change their mind about it," she said. In stand-up, the game is constantly cultivating the audience's surprise. Starting with what they know, and then taking them to some new place, and yanking open that window, and then, without their realizing what you're doing, planting in them a new idea.

After college, Shenker-Osorio had a brief, misbegotten stint as a business consultant. She quit before the year was out and pivoted to a more natural fit—the Peace Corps. Soon she was living in Honduras, in a village called San Juancito. Her assignment: helping local nonprofits write grant applications, their survival each year dependent on their word choices, on their ability to frame the realities of one place to people in other places.

In her later years as a messaging practitioner, she would become an expert at saying hard things in a way people can hear them. But, in spending time with Shenker-Osorio, I realized that this isn't her natural instinct; it's a skill she has learned through rigorous work. Her natural tendency is toward activism, not diplomacy. Which is why in Honduras she made a choice to call out corruption she witnessed—a nonprofit she was working with that was supposed to protect the environment was also, on the side, aiding logging firms destroying it. She called it out, and before long she had to relocate and change projects.

She also met her future husband in Honduras, encountering and traversing barriers beyond language. Donaldo Osorio was a woodworker from the village. On one of their early dates, they took a bus followed by a van and then hitchhiked to get to a hike to find a waterfall. Soon they were making plans to move to America and marry. When Donaldo arrived in Portland, Oregon, among his shocks was the idea behind parking meters. "What do you mean you have to pay for time? You have to pay for space?" he asked her. In that period, Shenker-Osorio worked in a program helping the children of Spanish-speaking migrant workers with reading and language. She also conducted research on how people acquire second languages.

Before long, she was back in school, studying public policy at Berkeley. She had never really been a numbers person, but now she felt more drawn to that side of things, adding quantitative chops to her wordsmithing skills, learning to conduct giant regressions. And she took a class with Lakoff, the cognitive linguist, who had done work applying his theories to electoral politics. He argued that political campaigns could do a better job of speaking to voters by understanding the metaphors that underpin their views—for example, the "nurturant family" model that is, for many liberals, a template for a justice-seeking state, and a "strict father" model that guides the sterner, tough-love vision of the state shared by many on the right.

Shenker-Osorio and Lakoff hit it off, and after grad school she worked for a time at the Rockridge Institute, a nonprofit think tank that Lakoff helped set up. The work was centered on applying Lakoff's insights about metaphors and other things to practical messaging problems. For example, Democrats often speak about "tax relief" or a "tax burden" or a "tax break." And that was fine and good, until your consultants helped you see that, metaphorically speaking, you were "talking about taxes in the language of an affliction," Shenker-Osorio said. "That's not good, because when people think of an affliction, they think of a thing they don't want. They want to get rid of it; they don't like it. When you say things like 'The tax burden on middle-class families is simply too high,' you're actually impugning taxes." In this phase of her career, Shenker-Osorio told me, she learned a great deal about what political actors *shouldn't* say. But Shenker-Osorio grew more interested in the question of what they should say, and here, she began to feel, empiricism—asking people—was essential and, in the circles she was in, lacking.

"I saw the truth of political comms or organizational comms," she told me, "which is that most of it is holding up a finger in the wind and being like, 'We'll put it that way.' Or, more recently, my favorite is, 'The URL was available.' *Why did you name your campaign that?* They were like, 'Well, the URL was available.' I'm like, 'Wow, that is strategic.'" And outside the realm of professional messaging, many of her fellow progressives seemed trapped in a communicative complacency. Do the right thing, fight for the right ideas, the rest will follow. Just speak the truth, and people will hear.

But comprehension couldn't be assumed, meaning well isn't enough, stimulus doesn't equal response, as Shenker-Osorio had seen over and over again.

To remedy the communicative failures she saw around her, she set out to forge her own particular methodology of message analysis and crafting, drawing on her own skills with language but also working with pollsters, focus groups, and surveys. The process that developed went like this: First, assessing a client's existing messaging. Then asking where they were trying to go. Then working on a new set of messages to get them there. And then testing the proposed messages. She conducted experiments around people's reactions or ran dial tests to see which phrases revved people up, which alienated people, which fell flat.

As she honed her method, she developed an ever more impressive roster of clients across the political left. She helped craft a Minnesota campaign called "Greater Than Fear," aimed at beating back white nationalist overtures, which received some share of the credit for sweeping Democratic victories across the state in 2018. In 2020, she had done that work in her home state of Wisconsin, which included helping local activists trying to reallocate public money away from police. "Fund our lives" was the slogan they employed. She worked overseas, providing early counsel to the campaign to legalize abortion in Ireland and conducting a massive research effort to reshape the debate over Australia's treatment of asylum seekers. During her stint in Australia, Shenker-Osorio also conducted workshops for communications strategists who would later help propel Jacinda Ardern and her Labour Party in New Zealand to victory in 2017. Shenker-Osorio was highly sought after around the world and within the United States, where she advised those in movement and activist and civic spaces, including the ascendant wave of groups led by people of color who are drawn to an alternative to traditional messaging approaches that they consider whitewashing. But there was one conspicuous absence in her roster of clients, and that was the Democratic Party and its associated organizations. The establishment kept her at arm's length. People sometimes said that she was the Democrats' Frank Luntz—the preeminent messaging consultant to the right—except that the Democrats didn't listen to their Luntzes.

Still, she plugged on with her work, gradually mining from the various different clients and situations and issues at hand larger insights and patterns. As I listened to her speak and read her presentation slide decks and watched her lead meetings for activists and organizers, I began to recognize these principles, grounded in data, which together amounted to a kind of philosophy. It was a philosophy that she couldn't help but think, if embraced by powerful actors on the political left, might kind of, sort of help save everything, maybe?

"ANIMATE THE BASE TO PERSUADE THE MIDDLE"

The cardinal sin of the establishment left—above all, the Democratic Party—was, in Shenker-Osorio's telling, its longing to be palatable to the middle.

For much of her career (until a recent turn among a subset of the party's candidates), the reigning Democratic theory of persuasion had been "You have your base, so don't worry about them; reach out to those moderates in the middle, and if you need to water down your ideas somewhat, so be it; that is the price of big-tent living." Much encouragement for this dilution came, of course, from the donor class that had an interest in shredding the safety net and keeping taxes low and pushing security spending. Thus you had Bill Clinton's triangulation and his gutting of welfare and his declaration of the end of big government; you had Barack Obama's abandonment of truly universal health care and his keeping on a Republican defense secretary to perpetuate a forever war on terror; you had establishment pushback against progressive insurgents, declaring that modest wealth taxes "penalize success." Time and again, the ultimate position of the Democratic leadership was the distilled version of an idea cut with so many mixers as to become juice. Or, as Shenker-Osorio once wrote, "There's a signature and unchanging brand of advice handed to Democrats for the last 25 years: be milquetoast."

The Democrats reminded Shenker-Osorio of the old miller in *Aesop's Fables* who heads to the market with his son to sell his donkey. At first, neither of them rides the donkey. People criticize that—*Why not use the donkey?* Then the son rides on the donkey, and some people criticize that—*Lazy boy, making the father walk!* Then the father replaces the son on the donkey. People criticize that—*Making your little boy walk while the adult relaxes!* Finally, they decide the only remaining solution is to carry the donkey. The donkey kicks out, though, and tumbles into a body of water and drowns. "By trying to please everybody, he had pleased nobody, and lost his Ass besides," the story concludes.

"It's deeply fitting," Shenker-Osorio has written, "that the animal in Aesop's 'Please All, Please None' fable was a donkey. This kind of 'let's meet people where they are and actually say nothing' approach is the best summation of current Democratic strategy."

Again and again, she saw Democrats reaching out in good faith to an opposition that was never, ever going to cave, in the hope that doing so would appeal to a still-undecided middle. Political persuasion was synonymous with reaching right in this doctrine, and even if it never worked, you would try it again next time.

In recent years, among some Democrats, there had at last been an insurgency against this thinking. Don't worry so much about changing minds on the right, the new theory went. Don't focus on winning ideological converts. Rather, focus on turnout: activate nonvoters and occasional voters. Try to rev up people who already agree with you. An influential *New York Times* op-ed in 2018 by the progressive pollster Sean McElwee and the political scientists Jesse Rhodes, Brian Schaffner, and Bernard Fraga suggested that Democrats fixate less on reclaiming Obama-turned-Trump voters and focus instead on those Obama voters who simply did not vote in 2016. "We would hardly urge Democratic strategists to abandon Obama-to-Trump voters," they wrote. "However, Obama-to-nonvoters are a relatively liberal segment of the country who have largely been ignored. They are mostly young and nonwhite, and they represent an important part of the Democratic Party's demographic future." As the journalist David Leonhardt wrote of the idea, "The missing Obama voters are overwhelmingly progressive in their policy aims—which makes it very tempting for progressive activists to focus on them. Doing so doesn't involve any policy compromises." This was the temptation of the ascendant turnout theory: instead of contorting yourself to change minds in the middle, you could be yourself and mobilize better.

"To Persuade or to Turn Out Voters—Is That the Question?" a headline on the website of Morning Consult, a leading polling organization, asked in 2019, referring to a common framing in politics in which persuasion was defined as wooing skeptical voters and turnout or mobilization was defined as getting people who already share your views to get off their couches and vote.

But in Shenker-Osorio's method, it was a bogus trade-off, because mobilization and persuasion were causally linked. One led to the other. "The battle that we've had on the left for a really long time is, 'Are we doing turnout or are we doing persuasion?' And this is, in fact, a false choice. Because I thoroughly believe that turnout *is* persuasion. And that canard that 'we're preaching to the choir'—the choir's where the trouble starts. And if the choir is not singing in harmony, then the congregation is not going to hear the joyful noise, if you will continue to accept this analogy from a Jew. And it's not out preaching and getting new adherents."

In Shenker-Osorio's vision of persuasion, you did indeed preach to the choir, so the choir would in turn conquer the hearts of the much broader audience in the seats—the moderates. She called it "engaging the base to persuade the middle." You didn't conquer the moderates by reaching out toward them and watering down your ideas beyond recognition. You won moderates over by so jazzing the base that they wanted to have what it was having.

"THE 'GOOD POINT' PEOPLE"

Shenker-Osorio believes that many on the left court disaster when they court moderates because they don't understand who moderates are.

People casually associate the "moderate" with the middle of the road, the center, but Shenker-Osorio thinks that is a fundamental mistake. When it comes to big issues and policies, moderates, to her, are confused, torn, not sure which pole is their pole. Which is different from saying they prefer the mean between the two poles. One way to think of this is that if I offer you a choice between a pizza and a burger, and you can't pick—you're an undecided voter!—it doesn't follow that you want a pizzaburger. Maybe you want a pizzaburger—the mathematical midpoint between a pizza and a burger. More likely, you will ultimately resolve the dilemma and go with a pizza *or* a burger. That might help us to reconceive of your 'moderate' stance at the beginning as a temporary state—a situation, not an identity.

In her research, Shenker-Osorio sees moderates not as possessing a fixed centrist identity but rather as being in a suspended state of mixed opinions. She believes the political left gets into all manner of trouble assuming the opposite. Democrats were like pizza sellers worried about growing the business who pivot to pizzaburgers to woo burger lovers and end up alienating their existing customers while gaining few new ones.

A better term for moderates, then, might be "persuadables." "Moderate" implies a taste for the tempered version of a thing. "Persuadable" implies malleability. The ranks of the persuadable change from issue to issue, year to year. But Shenker-Osorio thinks about it as a rule of 20-60-20. When you ask people to rate their support for various issues (as opposed to parties, about which people are far more partisan and tribal), a fifth of people are committed to your side; a fifth of people are reliably for the opposition; most people are "moderate," which is to say their minds are in play. This doesn't mean they don't succumb to partisanship and tribalism. It just means their commitments are less fully formed than others'. Persuadables, Shenker-Osorio and some colleagues wrote in a research report, "toggle between views shared by our base or by opposition."

"We've been taught that the middle-of-the-road voter, or the swing voter, or the conflicted voter—they get described in different ways—but essentially that mushy-middle voter, what they want is some kind of centrist position. They want something in between A and B," Shenker-Osorio told me. "In fact, what experimentation shows is that is not true. They are, by definition, nonideological, do not hold fixed ideological positions on policy issues. If they did, they wouldn't be persuadable, and they wouldn't be conflicted. They would have opinions, and those opinions would be fixed in an ideology. What we see is that they are the most susceptible to toggling back and forth, to having their conflicts be bigger and be more frequent. I call them the 'Good Point' People because they're like this: 'Good point. But, yeah, good point. But, also, good point.' And so they're capable of agreeing with things that are radioactively conservative, and they are capable of agreeing with things that are progressive."

The Good Point People believed that, yes, raising the minimum wage is essential for helping families survive and, yes, raising the minimum wage is going to crush small businesses and fuel inflation. They believed that, yes, immigrants enrich our lives and, yes, immigrants cost us jobs. In a survey of Minnesota voters with which Shenker-Osorio was involved, voters were asked if focusing on and talking about race is necessary for societal progress, and 85 percent of persuadable voters said yes. *Good point!* Then they were asked if focusing on and talking about race don't fix anything and in fact make things worse, and 69 percent said yes! *Good point!* The same survey asked if Black people face greater obstacles than white people to succeeding, and 74 percent of persuadables said yes. Many of those people then joined the 62 percent who answered yes when asked if Black people and Latinos who can't get ahead were responsible for their own destiny. *Good point! But also . . . good point!*

An almost comical illustration of this confused tornness is that "moderates" change their minds based on priming that seems far afield from the topic being polled. In one experiment, voters were asked their views on immigration. Some of the voters—this was before COVID-19—were put in the vicinity of hand sanitizer prior to the question being asked. The persuadable voters were more likely to turn in an anti-immigrant direction if they were among those put near the sanitizer. The sanitizer had presumably primed them to think of the threat of contamination. This was a strange but, to Shenker-Osorio, optimistic discovery. It didn't tell you that persuadables on immigration want some but not too much, or are fine with babies in cages but only babies who misbehave. Persuadables were hungry for clues from the world about how to think about the problem. If something as simple as being near hand sanitizer could change their minds on immigration, a good message might, too, but in the opposite direction.

Once you let go of the notion of persuadables as stuck in the middle, once you saw them as floating about, desperate for some hint about how to think, you could begin to ask yourself, how can I serve as the hand sanitizer in their lives—but for good ends?

"Between 'immigrants contribute to our culture, we're all the better for having them here' and 'we should put babies in cages,' there is no in between," Shenker-Osorio told me. "That's an on/off switch. What we actually see from persuadables is that they toggle between competing views of the way the world works, and whatever they hear repeated most frequently becomes 'common sense' and 'what everybody thinks.'" The persuadables she courted were malleable and contained many "fighting faiths," in Oliver Wendell Holmes's famous phrase, and were in a constant, unresolved process of meaning making, trying to alloy what they heard at work and on the news and from their friends into something solid like a worldview. "The work I do is about toggling people into the most progressive understanding they can have of the world, which is latent within them, and keeping that up, up, top of mind, so that that is their default," Shenker-Osorio told me. "The way I do that is by getting the base to keep repeating the set of messages that will activate those progressive narratives that already exist in people."

"REPEAT"

If Shenker-Osorio is right that torn persuadables aren't looking for an average of two positions but rather for what is normal, common sense, how the world works, then the way to persuade them of your view is by making it ubiquitous around them, inescapable. The way she advises campaigns to do that isn't just hawking the message yourself, over and over, via TV ads and candidate speeches and internet memes. It's also giving your most passionate followers something to talk about with their less persuaded aunts and brothers, co-workers and friends.

"Repetition is a really big deal," Shenker-Osorio once said in an interview with *The Forge.* "More familiar messages are rated more convincing. Never mind the content. Repetition creates cognitive ease, so people rate familiar ideas as more favorable, more convincing, and more positive." To put it another way, if one faction of cool kids in school is prone to shorts, and another favors pants, you on team shorts don't win over the undecided with Capri pants. You win them by getting as many people as possible to wear shorts in their presence.

Shenker-Osorio's term for this group of message repeaters was the base—everyday citizens who supported your ideas but may be more or less enthusiastic about them. This base is especially important in an age of widespread distrust in major institutions. "It is the job of organizers to get the base to repeat our narratives in order to persuade the middle, because the base is a more trusted source of information," Shenker-Osorio has written. "When your friend, your cousin, your neighbor, or your high school acquaintance posts something on their Facebook page, it is more persuasive than when you hear the same content in an ad—because of the level of suspicion."

So, Shenker-Osorio asks in her research, what makes people want to repeat a given message over and over? Not just believe it, but repeat it—talk about it at work, talk about it on the subway, talk about it at Sunday family dinners. This is a question, in Shenker-Osorio's analysis, that too many on the establishment left never ask. If they did, would their ideas come out the way they do?

Free community college, in addition to being a policy that would combat inequality and restore some measure of social mobility, is an easy and engaging and even thrilling idea for the base to repeat. Expanded community college access, with tax credits for families making less than $60,000, but phased out over three years, and only in states where governors supply matching grants, and on the condition that both parents are working full-time—in addition to being a less effective policy, this isn't something anyone is capable of repeating or would want to repeat. A campaign may go with the latter in an attempt to court the middle. But what it has actually done is leave the base cold while confusing the persuadables.

"What the middle is capable of believing is what the base is excited to keep chanting," Shenker-Osorio told me.

She gave the example of the effort to protect marriage equality in California against Proposition 8 in 2008. "The advice was, 'Oh, shit, people get all freaky-freaky if you actually talk about gay couples and you actually talk about these feelings, so here's what we're going to do: we're going to make a practical argument. We're going to talk about hospital visitation rights. We're going to talk about married couples filing jointly, taxes, stuff like that.' Stuff that does not make you think of gay sex at all. And because what our research is showing is that people are particularly freaked out about children—remember, this was back in the day—we're not going to show children. There won't be families in our ads."

Shenker-Osorio still remembers some of the ads that resulted from this advice. "If you look at the Prop 8 ads, almost none of them featured gay and lesbian people. They featured straight people talking about gay and lesbian people who presumably were so terrifying we couldn't even look at them." The strategy, as Shenker-Osorio saw it, was classic outreach by dilution: "We're going to make these super-practical arguments that are not going to make anybody think of children or sex. Filing your taxes. What is less sexy?"

That effort to save marriage equality lost. Afterward, Shenker-Osorio said, among political communications professionals and organizers who worked on the campaign, there was a reckoning: "Oh, what we're doing is we're just helping tacitly feed the opposition argument that gay people really must be terrifying because gay people won't have gay people in their ads. Can you imagine how terrible a group of people must be if they won't even make themselves the protagonists of their own ads?" Instead of flooding the undecideds with priming about how utterly normal gay people are, they had fed the opposite message. They had done so in the hope of reaching to the center, but they had presumably left their base cold.

To Shenker-Osorio, the problem wasn't just this political tendency toward outreach using the lure of milquetoast. Even when the left had a good message to repeat, large swaths of it behaved as though disciplined chanting of that message were beneath its dignity. "What is actually effective in persuasion is to say fewer things and say them more often," she told me. "When is 'Just Do It' not going to be Nike's slogan? Never. Not ever. And do we imagine that the PR people at Nike, every time they have to sit down and type 'Just Do It,' want to scream and throw their computer? Is it the most boring thing they've ever done? I'm sure it is.

"What the left does," she continued, "is, 'We're the smartest people in every room, obviously, and so we need to make up new things. We need to invent new things all of the time.'" She had noticed this tendency in center-left groups around the world, where intellectual rigor was prized. Repetition was for dimwits. People's self-image was of fresh thinking, creativity, innovation. In a meeting with an association of trade unions in Australia, she remembers hearing from someone in the group how, some years earlier, they had won a campaign called "Your Rights at Work." What, they asked her, should they call the new incarnation of their campaign to update those rights?

"Your Rights at Work," Shenker-Osorio said, almost not understanding the question.

"I think you must have misheard me," came the reply. "That's what we called it last time."

"What is it about winning that is distasteful to you?" was Shenker-Osorio's characteristically blunt retort.

In addition to the smarty-pants problem, there was a funding problem. The movement left was made up of countless nonprofit groups, each of which survived through fundraising. Every year, each group needed to apply for more grants, and you didn't get grants by saying the same thing every other group was saying. You needed to differentiate. "First of all," Shenker-Osorio said, "you're in competition, and, second of all, what you're showing off to funders is, 'We each have our own message, we're each beating our own drum,' and that is, by definition, the very opposite of what we know is persuasive, which is to have the greatest number of people echoing the same exact trope in order to break a signal through the noise."

"ALIENATE THE OPPOSITION"

Some years ago, Shenker-Osorio was working on a project looking at the results of dial testing—tracking a group's real-time, second-to-second opinion of messages they are hearing—on immigration policy. She was looking over various tests done by Democrats and by Republicans, including by the notorious Republican pollster Frank Luntz. Something struck her. On Luntz's tests, which tracked the attitude of base, opposition, and moderates listening to a message, the winning one was defined as that which raised base approval, raised moderate approval, and *reduced* opposition approval. Not the message that raised all three. The Democratic testers, on the other hand, gave the greatest weight to messages that made all three dials climb. When Shenker-Osorio asked about the difference, someone responded by citing a supposed Luntz mantra: "I dial for the red meat." He grasped what few on the left did: the power of generative alienation.

This insight went beyond Shenker-Osorio's "please all, please none" point. It wasn't just that you shouldn't focus on pleasing the opposition and persuadables, at the cost of dilution, in order to win. It was that you should seek out ways to please your base, get it chanting in ways that encircled and wooed the persuadables, and, at the same time, alienate and marginalize the opposition. The left needed, if you'll forgive the image, to dial for blue meat.

In one of Shenker-Osorio's and her colleagues' dial tests, from May 2018, you could see the difference between the pointed blue meat lines and the no less important kumbaya ones that would surround them. "Join together with people from all walks of life to fight for our future" made all three lines go up: base, persuadables, and opposition. But when the message made an appeal against oligarchic interests, saying that "certain politicians and their greedy lobbyists" were "handing kickbacks to the rich, defunding our schools, and threatening our seniors with cuts to Medicare and Social Security," that was some blue meat—the base and persuadables approved, and the opposition got angry, and by her lights that was good.

Another message they tested that month was titled "America's Strength":

> America's strength comes from our ability to work together—to knit together a landscape of people from different places and of different races into one nation.

Beautiful, touching, a little saccharine. Thus far, the lines on the graph rise together in tandem, giving the appearance of a range of mountains.

> For this to be a place of freedom for all, we cannot let the greedy few and the politicians they pay for divide us against each other . . .

Now, a divergence. The base and the persuadables continue to approve—the base actually climbing in this stretch, the persuadables holding steady, neither clapping nor sneering. But the opposition—it plunges. This is blue meat. And then,

> . . . based on what someone looks like, where they come from or how much money they have.

Again, a turn. The "greedy few" and the "politicians they pay for" lines earlier were tough stuff, actively alienating the opposition. But as the second half of the sentence unfolds ("based on what someone looks like"), the opposition grows more supportive again, even as the base and persuadables inch higher in their approval. Finally,

> It's time to stand up for each other and come together. It is time for us to pick leaders who reflect the very best of every kind of American. Together, we can make this a place where freedom is for everyone, no exceptions.

From around the words "stand up" onward, in response to the call for unity, we're back to three lines climbing up and to the right. So there was blue meat, there was a place for it, and it was sandwiched between inspiration.

Shenker-Osorio had developed an instinct for "good riddance" phrases—blue meat that did the wooing she wanted but reliably drove away the roughly 15 percent of voters she didn't want. Phrases like "immigrant Americans moved here for the promise of freedom and opportunity in this country" and "a greedy few rigged the game in their favor, now too many jobs don't pay enough for our needs, let alone enable our wants." These were generatively alienating lines. She sought them out.

Part of why blue meat worked is that it clarified things. It distinguished. Everyone wants everyone's kids to have a better life. But speaking of a greedy few rigging the rules explains how and why many kids don't have that. And it pushes some voters away. But generative alienation also worked for another reason. A message that merely left your opposition cold was one thing. But a message that alienated them could throw them off their game. It could make them call you out and talk about you incessantly. And, yes, the talking they would do wouldn't be flattering to you. But they would be talking about your idea, repeating it ad nauseam, your phrases would fill the air, helping Shenker-Osorio with her goal of a much-repeated message encircling the persuadables.

This move, she told me, is where right-wingers excel: making provocations they know will cause the left to engage in days of outrage parroting. "We get off our game, and we start repeating them in the guise of 'Can you believe they just said immigrants are animals?' " she said. " 'Can you believe they just said that you won't be able to eat a hamburger? Can you believe they just said that Jews fired space lasers? Can you believe they just said this virus is because of China? Can you believe they just said *fill-in-the-blank*?' And we thereby repeat it."

"THE PROBLEM WITH PROBLEMS"

To sum up the Shenker-Osorio method thus far: Don't dilute the vision to reach out to a middle that isn't in the middle but is confused. Thrill your base; alienate the people who aren't going to vote for you anyway but will do you the favor, if you're setting the rhetorical agenda, of yelling your ideas all over town. Don't be afraid to call out, to woo the right people and drive away the right people. And there was more. These callouts, she argued, needed to be nested within a positive, galvanizing mission that her allies on the left too often forgot to include while deploring problems.

Problems. Oh, how her fellow progressives loved problems. Couldn't get enough of them. Problems were, after all, their reason for being.

"Many progressive and Democratic messages," Shenker-Osorio told me, "basically boil down to 'Boy, have I got a problem for you!' Or, 'This is the *Titanic;* would you like to buy a ticket?' Or, 'We're the losing team. We lost recently, so you should join us.' That's progressive messaging in a nutshell, which is what I've been fighting and screaming to overcome."

In one of the messaging reports she worked on with colleagues, she wrote,

> Right now, most progressive messaging follows a familiar order: lead with problems, move to solution, end with a call to action. Americans got 99 problems and they don't want yours. The desire to sound the alarm about the egregious, systematic and growing harms to our communities is understandable. But that doesn't make it compelling. The problem with problems is that people don't want more of them.

Progressives' problem fixation had many sources. One was a laudable desire to use the political process to teach voters—about climate, about the subjugation of various populations, about double standards. "Frequently, we have an understandable desire to do what I would call nonstrategic political education," Shenker-Osorio told me. "There are so many terrible true things in the world, and we un-strategically desire to tell people about all those things. But it does not actually move people or build power. We need to think through the lens of 'What do I need this person to believe, and what do I need them to do?' as opposed to 'I need to tell them this terrible truth.'"

But she also wanted to make clear: "I also don't believe in a narrative in which we don't name problems." It was all about how.

Another factor in the problem obsession, she said, is the confusion of activists with the base. The activists she defines as people like her. Of that group, she said, "We never met a problem we didn't love. 'Boy, have I got a problem for you'—that's our love language. 'Sign me up! Cool! Could I please have more problems? Awesome. There. You had me at "fucked-up situation." You had me at "horrifying photo."'"

Then there's the base—or, as Shenker-Osorio calls it more precisely, the unengaged base. They're with you, but they're not as hyped up, and there is a decent chance they don't make it to the polls in any given year. "They are all set for problems," she said. "You know why? Because their job sucks, and they can't get their kids to school, and they can't pay for their health care and life. America has made life suck for them, and they're not out shopping for new problems."

And here's where the confusion occurs. It's the political activists who write the Democratic National Committee fundraising emails, who dominate Twitter, who make the ads, who put lives on hold to work for candidates. Those people get into what Shenker-Osorio calls a "continuous, incorrect feedback loop, where harms-and-horrors messaging" gets broadcast to the public, and they confuse the adulation they get from their fellow activists with adulation from the actual unengaged base. "Every DNC email, every candidate email, and, let's just be honest, every email from the left is like, 'This is a new crisis. This is terrible. It's very horrible.'

"So what happens is we retweet that shit, and we share that shit, and we 'like' that shit, and we even give $27 to that shit," she went on. "And so the activists are in a feedback loop where they're like, 'This is working.'" And that has to do with the financial incentive: "I've had this conversation 657 times with colleagues that run these big movement lists. It is considered canon in political fundraising that you've got to scare the shit out of people." (As I wrote this paragraph, I received an email from MoveOn with the subject heading "This is really, really bad." The sender's name had been temporarily changed from "MoveOn." It was "Wake-Up Call for Democrats." The email's first sentence read, "Democrats are in big trouble.")

"It keeps getting you hits," Shenker-Osorio told me, "but what it does not do is grow the base. It does not increase the number of people who want to join your cause. You keep getting hits off of the same people. And, in fact, there are diminishing returns to fear. You're poisoning the commons. Because what we see is that making people more fearful over time makes them more conservative.

"Our opposition is not the opposition," she said. "It is cynicism. So when you say to people, 'Here's how shitty everything is. Also, it's *this* shitty. Also, did you know it was *this shitty*? Here's some additional information about how shitty it is,' most unengaged people's response is like, 'You know what? I might just hang out over here and watch *90 Day Fiancé*.'"

Voters aren't stirred to reduce harm, Shenker-Osorio said. They're motivated to create good. "As many have remarked, Martin Luther King did not get famous for saying, 'I have a complaint.' He certainly did not get famous for saying, 'I have a multi-bulleted list of policy proposals.' There has to be a dream." Another mantra: "You've got to sell people on the beautiful tomorrow."

"PAINT THE BEAUTIFUL TOMORROW"

Shenker-Osorio tries to explain to clients that people already know Trump is bad. They know the health-care system sucks. They know their employer has too much power over them. They know Immigration and Customs Enforcement officers behave cruelly. But all of these criticisms, Shenker-Osorio argues, translate into negative demands: things to stop doing, things to abolish, things to rein in. What is missing is to show people, vividly show them, what the world would look like if you won. "Democrats," Shenker-Osorio has written, "are deeply, deeply comfortable with being against things, and they are far less comfortable with stating what they're for. The entire premise of my work is, 'Say what you're for.' The rest is commentary."

"Let me take a super-specific example—'Abolish ICE,'" Shenker-Osorio told me. "I am a person who supports abolishing ICE—I'd like to establish that for the record. But I also think that 'Abolish ICE,' like 'End family separation,' like 'End deportation,' like 'Stop climate change,' like 'End homelessness'—all of those things are negative demands." They focus the listener's attention on what you don't want. Shenker-Osorio had run various message tests of that kind of phrasing compared with a message like "Let's create a fair immigration process that respects all families."

"There's no comparison," she said. "'Create a fair immigration process that respects all families' is more persuasive, it is more mobilizing to people who ideologically are aligned with us, and it opens up a much broader array of possible policy solutions.

"I genuinely believe," she continued, "it is a Republican wet dream that they have us talking constantly about everything that we oppose because (a) it gives them more airtime, (b) it scares the shit out of people, and when people are afraid, what they seek is a more authoritarian, more restrictive, more conservative kind of leadership and structure, (c) it has us not speak about what we're for." She joked with colleagues that despite all her research into the nuances of different messages, there was really just one winning message for her side: "That message is, 'We can have nice things.' "

Thus Shenker-Osorio advised her clients to speak of ensuring clean, safe air to breathe and water to drink instead of just mitigating climate change. Of paying people enough to provide for their families instead of just fighting low wages and poor working conditions. Of helping people be there for those they love instead of just condemning arbitrarily shifting work hours and the lack of paid leave.

It made me think back to my time on the campaign trail with Sanders. How many times had I heard him forcefully excoriate the health insurance apparatchiks who deny people care, or the greedy drug company executives, and how many times had I heard him movingly declare health care a "human right"? But I'm not sure I could recall him painting any kind of picture of what life would look like if universal health care arrived. What awful jobs would people quit, no longer handcuffed to the employer insurance? What businesses would they then start? What stresses would lift from their marriages? What would they do? Who would they be? This was all but absent from the advocacy for Medicare for All. Yet it was what it would actually translate into in people's lives, and in Shenker-Osorio's view it was what might actually persuade.

And it wasn't only problem fixation that obstructed the painting of tomorrow. It was also, for many on the left, process fixation. Democrats could not shake process. They unself-consciously referred to a historic legislative proposal formally known as the Build Back Better Act as "the reconciliation package" when they went on TV, as if they had never met a real person. "Advocates tend to describe concerns by naming processes," Shenker-Osorio wrote in one of her messaging memos. "For example, characterizing the decimation of Medicaid as 'moving to block grants for states' brings the *means* front and center and sends the *ends* into the shadows. At the same time, we tend to label our desired solutions in terms of policy, not outcomes. For example, 'minimum wage increase' and 'paid family leave' instead of 'people are paid enough to make ends meet' and 'you're at your new baby's side,' respectively."

As an answer to this tendency, Shenker-Osorio had another of her catchphrases: "Sell the brownie, not the recipe."

"OUR CONVERSATION, NOT THEIR CONVERSATION"

Over the course of my conversations with Shenker-Osorio, I noticed her to be hyper-attuned not only to what is being said but also, perhaps even more so, to what conversation is being had, and, even more than that, whose conversation is being had, whose terrain you are on.

Sometimes in politics, you can be saying the right thing in the conversation you find yourself in, but you may be in the wrong conversation, which is to say a conversation that has you losing the war even when you win the battle. As Shenker-Osorio sees it, to be arguing on your opponent's conversational turf, on their terms, through their frames, is to concede before you open your mouth.

For example, when the right argues that they and their tax cuts are best for the economy, some on the left might answer, "No! Our program of raising wages is best for the economy." In one sense, it is a good, logical answer. But, in Shenker-Osorio's way of thinking, you have made an error. You have agreed to enter a debate about who is better for the economy. This, Shenker-Osorio has said, "is a terrible conversation to have. It is irrelevant. The economy is not real; it's a convention. The conversation progressives ought to have is, 'Who loves people best? What is best for people? What will we do to meet people's economic needs?' "

The problem with joining the "Who's better for the economy?" debate is that you have accepted the right's frame. Now you're having its conversation. "Republicans' brand strength is that they're better for the economy," Shenker-Osorio told me. "And of course that's bullshit. It's not true. It's disproven. But it doesn't matter. Just like Coke is 'classic,' and Pepsi is the 'next generation,' if you want good for the economy, you go with a Republican." So even as you advocate for why your side is actually better for the economy, you're validating a turf that is in fact questionable: that what is good for the economy, rather than people's economic well-being, is what we should be talking about.

This adoption of the right's framing didn't happen accidentally. It often grew out of those attempts at outreach. Candidates on the left felt they were weak on, say, border security. Migrants were streaming across the border, camps were filling up, the right was making a fuss about it, something had to be said. So the candidate on the left gives a press conference and says, "We also want to secure the border. And to secure the border, we need to give people a legal road map to citizenship," and so on. The problem, Shenker-Osorio said, is you have now echoed the right's idea that the border is insecure—which you didn't have to do. But as soon as you validate that frame, you become a runner-up on the issue whose salience you just raised. "If you tell people the border is insecure by saying, 'We need to secure the border,' then they're like, 'Oh, the border's insecure? I better go look for Robocop, not the B-minus, flabby alternative,'" Shenker-Osorio told me.

To speak in politics is not only to express your view of a particular issue. It is also to participate in voters' constant, often unconscious internal re-ranking of which issues matter.

On health care, this is what it sounded like to live on your opponents' turf, inadvertently having their conversation: Medicare for All, or just universal health care in general, will be cheaper; it will save us money. It was true, this claim. But what you were assenting to without assenting to it was the idea that the highest value is saving money, is economic efficiency. This is not a winning conversation for you if universal health care is your goal. It was, however, the dominant message of the Obama administration in selling the Affordable Care Act: "Bend the cost curve down."

However, Shenker-Osorio said, when instead you tell voters something like "No matter what you look like or where you come from, when someone you love is ill or injured, you want them to get the very best care without going bankrupt to do it," you are not only advocating for your position; you are also forcing the discussion onto the terrain most favorable to your side—in this case, what is good for people, not what is good for cost control.

For Shenker-Osorio, the most flagrant illustration of the whose-conversation problem came in response to Donald Trump's presidency. To be sure, Trump gave people a lot to react to. But from Shenker-Osorio's point of view, all he was doing was forcing the entire country, especially his opposition, onto the turf of his conversation, whatever it was. Pro–kids in cages or anti–kids in cages, you were talking about a chaotic border, the very thought of which benefited him. Then Trump began doing authoritarian things, and pundits and laypeople alike began incessantly referring to him as an authoritarian, a strongman, a wannabe dictator. It wasn't untrue. The problem, as Shenker-Osorio saw it, is that the perception of strength worked for Trump. The 2016 Trump voters who had become persuadable in 2020, up for grabs, still had a "lingering attachment" to Trump, she said, and are attracted to the idea that "he gets stuff done, he doesn't care what people think, he's brash." Labeling him a strongman risked backfiring. Instead, she told me in the fall of 2020, "Democrats should call him a weak loser, a bumbling idiot who is trying to steal the election." This was meant not to minimize the very real danger to democracy in that moment but rather to suggest that the dangerous thing that was happening was because of weakness, not strength.

"What you fight," Shenker-Osorio likes to say, "you feed."

Avoiding the pitfall of having someone else's conversation isn't easy. Especially now, many on the loonier fringes of the right make claim after outrageous claim, and they beg for refutation. But the refuting, if done carelessly, risks validating their framework. "The vast majority of Muslims pose no threat to our security" was an accurate sentiment heard often in the wake of 9/11. But it was a sentiment that reified the discussion about Islam as intrinsically problematic. Better, Shenker-Osorio says, to say, "Muslim Americans are our neighbors and our co-workers; they are the kids in our schools and the parents in our parks."

The Fight for $15 struggle was one of Shenker-Osorio's favorite examples of a campaign that had gotten it right. "The traditional way that we have fought a wage argument has been, to my horror, some permutation of 'We love the economy best.' A standard minimum-wage message would be, 'We need to pay people more because that will grow our economy. When you pay people more, they can be customers in our stores, and we have a consumer-driven economy where spending needs to cycle through.'" This was, for Shenker-Osorio, validating the wrong discussion. It was, she said, "the classic example of the milquetoast, please all, please none, find the thing to say that all three lines track more or less upward, because you're not offending anyone, right?"

Among the problems she had with that message was this: "The base isn't going to repeat it, because—are you kidding me? That's not why people care about getting more money. They care about getting more money so they can feed their fucking family." And it deepens the confusion of the persuadables you're courting, who are already torn and in the market for a worldview. The message you send them, Shenker-Osorio said, is that "the higher-order principle here is, how do we grow the GDP?"

What Fight for $15 did was seize the moral high ground. The message was that people who work for a living ought to earn a living. While making the case, it focused attention on the right discussion to be having, about what makes people thrive.

What maddened Shenker-Osorio was when someone on her side got it exactly right, showed their savviness at navigating conversational terrain and forcing people to have theirs, and then got attacked by their own allies for it. That was what happened when, in the fall of 2021, Representative Ocasio-Cortez made a splash by attending New York's Met Gala wearing a white dress on which the words "Tax the rich" had been printed. Instantaneously, everyone had feelings about it. The right attacked her idea of taxing the rich. Centrists attacked her as a hypocrite for attending a fancy dinner that cost some attendees $30,000 a plate while professing her tax ideas. Some of her own cohorts on the progressive left criticized her for engaging with a problematic institution at all, and for an empty gesture that did nothing to move the needle, even as Black Lives Matter protesters outside the event were getting arrested for calling out its hypocrisies. And, of course, a whole bunch of people simply loved it. When I attended a Halloween dog costume parade in Manhattan the following month, dogs in white dresses emblazoned with "Tax the rich" in red letters were among the few costumes repeated more than once. More important, the dress spawned millions of impressions on social media, became a near-hegemonic trending topic for a few days, forced television pundits and lawmakers to comment, drove cable news discussion, inspired think pieces and newsletter posts, and so on.

As everyone offered their unique and urgent take on the dress,

Shenker-Osorio was, as is her wont, watching the conversation they were collectively having. And she saw so many smart people missing the obvious: "You know what folks are repeating today, regardless of their take on the messenger, medium and setting? 'Tax the rich,'" she wrote on Twitter. "@AOC made that happen, surely knowing she'd face both left & right criticism for doing so." She called the dress moment "a master class in setting the narrative frame."

"CLAIM FREEDOM"

In recent years, there has been some debate on the political left about marketing ideas to a much wider audience by making alternative cases for them—cases that center what various target audiences care about more than what the speaker does. Examples include making a Christian case for protecting the environment, to make inroads on the climate-skeptic right, or making a pro-business case for universal health care, arguing that liberating people from employer-based health care will unleash a thousand start-ups. Was this savvy politics, growing the circle? Or was it what Shenker-Osorio warned about in having the wrong discussion?

Her answer here was nuanced. You never want to be having your opponents' conversation. But you also don't want to leave your opponent alone on moral ground that remains vital to claim.

Worrying about what's good for Mr. Economy—that is the right's issue, the right's conversation, the right's question. Shenker-Osorio drew a contrast between that and, say, the concept of "freedom." That idea was contested. People on the right spoke of freedom from taxation and regulation and vaccines. But people on the left spoke of reproductive freedom and freedom from police violence and freedom from want. To frame your ideas in the language of freedom wasn't validating the right's frame. It was staking a claim to the idea of freedom as being as much yours as theirs. It was participating in the debate about what freedom is and who guards it.

"The right wing has named and claimed freedom for a very, very, very long time," Shenker-Osorio told me, "and I have argued that it is just utter stupidity for the left to let go of freedom." She put this view to work as she worked on campaigns to pass voting-rights legislation in Congress during President Biden's first year. She told everyone who would listen, on the Zooms convened for organizers, advocates, and activists, that the fight should be characterized as seeking "the freedom to vote."

She felt similarly about the frame of family. For a long time, the left had given it up to the right, but for no reason. There was no reason for the right to own family. Its ideas weren't intrinsically pro-family in a way the left's weren't—whereas, on the economy, the right was genuinely more interested in what was good for the economy, as an entity unto itself, even if at the expense of the interests of human beings, than the left was. A Christian appeal to care for the earth struck her as similar. Christianity has a lot to say about the proper way of living on the planet. To cede the discussion of climate change to those Christians who don't believe in it was to fritter away political opportunity.

So where does making these crossover pitches curdle, for Shenker-Osorio, into having someone else's conversation? The line wasn't entirely obvious to me, but she said it becomes capitulation when the conversation you're having isn't authentically yours, isn't something you could equally claim. For example, she said, making a case for environmentalism in terms of honoring tradition for tradition's sake: "We should care for our land, we should care for our earth, because it's the American way. And it's what we've always done." To her ear, this sounded off, because tradition, doing something because it's what we've always done, is a frame that will never benefit the progressive left. To make a case for protecting the planet, while endorsing the notion that things should be done because they've been done, gets into that winning-battle-losing-war space.

Why did this discomfit her where making a biblical case for environmentalism did not?

"It's because the Bible, I would argue and some other people wouldn't, is still up for grabs," she said. "In terms of what the Bible is actually teaching and preaching. Because I come from a faith tradition, I'm Jewish and religious, I have familiarity with the Hebrew Bible and an understanding of scripture that tells me that women are equal to men and that tells me that gay people are good and godly. And so what I'm saying is that religion, spirituality, being a good steward of the earth, is like freedom. It's a contested concept, where there is a right-wing version of it, and the right-wing version may even be dominant. But that's not the only version that exists. Whereas being good for the economy or tradition for its own sake, to take two different examples—or we should protect the immigrants because they will mow our lawns and clean our houses—there is no progressive version of that." To make arguments along those lines was to accept the underlying frame as correct. Thus when you argued in these other terms, you were accidentally working for the opposition.

"MAKE A PROBLEM SANDWICH"

So, in Shenker-Osorio's methodology, you have the idea of enchanting your base to woo the persuadables, of generatively alienating your opposition, of painting the beautiful tomorrow, *making them see it,* of being sure to have your conversation, not inadvertently theirs. If these were the elements of a good message as Shenker-Osorio saw it, how did you put one together? What was the beginning, middle, and end?

A common problem with message ordering, from Shenker-Osorio's standpoint, is starting with the problem. She rattled off examples: "We look around today and people are struggling like never before; they're suffering and dying from COVID. Or today we look around and the scene is one of unrelenting violence and hardship. Basically, the first sentence is like, 'The climate is fucked, union density is at its lowest in however many years, there is destruction, everyone is dying.'"

As with many common messaging errors as she saw them, the instinct came from a good place. It originated in labor organizing, where the standard arc is A-H-A—anger, hope, action. Before your colleague at Starbucks or Amazon or Tyson mentions a union drive to you, they might ask, "What's not going well at work? What pisses you off at work? What's fucked up about this place?" From there, they build toward a solution.

But Shenker-Osorio had found that, outside the workplace context, the opening salvo of anger didn't work as well. Perhaps it was because people go to their jobs every day and have pain points that are clear and present to them, and they have also seen their workplace tangibly change over time, for better or worse, when a new regulation or new boss or new management mantra came in. In the more abstract realm of electoral politics, there are many more intermediary layers between the clear and present problems in people's lives and what might change. Starting with anger doesn't seem to make people believe things can change. It turns many people off of the political process. And when Shenker-Osorio crafted the actual messages, the angry opener also made it harder to pivot to a closing message of hope. You reinforce the cynicism so many voters were already feeling. You ratify the attitude many already had: that nothing will ever change. "When you open with that salvo, what you can't achieve is the second step—the hope," she told me. "It's not that people don't think our ideas are right. It's that they don't think our ideas are possible, and so why bother?"

The message ordering Shenker-Osorio suggests instead goes like this: shared value, problem, solution.

If you were pushing to increase the minimum wage, for example, you might begin by framing this as a shared value: "No matter what we look like, where we come from, or what's in our wallets, most of us believe that people who work for a living ought to earn a living." If you were getting into police reform, you might launch with "Whether we're Black or white, Latino or Asian, Native or newcomer, most of us want to move through our lives and our communities without fearing for ourselves or our loved ones." It could be as simple as "No matter our differences, most of us want pretty similar things."

Shenker-Osorio's reason for starting this way reminded me of something Loretta Ross had said. A fundamental thing many people who disagree with you share with you is the desire to feel like good people. If the message is venturing into challenging territory, it helps to ground it first in a shared belief. "You want to call people into their higher angels," Shenker-Osorio has written. "Here's a principle that you want to believe that you believe in. Here's how it works. Here's this thing happening today that is making this principle impossible. Would you like to resolve that dissonance?"

With the shared value articulated, you move to what is preventing the principle from being honored. And here, Shenker-Osorio said, it is important to name villains, and important to identify not just what the villains are doing to obstruct the fulfillment of the principle at hand but also their motivation in doing that. What is the payoff for them? So if you're continuing with that minimum-wage message in a moment of continuing racist appeals from the right, you might say, "But today, a wealthy and powerful few try to divide us from each other" (the obstruction and the naming of names) "so that we'll look the other way while they pick our pockets and hand the spoils to their corporate cronies" (the essential why). Or, "But today, a handful of politicians try to shame and blame Black people, new immigrants, and people struggling to make ends meet for our problems because they hope to distract us from their failure to prevent and treat COVID." In other words, they're not just being jerks. There is a crime, and there is a motive.

"It's a movement away from just saying Trump is a fucking racist, Trump is an asshole, Trump is inciting violence, Trump is evil—to pulling back the curtain and saying the why," Shenker-Osorio says. "You have to say the why. Otherwise, you're not providing an origin story."

And then the solution. Here, again, after naming names and chiding villains, we're pulling the nose back up to inspiration. "So we all believe in this thing, here are the people getting in the way of our thing, and here is why they benefit from obstructing progress." And now: "By joining together across racial differences, we can swear in new leaders who work for every one of us, no exceptions." Or, "By coming together, we can rewrite the rules so that the wealthiest few pay what they owe and all of us have what we need for generations to come." The details vary depending on the policy in question—health care, taxes, the minimum wage. But the arc is the same.

The result is what I would call a callout sandwich: a generous heap of callout between two thick slices of call in. Call people—all people—in with that universally appealing paean to values. Call out the people getting in the way of those values translating into better lives. But neither start nor finish there. Remind people that if they come together, things can change and other worlds are possible. One way that I made sense of Shenker-Osorio's advice to Democrats in particular is that she was urging them to do both their calling in and their calling out more sharply than they often did. At present, their callouts often seemed tempered by the feeling that they should be calling in persuadables. Their call ins were limited by the reluctance to use terms or concepts like freedom or family that the right had claimed as their own. Shenker-Osorio longed for a party that called voters in with sonorous invocations of their own definitions of freedom and family, framed as universal aspirations of having each other's back and wanting the same things for our kids, and then followed that up with fearless naming and shaming, recognizing no contradiction between these things, and finally moved to transcending the cynicism the callout might engender by saying, "We can solve this!"

When these various elements were assembled, here is what they sounded like. Consider a sample message Shenker-Osorio drafted on immigration during the Trump presidency:

> Most of us believe that family comes first.

That was the shared value. And not just any shared value, but family—one of those claimed by the right that Shenker-Osorio felt shouldn't be ceded.

> But today, certain lawmakers want to forcibly separate mothers from children, husbands from wives, and sisters from brothers. Anything that tears apart our families threatens our nation.

Now the problem was introduced, as well as the people behind the problem—the obstruction to the fulfillment of the shared value. And there is a further twist: a hint of national-security language applied to the earlier language of family. The message is contesting not one but two turfs of political discussion that the right claims but hardly owns.

> In opposing this new executive order, we affirm our belief that having "family values" means valuing families by keeping them together and honoring the contributions immigrant Americans make to our country and communities.

In this case, the message returns to a shared value and doubles down on contesting the right's family posturing by claiming the mantra of "family values."

> That's why American families are [solution/call to action].

And then the call to action, presented as a thing that is already going on, not a thing that should—thus making the defense of immigrants normative, the thing that's happening, the way the world is.

Or consider this message on voting rights:

> Whatever our color, background, or zip code, most of us believe that voters pick our leaders—our leaders do not get to pick their voters. When it comes to our elections, we want a transparent process we can trust, where Americans have equal freedom to vote, whether we live in a small town or big city, the South or the North.

The shared value first. And here a sly, even slightly manipulative effort is made to take a contested and divisive issue—gerrymandering and other forms of electoral rigging—and present the opposition to them, somewhat falsely, as a widely held value. We all think voters should pick their leaders, right, guys?

> But today, a handful of politicians put up barriers to silence our voices based on what we look like or where we live.

Now the problem, the obstruction, the obstructors, and the barest hint that they're weaponizing identity to pull this con off. Which might help explain all the identity warfare around you.

> We make the future, and it's time to enact national standards for voting to ensure all of us have a say in key decisions like pandemic relief, health care, and bolstering our economic well-being.

Now the proposed solution, but a policy prescription that is quickly followed by the proposed payoff to you. You need a say in the everyday, basic things in your life. This will give it to you. You are not being lectured on democracy as a lofty end in itself. You are being met where you are, in the daily grind of your life.

> Together, we can ensure Americans can safely and freely cast our ballots so that every voice is heard and our elections reflect the will of the people.

Now a sense of "we can do this" with a dash of the beautiful tomorrow, inflected once again by shared values: "so that every voice is heard."

Shenker-Osorio's most influential work along these lines is an undertaking called Race Class Narrative Action. The project took root in 2017, asking a question that felt acutely relevant in that first year of the Trump presidency but also wouldn't go away, rising to the fore every time the left came face-to-face with racist dog whistling from the right and was flat-footed: How do you push back on racist appeals?

Shenker-Osorio came to the project at the behest of a Berkeley law professor named Ian Haney López, author of the book *Dog Whistle Politics.* The pair teamed up with Heather McGhee, who then ran the think tank Demos, to test a range of ways of putting forward a progressive message in the context of constant race-baiting from the right. What they knew going in was that there tended to be two dominant approaches to the problem on the political left. Some leaned into race in combating racism, calling for the dismantling of white supremacy, chanting "Black Lives Matter," calling out Trump and the Republicans' overt racism. Their challenge was that they risked turning off those so-called moderates, particularly women, who, for better or worse, were so pivotal in so many elections. Others put forth a more class-centric narrative that at times ignored and papered over the racist appeals, which risked demoralizing the people of color in their base.

The error Shenker-Osorio and her colleagues saw Democrats making was assuming that silence about race could broaden the tent, could be its own form of outreach. Why provoke white voters? Why answer explicit racism with the explicit embrace of antiracism? The problem with such thinking was that, to cite another of her mantras, "politics isn't solitaire." Joe Biden or Bernie Sanders avoiding the subject of race didn't drain the subject from the campaign. The right was still doing its thing, still shouting these messages into people's ears.

The problem with going silent on race, Shenker-Osorio said, is that "they're hearing from the other side, 'You know why you don't have a job? You don't have a job because of immigrants.' 'You know why things are bad? Things are bad because that lawless mob is out wreaking havoc in our cities because Democrat mayors are not preserving law and order,'" Shenker-Osorio said. "You have to have an explanation and a rejoinder for what the other side is saying. Otherwise, your economic promise has no way of breaking through." The dog-whistle appeal that has now entered a voter's mind, or grown louder within it, has sown the idea of a problem the left isn't proposing to solve.

So the team tested an approach integrating honesty about race with a broad-based appeal to economic inclusion. And when their results emerged, they summed up their finding this way:

> Arguments for courting white working-class voters are bound up with a corollary, often unspoken, claim: Democrats must choose between non-college white voters and voters of color. Baked into this is the conviction that appealing to one group necessarily imperils Democratic chances with the other.
>
> We have important new evidence that we discuss below that shows this is wrong.

The secret to building "a multiracial progressive coalition for economic and racial justice," they found, was talking explicitly about race—and talking about it as a thing opportunistic politicians exploit in order to avoid giving you those nice things they could be giving you. In one field experiment, Minnesota organizers showed potential voters a flyer with this text:

> Whether white, black, or brown, 5th generation or newcomer, we all want to build a better future for our children. My opponent says some families have value, while others don't count. He wants to pit us against each other in order to gain power for himself and kickbacks for his donors.

Shenker-Osorio and her colleagues conceived of this preemptive naming and interdiction of racist appeals as a form of intellectual vaccination. "To inoculate against our opposition's narrative, we must expose the right-wing tactic of deliberate division and racialized scapegoating that keeps us from demanding the rules and resources all of us need," the group wrote in a report. A politician running against someone making these racist appeals might assume that simply offering a distinct and positive vision—typically one focused on economic uplift for all races—was enough. What Shenker-Osorio and the others were arguing was that racist appeals were a virus whose particles hung in the air. It wasn't enough to pump your own, healthier ideas into the air. You first had to prevent voters from being infected by racist appeals, and only then try to win them over to your ideas. You did that by warning people about the incoming hate, explaining why and how it was being used, who was benefiting, how it hurt them regardless of who they are. Then you could limit the virus's infectiousness. Over time, the team found that messages that sought both to defang a racist appeal and to talk about shared economic solidarity outperformed messages that centered race and minimized economics, as well as messages that centered economics and minimized race.

What was important, Shenker-Osorio and her colleagues found, was to link the fight against racism to the cause of life betterment, which language like "dismantling white supremacy" didn't do. "Calling out intentional divisions and outcomes is not enough by itself," they wrote. "A positive call to action that recognizes 'we are stronger when we work together' is more effective with base adults and persuadables than focusing solely on the politics of division." What they were after was a delicate threading of a small-eyed needle: being true to the problems of the country, being true to the challenges of people of color, being empathetic to those white working-class voters who shared some of the economic challenges and who feared that solving the racial challenges would come at their expense, and somehow finding words to forge them into a broad, multiracial coalition.

Their approach, rather novel within Democratic strategizing, was then translated into very specific guidance for politicians and movements. If you paid careful attention to American politics in recent years, you would have noticed that a great many political figures on the left increasingly spoke along the lines of the Race Class Narrative project's guidance. Bernie Sanders adopted that language in his 2020 campaign, distinguishing it from his 2016 run. His Senate colleague and erstwhile rival for the presidency, Elizabeth Warren, put the language into practice to such powerful effect that *The Nation* proclaimed her "the First Intersectional Candidate for President." Even Joe Biden, Scranton Joe, whose entire political brand was his appeal to those white moderates, changed his tune. In his first speech on race as president, while signing an executive order on racial equity, he said, "For too long, we've allowed a narrow, cramped view of the promise of this nation to fester. You know, we've—we've bought the view that America is a zero-sum game in many cases: 'If you succeed, I fail.' 'If you get ahead, I fall behind.' 'If you get the job, I lose mine.' Maybe worst of all, 'If I hold you down, I lift myself up.'" After McGhee, who had seeded the project while at Demos, heard that, she told an interviewer, "Calling out that we are all on the same team and that racism is holding the entire country back is groundbreaking for a U.S. president." Biden hadn't just portrayed racism as bad for its victims. He had portrayed it as bad for white people, too. For her, the speech had all the suggested elements: calling out the racism, and explaining how it is weaponized to deprive all Americans of nice things.

Beneath the philosophy of this approach were simple shifts in language. Instead of saying "United we stand, divided we fall," airily and Pollyanna-like, Shenker-Osorio and her colleagues encouraged a race-conscious formulation like "No matter our differences, most of us want pretty similar things": naming the fact of differences in order to inoculate against the exploitation of differences. Instead of "working people," they pushed "working people, whether Black, white, or brown." Instead of "come together in the hopes of a better future," they suggested "come together like we did in our past," to remind people that creative cross-racial solidarity is not an abstraction but has happened before and could happen again.

As Shenker-Osorio's star rose and her mantras spread, she was part of a broad, strategic effort widely credited with helping to protect the 2020 election results and ensure a peaceful transition of power.

Throughout that election year, a vast and unwieldy coalition of organizations on the left (and beyond) set aside their usual differences and collaborated around the common goal of ensuring a free and fair election and, presuming Donald Trump's loss, a successful transition of power. *Time* magazine later described the effort as "a vast, cross-partisan campaign to protect the election—an extraordinary shadow effort dedicated not to winning the vote but to ensuring it would be free and fair, credible and uncorrupted." The article's headline read, "The Secret History of the Shadow Campaign That Saved the 2020 Election."

On regular Zoom calls, Shenker-Osorio gave the group messaging guidance, dealing with hard and contentious cases like "Abolish ICE" and "Defund the police," seeking ways to honor the radical aspirations some parts of the coalition had while being careful not to squander the election. Election Day came and went, and Trump, having lost, began looking for ways to stay in office, and then the January 6 insurrection exploded. On a call with more than nine hundred members after that attack, the group listened as Shenker-Osorio advised against calling what had happened a "coup." Not because it wasn't. But because, as Alexander Burns of *The New York Times* put it, making mention of her counsel, "the word could make Mr. Trump sound far stronger than he was—or even imply that a pro-Trump militia had seized power." For her, the word "coup" implied strength and organization. It risked turning a dangerous thing into an even more inevitable-seeming thing. It was important to warn people about Trump while giving him the aspect of foolery rather than evil genius.

After the coast was clear of him in January 2021, Shenker-Osorio and some colleagues continued hosting Zooms, now focused on getting things done in the Biden era and beating back resistance. Though they were private sessions, I was allowed to watch them, getting a glimpse of the phrasemaking and coordination behind so many of the messages I was used to hearing in public.

On July 28, she spoke, along with her colleagues Mike Podhorzer and Jiggy Geronimo, on a Zoom titled "Turning Up the Heat Before the Congressional Recess." They had new data to share on what messages were working on members of Congress and which weren't, especially on the subject of the democracy and voting reforms languishing in Washington. The problem, their research found, was that in a time of economic hardship and a punishing pandemic voters were focused on personal well-being and highly immediate issues, not on seemingly more abstract concerns like democratic decay. In fact, language about a "fair and effective democracy" proved to be the least effective message they tested. The challenge they faced was how to give democracy problems, which of course imperiled efforts to improve people's lives, more here-and-now salience to people.

Part of the answer, Shenker-Osorio said on the Zoom, was framing democracy reforms in a language of agency over the kind of health care you have, the kinds of roads you have. Don't make the mistake too many on the left do, she said, in assuming that people will value eliminating the filibuster as an end in itself, or cracking down on gerrymandering, or creating national voting standards. Frame each as a tool to give people more say in the shape of their lives. It was vintage Shenker-Osorio: Don't be wonky; don't assume everyone is one of your activists; paint the beautiful tomorrow; sell the brownie, not the recipe. Don't rally people to care about some arcane word they probably don't understand. Make them think of a pain point in their life—that expensive diabetes treatment—and tell them how giving the federal government supervision of elections and cracking down on gerrymandering and allowing mail-in voting would empower them to solve their problems.

Now, all warmed up, Shenker-Osorio made a point she had been eager to share—about freedom. What the recent surveys showed was that when you asked Americans of all persuasions what values they most cared about, freedom consistently topped the list. It was the top-ranking value for strong Biden voters, tepid Biden voters, tepid Trump voters, and strong Trump voters. A whole country, agreeing on something, at last! "This really, truly is, over and again, the core value that Americans associate with this country," Shenker-Osorio told the group, which consisted of progressive activists and organizers and staff members.

"So we cannot lose the freedom debate," she continued. "We cannot afford to be in a place where we just sort of shrug our shoulders and say, 'Freedom is a right-wing concept.' Freedom is not a right-wing concept. It's a contested value."

She knew whom she was talking to, and she knew why they might squirm at using language like freedom. What was next? Wearing an American flag pin? But she wanted to reassure them that freedom was contested terrain, and they needed to stake their claim. Freedom feels "corporeal," she said at one point. It feels as if it has something to do with your life—unlike the more abstract idea of democracy.

Two weeks later, on another Zoom, Shenker-Osorio was making her case again. She was sounding an alarm. The saving-democracy talk simply was not working. She wasn't saying it shouldn't be working. It just wasn't. It was too intangible for people, evidently. For better or worse, large numbers of voters do not sit around fretting about democracy. They were fretting that summer about crime and rising prices and work conditions.

But, Shenker-Osorio observed, her allies on the left had what she called a responsibility complex. Voters might clearly be telling them, as they were that summer, that voting reforms were not at the top of their priority list. And the political professionals would take that as a challenge to explain why voting reforms are more important than they think. Throughout the summer, as voters spoke of rising gun violence and inflation and strikes, the political class on the left was warning of dire threats to democracy, and of the siren of authoritarianism around the corner, and of gutted voting rights. They were trying to get voters to re-rank their priorities, often by suggesting that the issues voters cared about wouldn't matter if the country lost its democratic institutions. Shenker-Osorio was suggesting a more empathetic and effective path: instead of the "No, pay attention to *this*!" vibe, she wanted the left to reframe voting reforms as a mere tool to give people the power to solve the problems bugging them that summer—a tool to improve their quotidian lives tangibly.

I tuned in to another session a month or so later, in mid-September 2021. At the outset, Shenker-Osorio called for "a moment of palate-cleansing celebration." "The Democrats are on message!" she said, sounding surprised at her own words. What she was referring to was the sudden and unexpected adoption of her "freedom" advice by the Democratic Party. "We have been pushing this freedom thing very hard," she said. And the day before, September 14, a group of senators had introduced a new legislative proposal titled the Freedom to Vote Act. It was the product of long negotiations between voting-rights hawks and moderates like Joe Manchin of West Virginia, who had trouble with an earlier, more far-reaching proposal known as the For the People Act. The new proposal, while diluted, was still regarded as offering the most thorough democracy reforms in a generation. And, for once, the Democrats had listened! Even Joe Manchin had listened. They had recast democracy reform in the language of freedom.

In the Zoom chat, people thanked Shenker-Osorio and her colleagues for their work and beating the freedom drum. It was an encouraging day.

On days like this, Shenker-Osorio allowed herself to feel as if her way of messaging were on the rise. "I would say that the kind of thinking that I do about language, and the kind of thinking that I do about persuasion, and my theory of change—engage the base, persuade the middle, alienate the opposition—that is certainly what I see in the messaging architecture and approach of the new crop of Democrats. It's how folks in the Squad message," she said, referring to the growing contingent of progressive lawmakers that included Representatives Ocasio-Cortez, Ilhan Omar, Rashida Tlaib, and Ayanna Pressley. Her methodology was ascendant "in the movement spaces, the outside spaces," she said. Elected officials, but for the Squad types, were harder; the Democratic Party bosses, harder still. From time to time, she was called in to brief the White House or the party or a group of senators. But she knew that being invited to the table or the panel, where a comic turned message guru added some spark, didn't mean her lessons would be heeded. Because everything she said, she knew, was being countered by a vast apparatus of Beltway advisers who habitually hawk the most milquetoast, safe, bipartisan, please-everyone-and-please-no-one scripts, largely for the benefit of the donor class and the oligarchic interests they seek to defend above all else, and who relentlessly break all her rules.

September turned to October, and the focus of national politics turned to Biden's two-track agenda: his effort to pass a bipartisan physical infrastructure bill and a social policy bill that Jonathan Weisman of *The New York Times* called "the most significant expansion of the nation's safety net since the war on poverty in the 1960s," touching "virtually every American's life, from conception to aged infirmity." And Shenker-Osorio's brief celebratory moment of being listened to the month before had given way to the more familiar pattern of watching all her lessons ignored.

Somehow, a dramatic and humane proposal to improve daily life for tens of millions of people was getting lost in the weeds of process and shop talk and inside baseball. Reconciliation. BIF. BBB. Three point five trillion dollars. Manchin. Sinema. The filibuster. The debt ceiling. This was the language employed even by the advocates of these proposals. What was falling away was the substance of what the plans would do for people's lives.

There were elderly people who could not see because they could not afford the eyewear, and if some of these proposals passed, they would regain sight. There were cousins and spouses and neighbors of theirs of similar vintage who could not hear but, if the full program were to be enacted, would. There were grandpas and grandmas who would, if present realities continued, have no teeth in a few years. Under some of these policies, they would keep their teeth—and their independence. If the most sweeping version of these proposals passed, there would be children who soon tasted clean water for the first time in their lives.

But voters could have been forgiven for forgetting, or never knowing in the first place, that the shape of their lives was up for debate in Congress, because no one was presenting it this way. In a Zoom session, Shenker-Osorio reminded her colleagues about selling the brownie, not the recipe. Once again, so many of the advocates on her side had forgotten about outcomes. "When I say 'outcome,' I mean in whatever space you have it, what it sounds like in terms of lived experience, what it feels like to walk into the doctor's office, get the care you need, and not wonder about the bill that's going to arrive later. So when you have the room, don't name even the policy subcomponents. Name how it would feel to actually experience those things in people's lives."

Now she offered a friendly chart advising Democrats on what language to "replace" and what language to "embrace." Stop talking about $3.5 trillion. Stop talking about infighting between moderates and progressives. Start talking about "some lawmakers siding with the rich against the rest of us." Start talking about "air we breathe, water we drink, paid time to care for our loved ones." Stop talking about the filibuster. Start talking about "schools that nurture our kids' dreams."

Election Day 2021 was a few days later. Around the country, many voters turned on Democrats. It wasn't unexpected; in fact, it is the general pattern of American politics the year after one party takes over. Suddenly reporters and pundits were on the air asking why it was so hard for Democrats to show voters what they had delivered and why they had been, as always, too shy to get their existing agenda through and to propose even more. In Virginia, the Democratic candidate for governor, Terry McAuliffe, struggled to respond when in the final days his Republican opponent stoked resentment about the teaching of race in Virginia schools. "One thing is clear," the *New York Times* journalist Mara Gay posted on Twitter the following day, "if Democrats don't learn how to talk about race, Republicans will do it for them." I could hear the sound of Shenker-Osorio huffing that week on the far side of the country.

A few weeks later, President Biden was on the road selling his achievements, standing in front of giant signs that read, "Bipartisan Infrastructure Law." Shenker-Osorio, irritated, posted online, "The reflexive obsession among mainstream Dems with calling the infrastructure bill 'bipartisan' is proof positive we're willing to campaign for our opposition." Shortly afterward, she vented to me, "We don't have time for this shit. We don't have time to be genuflecting at the altar of bipartisanship, and pretending that Republicans are a party, that they are anything other than an authoritarian faction. We do not have time." The stakes, she said, were plain enough: "the survival of the planet—water to drink and air to breathe."

She licked the wounds of her annoyance and got back to work.

6

THE VACCINE AGAINST LIES

Among the newer difficulties Shenker-Osorio faced was that the modern right in America was no longer just animated by extreme ideas. An ever larger slice of it functioned in the manner of a cult, providing supporters with their own fully baked alternative reality, a world of fictions—voter fraud that wasn't happening, made-up pedophile rings involving a pizza restaurant, conspiracy theories about the climate and vaccines—that whet the appetite for its very real policy agenda. This development added an epistemological aspect to the challenge of persuasion in an age of fracture. There is persuading those with different beliefs. Then there is persuading those with different facts.

In recent years, as this crisis of disinformation and political cultism grew, a former cult member turned cult deprogrammer named Diane Benscoter began to receive emails from relatives of Americans being sucked down these rabbit holes.

Meegan wrote of being her mother's only child and caretaker. The mother lived on her property. But she was baffling Meegan and her husband with her ever more outlandish beliefs. She was anti-vaccine, antigovernment, but pro-Rapture. She believed the people in power were on a mission to kill everyone. She had become a fountain of misinformation, sending articles, posting nonsensical things online. She believed Meegan and her husband were the brainwashed ones. Meegan had concerns both practical and existential: What happens when you can no longer bear your own mother because of what she believes? And what happens when this radicalization happens while she lives on your property and is refusing to pay her bills because the Rapture is due to arrive any day now?

Jad wrote Benscoter about his mother. For her, the gateway drug had been MAGA. Now the mother was full QAnon and beyond. Everyone dead was not dead—Marilyn, Elvis, JFK. Everyone alive was not, in fact, alive—Joe Biden, Mike Pence, Hillary Clinton. You had to be vigilant, the mother felt, because of all those celebrity baby kidnappers. The day before the email was sent, the mother had canceled plans with the family. Why? To fill her bathtubs with water and obtain a propane stove because of the impending utilities blackout that, like all her other predictions, never came true. And this mother, too, thought her children were the brainwashed sheep, dupes of power. What was Jad to do?

Tina wrote of how her husband now basically lived online, bingeing on videos about how George Floyd is still alive (paid actors), how Hillary Clinton was killed by a firing squad (human trafficking), and how all the debt was about to be erased. Because of this last fact, her husband thought it was a great time to get a new truck—financed, of course. Already morbidly obese, the husband was gaining weight because his binge-watching of conspiracy-promoting videos was accompanied by binge eating. His hygiene was declining. What could be done?

One letter writer's mother-in-law had lost a relationship with her own increasingly mentally ill twin sister because of QAnon. Someone else's seventy-year-old sister had joined a cult with its own language and its own regular phone conferences, and she, too, had succumbed to Q beliefs, in addition to falling ever deeper into debt. One woman wrote to Benscoter about her mother having become a conspiracy theory messaging fiend online. The daughter had lost a relationship with the mother and was desperate to rebuild it, and she didn't have much time: she had terminal cancer, and getting through to her mother was her dying wish.

What can I do? these correspondents asked Benscoter. How could they save relationships with people they had lost? How could they bring back loved ones who had become strangers to them, having found new homes for their minds that were incompatible with their former lives?

Across the country an epidemic raged, a plague of grief without deaths. People mourned the lost living, whose minds had passed on to some strange beyond. Families cracked. People in the sunset of their lives chose YouTube over the children they had lovingly raised. An astonishing 17 percent of Americans were said to be QAnon believers now. And a number of their loved ones wrote to Benscoter, because she knew a thing or two about how people get sucked in to cults and how some get out.

As she returned to the anti-cult work she had sworn off long ago, Benscoter had two realizations: One, this problem was everything she had been preparing for her whole life. Two, nothing could prepare anyone for this problem. It's one thing to help one person, or thirty, get out of a cult. But what do you do when your deprogramming target is forty-three million of your fellow citizens?

Diane Benscoter came to the work of extracting people from cults in a relatively common way: being a cult victim herself.

She grew up in York, Nebraska, in the 1960s and felt everything around her was bland. From the sky, her hometown was a quilt of greens and browns and yellows, full of farms bounded by roads spaced a mile apart. Entertainment options were limited: young people partied with Budweiser binges at the corner of one mile marker and another. Growing up, Benscoter had loved her family, but as she hit adolescence and felt a growing sense of self, she recalled her attitude changing. Her family began to grate on her. She didn't want for herself what she assumed they wanted for her—to carry the staid traditions of their social universe one generation further, marrying a man from the area, living a conservative, predictable life. No one seemed to understand her. Her parents' generation was sending their children to their slaughter in Vietnam. She didn't understand how no one seemed to care, at least no one around her. She found little solace even among her own age-group in York. There was more relief to be had in drugs and music and the counterculture. If those around her didn't seem to get her, Bob Dylan sure did.

In 1973, at the age of sixteen, Benscoter dropped out of high school. She moved to the more cosmopolitan environs of Lincoln, Nebraska.

One day, she was on the way to a job interview at a local alternative newspaper, when a white van pulled over. Several people popped out and began to distribute bananas. The bananas were wrapped in flyers, clinging to the fruit with rubber bands. Benscoter opened the flyer, which read,

> WALK FOR WORLD PEACE. PLEASE JOIN US FOR A 3-DAY WALK TO HEAR REVEREND SUN MYUNG MOON SPEAK IN DES MOINES, IOWA. FOOD AND HOUSING PROVIDED. BRING A CHANGE OF CLOTHES, A SLEEPING BAG, GOOD SHOES AND GOOD CHEER.

Benscoter had not heard of the Moonies. At first, she had the idea of covering the walk for the alternative newspaper, whose editor had told her to submit a trial piece if she wanted a job. Off she went on her first assignment. She never did file that story.

She rode in a van to Omaha, where the walk would launch. Her hosts were members of the Unification Church, which was founded in South Korea by the Reverend Sun Myung Moon. Moon was regarded by his disciples as a new messiah who had been sent to finish the mission Jesus had failed to complete. The Moonies constituted a fast-spreading cult, perhaps best known for their mass weddings, at which Reverend Moon picked supposedly compatible partners from the audience. In the van, and then at the house where they arrived, and then day after day on the walk to Iowa, Benscoter's hosts focused intently on her, showing a genuine curiosity that her family and friends seldom had, empathizing with her inchoate visions of living in a commune, reassuring her there was a divine plan for her.

Before long, she overcame her aversion to all the talk about Jesus and his failed mission and began to warm to the idea that maybe a new messiah had been born in the early twentieth century. She even cut her hair as a sacrifice for this new savior. She was no longer an aimless kid from York who might find a job in a department store and cruise control her way through life: a husband, kids, the works. She was now a disciple of a great messiah. "My dedication to the cause was so immense, just overnight," Benscoter later wrote.

Among the attractions of a cult like the Moonies is that it offers a totalizing, all-explaining, all-inclusive home. Because it offers a logic to explain everything, everything suddenly makes sense. No wonder her parents had been so difficult, Benscoter realized. If it was true that Satan works through those you love, not just through the outright evil, then it was only natural. She would have to push past their worries about her. Life was full of uncertainty, but Benscoter felt the discomfort of uncertainty being eliminated. You didn't have to think about the kind of sexual life you wanted, or the kinds of books you wished to read, or what entertainment you liked, or what kinds of friends were good for you, or how to spend your time. This home for the mind provided all. Bob Dylan and sources of comfort like him had been great, but they touched only particular aspects of one's life. The cult wrapped all of you in its warm embrace. Nothing had to be wondered about anymore.

In the warmth of that embrace, she found new comforts: the reading of pledges, the unison prayers, the falling on knees, the singing, the crying, the fasting, the fundraising without asking too many questions about the destination of the money.

A few years in, her beliefs still strong, Benscoter, having dropped out of high school, felt an urge to resume her education. She moved to Iowa and lived with her brother and his partner to study some more. Her mother took advantage of the situation, finding a pair of women willing to attempt something called a deprogramming: a surprise intervention in which, typically, a mix of family members and outside helpers try to persuade people out of their membership in a cult.

When the two deprogrammers turned up at the door, Benscoter was furious. "There's nothing you can say to change my mind," she told them. But she sat down with them anyway.

At first, these deprogrammers had limited effect. One of their strategies was reading passages from the Bible that contradicted Moonie teachings, and while Benscoter couldn't rebut them herself, she felt what she was being told could be rebutted. They were trying to replace what was in her head with other, better information, a strategy that has doomed the attempts of many persuaders in various fields. But then they tried something different—attempting merely to displace what was in her head, simply by planting a seed of doubt, suggesting to Benscoter that she might have been tricked. The two women played a tape by an ex-Moonie talking about his experience escaping the cult. "He said that as he began to open his mind to the possibility that just maybe he had been lied to, another thought began to take over," Benscoter writes in her memoir. "He started to realize that it was possible that he had just spent four years of his life working for a lie. That sentence made me lose my appetite." The approach of displacement had broken through.

Benscoter felt the floor falling out from underneath her. "*My God, what if it's a lie*, I thought to myself, and begin to feel cold inside," she wrote. The deprogrammers continued with the displacement approach, reading from another book about brainwashing techniques in revolutionary China. Once again, they weren't trying to make her believe anything particular in that moment. They were illustrating the anatomy of brainwashing in general. It was helpful that the manipulation in question had nothing to do with the Moonies, belonging to a completely alien situation. People have less elaborate fencing systems to protect them from ideas on subjects they have little investment in. So she could see the art of manipulation more clearly and objectively. And then, having seen it, she could begin to make connections herself. The book on Chinese brainwashing soon had her reeling, because she recognized many of the techniques:

> The words, "*What if he's not the Messiah?*" were screaming in my mind so loudly that I began to hear the sound of glass breaking around me. I could hear it crashing down in a million pieces from every direction. Something was wrong inside my brain. I screamed. It was a wordless scream. I just screamed, covering my ears to stop the sound of the glass.

Attempting to persuade her of new beliefs—of better, truer biblical interpretations—hadn't worked. But making space for new beliefs to enter by deflating the old ones—that was more effective. In a flash, Benscoter knew she was out. She needed to sleep. She told her Moonie family she wouldn't be returning. She felt fear, then emptiness, then relief, a burden lifted from her. "I just can't believe all that was for a lie," she kept saying.

After she left the Moonies, Benscoter worked for a time in a rehab home for recently escaped cult members in Minnesota. She also got involved in a controversial side hustle that had its temptations for someone angry about having been conned: helping families perform a particularly fraught kind of deprogramming—involuntary ones.

Families pining for gone-but-not-dead loved ones would hire a team to stage an aggressive style of intervention. It generally involved some variation of kidnapping the cult member, bringing them to a safe house where loved ones would block the exits while seeking to reassure them, and then trying to talk them out of their cult over a few days.

Some of the missions were easy: as soon as the kidnapped cult member saw their family members, they began to crack. Others were harder, with a whiff of violence hanging in the air and uncooperative subjects. Sometimes the police got involved. Because of the strain and legal risk of the work, Benscoter drifted in and out of it, taking on assignments, deciding she was done with the whole thing, getting back into it, saying yes one more time, falling away, succumbing again.

At one point, Benscoter vowed for real: no more involuntaries. She was done with the kidnapping. Then, in 1984, a request came in from a family in Sweden. Their daughter was a Moonie in Colorado. The case touched Benscoter personally. Plus, she admitted, she needed the money. She told herself she would do this one last case.

The target, Beatrice, was yanked off the street by security guys, then put into a car with her parents. They drove to a remote location. They switched cars to evade police. But in this case the target wasn't making it easy. She refused to eat. And the team got word that the police were onto them. The group split up, the parents going to the police to reason with them while the deprogrammers took Beatrice to another isolated location. And then Beatrice managed to escape. Benscoter and her partners fled. She vowed to be done with deprogramming for good.

A few years later, she was living a peaceful new life in Portland, Oregon, working as a switchboard operator at Oregon Health Sciences University. One day, there was a knock on the door. Two men in suits greeted her. They were from the Federal Bureau of Investigation. She was under arrest for kidnapping Beatrice and was considered a fugitive from Colorado. A mug shot from August 1, 1988, shows a woman at once defiant and chastened. Since the day she met the Moonies in 1974, she had been on a long, strange adventure with cult life, and then with anti-cult work, and she had finally left it all behind for some normalcy, answering phones and dispatching hospital public safety officers on the graveyard shift, but it had caught up with her at last. She could go to prison.

Her allies in the anti-cult movement posted her bail. She took a plea bargain and wiggled out of hard time. At the pleading in Colorado, the mother and father and sister who had bored and frustrated and misunderstood her back in York were the ones who turned up for her. "That was the last time I had anything to do with the anti-cult world," she wrote in her memoir. But it wasn't.

For the next many years, Benscoter mostly stayed away from anti-cult activity. She was promoted from answering phones at Oregon Health Sciences University to running race trainings for its affirmative-action department. Then, in the late 1990s, she reinvented herself again. She became a technology-company headhunter in the go-go years of the early internet.

When the financial crisis of 2008 hit, it was a bad line to be in. She felt as if she were at a natural transition point, with her daughter going off to college and with the therapy she had done leaving her with questions she was ready to confront. For years, she had been plugging away on the side on a book project about her experiences. Now, she felt, it was time to commit to it. The book would become a forum to ask and answer some of the many questions still haunting her: How could people like her be so casually and easily persuaded to abandon a whole existence and family and life? Did they have some intrinsic quality that made them vulnerable to these entreaties? What did recruiters say and do to make people lose themselves? She thought back to her work at the rehab house and remembered that while it took in people from different kinds of cults, she had seen deeper patterns, a common arc of manipulation.

As Benscoter left the world of headhunting for that of the aspiring writer and theorist, she read avidly in psychology, brain science, neurology, feminist theory, and an emerging field called memetics, which studied the virus-like ways in which ideas spread—a subject the internet had made more urgent. In a 2009 TED Talk she gave and in her subsequent memoir, she began to put together her personal experiences and her reading to articulate her own particular view of the cult problem.

One of the propositions she advanced was that the discussion of cultlike behavior and extremism focused excessively on the people propagating the ideas, not the people consuming them. It was still the heyday of the war on terror then, and Benscoter was trying to make connections between her recruitment and other forms of radicalization. "Tens of thousands of troops cannot stop extremism," she wrote. "It is time we stopped looking for some vague enemy called 'evil'—which we will never find—and start looking at the real cause of extremism: human vulnerability." Any serious effort to defeat cults had to focus on interrupting the conditions that caused the buyers to buy, not just on clamping down on the sellers. If you wanted to understand why the Taliban had taken over Afghanistan, you had to understand what was going on in millions of Afghans' lives, not just the military strategy of the Taliban. If you wanted to understand how the Moonies had taken over Benscoter, you had to understand what it was like to be a teenager in York, Nebraska, in 1973, not just how they recruited people to walks. Where cults thrived, something in the society wasn't working right.

Another of her main theses was that cults were driven by their leaders' talent for "psychological manipulation" and that this ability wasn't going to go away. "The core of the problem is that there will always be someone who figures out how to take advantage of people on a psychological level for their own benefit," she said. The internet, she said, had only made this easier. So much breath and treasure were spent thinking of how to disrupt and dismantle specific webs of extremists. But you could never disrupt or dismantle the human ability to prey on people in need.

A third idea built on those two: if human vulnerability and the grasping for easy answers are widespread, if there will always be cynical actors hoping to lead the lost into phony promised lands, then cults and their lies can never be beaten back. The attempt to pull people in will be endemic to societies. The internet, which brings the manipulation into your bedroom and your pocket, will make it easier. You don't even have to leave home anymore. If all this was the case, was the proper answer to endemic manipulation and deception something like inoculation? Could the public in effect be vaccinated against these techniques of brainwashing?

Benscoter's understanding of manipulative ideas as having potentially epidemic qualities drew on her reading about the concept of memes. Developed by the scientist and author Richard Dawkins in his 1976 book, *The Selfish Gene,* "memes" were explained by the author

> as the cultural equivalent of a gene. So anything that gets passed from brain to brain, like an accent, or a basic word, or a tune. It's anything that you can say spreads through the population in a cultural way, like an epidemic. So a craze at a school, a clothes fashion, a fashion for a particular way of speaking, all these things are memes. Anything that could be the basis for an evolutionary process is a meme, simply by becoming more frequent in the population, in the meme pool, in the same way the gene becomes more frequent in the gene pool.

Benscoter applied this idea to cult manipulation. "How I've come to view what happened to me is a viral, memetic infection," Benscoter told her audience at TED. She added, "The way a virus works is it can infect and do the most damage to someone who has a compromised immune system." She was suggesting a reorientation in the battle against cults: building the immunity of a society toward what she saw as inevitable. If it's not Fox News, it will be Facebook. If it's not Facebook, it will be QAnon via email forward. What if we gave up on shutting the spigot of cons and focused on protecting people from them?

With this new understanding, the problem of disinformation and cultism could be seen almost as a public health problem. As Benscoter pursued this idea, Donald Trump had paved the first stretch of his long road to the White House by spreading disinformation that the nation's first Black president had been born outside the United States and thus was illegitimately elected. Trump would ride the resulting notoriety into a presidential campaign in 2016 that was marked by distinctly cultlike adherence and the very kind of cynical manipulation from above that Benscoter had spoken of. And few in the media or in politics had any idea how to stanch this dangerous meme epidemic of racist, authoritarian ideas.

Then, in the tenth month of Trump's presidency, with the conspiracy theorist in chief in the White House and the roiling, delusional movement he had cultivated seething across the country, and with other forms of disinformation making the rounds, an anonymous post on an internet message board called 4chan appeared. Its author was one "Q Clearance Patriot." The poster claimed to be a government big shot who knew things. And what this big shot supposedly "knew" was that there is a vast global cabal dedicated to raping little children, that this cabal involves many household names in the political and business worlds, and that Trump's purpose and mission were to defeat it.

The messages, known as drops, continued. They were cryptic and strange, and they gave the growing number who followed them the sense of purpose that many found in video games:

> PANIC IN DC
> [LL] talking = TRUTH reveal TARMAC [BC]?
> [LL] talking = TRUTH reveal COMEY HRC EMAIL CASE?
> [LL] talking = TRUTH reveal HUSSEIN instructions re: HRC EMAIL CASE?
> [LL] talking = TRUTH reveal BRENNAN NO NAME COORD TO FRAME POTUS?.................
> FISA = START
> FISA BRINGS DOWN THE HOUSE.WHEN DO BIRDS SING?
>
> Q

These drops framed the world in mysterious, uncertain terms, but the uncertainty could be lifted if you put together the clues, which were all around you, and figured it out. If Benscoter had been taken in by the enveloping hold of easy, totalizing answers, QAnon followers found something different but analogous in this dramatization of existing uncertainties and the promise of resolution. The world was bewildering. It didn't have to be.

Benscoter watched from the margins as the headlines piled up and as various institutions tried, and failed, to cope. Facebook made pronouncements about blocking content from hundreds of pages and groups and more than 10,000 Instagram accounts. QAnon grew. Twitter said it took down 150,000 accounts at one point. QAnon grew. In the 2020 elections, one outlet counted more than two dozen QAnon-embracing candidates for Congress running from the right across the country. There were calls by some in the Republican Party to distance itself from the crazies. QAnon grew. A poll by National Public Radio and Ipsos captured a steady onward march. In 2019, 5 percent of Americans said they thought the foundational lie of QAnon was true: that "a group of Satan-worshipping elites who run a child sex ring are trying to control our politics and media." In 2020, it jumped to 10 percent. By 2021, the figure had grown to 17. That implied some forty-three million American adults. And they made their growing presence felt when, for the first time in American history, an armed insurrection—egged on by QAnon—marauded through Washington and, with White House backing, attempted a coup.

The scale of this crisis reinforced Benscoter's growing feeling that the cult problem itself needed to be recast in the public imagination. This was a collective problem wrongly understood and experienced as individual family tragedies. The rise of QAnon wasn't a problem you could kidnap your way out of. It wasn't a problem parents could sweet-talk their children out of, or, as was often the case, vice versa. If the country was to have any chance of solving it, it needed a public health response to a spreading pandemic of lost minds.

Benscoter began to think about what the deprogramming she had done on an individual level might look like on a mass scale. She talked to public health experts, developing a vision of a societal solution. She compared what she was after to the work that had happened on cigarettes. They were once regarded as a matter of individual choice. And, at first, even when they came to be seen as dangerous and lethal, the consensus remained that people had to figure it out, listen to the advice of doctors, find the willpower to quit. Then a growing chorus agitated for a public health response, and there were labels and education and advertising and indoor smoking bans, and at last things began to change.

Benscoter set up a nonprofit called Antidote, and these days it is in the early phase of a potentially vast project on how societies can vaccinate citizens against the virus of cults, disinformation, and manipulation. The approach is rooted in her own experience of the limited efficacy of trying to persuade people with better information, as well as her understanding of the real potential of trying to warn people of attempts to manipulate them.

As with other public health campaigns in other areas, she envisions a multipronged approach. She wants to develop educational videos that might wake cult victims up, by playing on the only desire she has found can compete with the desire to have the world explained simply and totally—the desire not to be conned. She imagines video listicles like "Ten ways to tell if you're being psychologically manipulated." Other videos will target family members, to help them detect the signs of a manipulated person in their household more quickly and to help them talk more effectively to those loved ones. Popular television shows and movies might be encouraged to create story lines involving family members subject to psychological manipulation and smuggle into the narrative some of that anatomy of brainwashing that so moved Benscoter—just as earlier generations of artists brought crises like HIV/AIDS into their projects, forcing the public to grapple with the problem. The object of all this would be to build up collective immunity to disinformation and manipulation.

In the educational arena, Benscoter envisions a "curriculum for all levels, starting very young with children, basically to understand how to be more resilient. Because there's no way to make a world where there's not people who will try to do this, take advantage of people's vulnerabilities. That's crazy to think you can stop that. But what we can do is make people resilient to it."

I asked if it was an exaggeration to say that her vision was a deprogrammer in every home.

"Well, yeah," she said. If the educational mission succeeds, millions of people might gain skills they now lack to recognize when the teenager coming down for breakfast keeps bringing up the secret files on Hillary Clinton. Friends might be able to reach down into the rabbit hole and grab their friends before they fall out of grasp. (One could also think of the unintended consequences of training millions of people to grow even more suspicious of one another than they already were, constantly scanning for signs of manipulation.)

Benscoter wants to create support groups, modeled on Al-Anon, to give families wrestling with cult members a space to be heard and to compare notes. She also envisions a forum for cult members themselves to come in from the cold if they break out. "Right now," Benscoter said, "there are more people coming to us saying, 'I made a mistake. I need to put my life back together.' We need to help people who are walking out and need to understand why this happened to them and how to rebuild their life." She imagined large support groups on Zoom, of the kind that have taken off for other varieties of addiction. Some formers are also suddenly in need of more practical help to deal with the ruptures they have suffered as a consequence of following their totalizing obsession—a job, a place to live, a life coach or therapist, maybe a chance to go back to school. Without a massive program providing such resources, a great many risk backsliding into the belief systems that have given them a home.

Then there is the challenge of retraining mental health professionals. Benscoter believed that every therapist and counselor needed training in recognizing and redressing cult manipulation. A therapist, properly trained, might be able to see that a couple sparring over political beliefs isn't merely sparring over political beliefs, but that one of them is in the midst of a brainwashing that requires a separate therapeutic intervention. She wanted these practitioners, and lay citizens as well, to stop thinking of the more serious cases of people falling down rabbit holes as people falling down rabbit holes. She wanted people to understand many of them as succumbing to cults.

As I listened to Benscoter, I understood her to be advocating for one of those shifts in education that take place every generation or so. Changes in social conditions—in the economy, in technology, in the world situation—lead to changes in what every person is thought to need to know. Sex education was once considered a private matter and then came to be seen as a public responsibility. Typing, and googling, and the discussion of race, and speaking a foreign language, and algebra, had all traveled a similar path of becoming core to an education.

Benscoter was arguing that, given the present situation, the resistance of the cultlike psychological manipulation that flourishes on the internet needed to become a rudimentary part of human development.

"People think, 'Oh, there's only six deprogrammers in the world that can do this.' And that's just so not true," Benscoter told me. "There has to be a democratizing of deprogramming."

On the other side of the country, a cognitive scientist named John Cook was coming around to his own idea of a public health solution to lies.

As COVID-19 began to spread, Cook watched the flaring up of arguments—the minimization of the virus, the refusal of masks, the resistance to closures—with a sense of déjà vu. Cook's academic specialty is the workings of disinformation and how to fight it. He was based in those days at George Mason University, in the suburbs of northern Virginia; he has since returned to his native Australia, to Monash University in Melbourne. Though his focus is climate change, as the virus exploded in early 2020, along with a growing volume of potentially lethal fake information, Cook found himself doing what came to him naturally: mapping out the arguments and trying to deconstruct the dark art of misleading others.

Guiding people to be able to navigate fallacies is Cook's life's work. "Often, you'll see an argument and think, 'That doesn't seem right.' But it's difficult to put your finger on exactly where the argument goes wrong," he told me. So he and his colleagues had developed what he called a "systematic, step-by-step process for identifying fallacies," to help people more easily combat disinformation. When someone went viral claiming that masks don't work because their friend wore a mask and still got sick, Cook didn't need an epidemiology degree to recognize No. 3 in his list of the five common signs of science denial—impossible expectations: a standard of proof so high that virtually no phenomenon, however well established, could meet it. Or when Trump seemed to blame an intentional plot by the Chinese, Cook could detect No. 5 at work—conspiracy theories.

Disinformation nerd that he is, Cook built a spreadsheet of all the false claims he was picking up on, with an analysis of their underlying fallacies. What struck him was how familiar it all felt. Whether in his area of climate change or now on COVID, the political actors who spread disinformation about these problems used the same moves, over and over. As Cook put it to me one day, "The human capacity to deny and act in a boneheaded fashion is seemingly infinite."

Climate change was slow moving, long simmering, still abstract for many. But COVID was here and now, urgent and acute. That the same tactics of sowing disinformation were capturing minds on both problems validated one of Cook's deepest suppositions: that it was a fool's errand to respond to each crisis of disinformation, each new fake fact, on its own, one by one. As soon as you beat back one outbreak of lies, there would be the next. In those first days of the pandemic, the great challenge was getting people to wear masks and socially distance and wash their hands. Before long, however, the world's eyes would turn to vaccination. In the United States, vaccination would become one of the most grueling tests in history of the government's and other actors' ability to persuade skeptics of facts beyond dispute. Once again, the same techniques of denial would arise, the same fallacies would flourish, along with the same questionable efforts to beat them back.

Because of the Whac-A-Mole nature of disinformation, Cook had long been in search of a more general-purpose solution, a remedy that would work across different varieties and topic areas of fraudulent messages. But with COVID, the work took on a special resonance, because vaccination was more than just the latest obsession of the disinformation agents. It was the central metaphor underpinning Cook's approach to fighting deception.

Cook believed what Benscoter had discovered in her own way but what few of the rest of us were ready to admit: that a world awash in disinformation had grown inevitable. And that amid such a pandemic of lies, the only remedy was to inoculate everyone against organized manipulation.

Cook had first come to this work of equipping people against disinformation from their friends and relatives and colleagues as a young man in Australia, arguing with his father, and then his father-in-law, about climate change and failing to persuade them. He had always been an outlier in the Cook family, the studious brother among tough guys. In his final year of high school, Cook was the top student in the whole class—the dux, as it's called in Australia. He became the first in his family to enroll in college, at the University of Queensland.

At UQ, he majored in physics. In explaining how he fell for it, Cook drew a connection between his own feelings back then and the attraction to disinformation of those he now studied. "I've been thinking a lot about that human tendency toward pattern detection and ascribing meaning to randomness," he told me. "Probably because of all the conspiracy theories that are happening at the moment. And, in a way, physics is that, isn't it? It's ascribing meaning and causality to the world we see around us." Cook's ability to see in those who believed in reality and those who didn't the same human needs was among the advantages he brought to his eventual scholarship.

After college, Cook worked as a cartoonist—successfully enough to pay the bills. When he had been a physics student, he had tinkered with drawing on the side. Now cartooning was his livelihood, and he found himself dabbling in science. In addition to doing his own reading, he played the role of science defender at family gatherings.

His new father-in-law was a climate denier. Climate was not yet Cook's issue, apart from his general adherence to science. But the denials he encountered bothered him. "We would have a family get-together, and he would start arguing his climate-denial arguments. Then, at the end of the third time we got into one of these arguments, he gave me a printout of a speech by Senator Inhofe from Oklahoma. It's kind of surreal that we're an Australian family in Australia, and he's giving me a speech from a senator from Oklahoma."

Dutiful son-in-law that he was trying to be, Cook took the time to read the speech by Inhofe, a man whose best-known contribution to the climate issue is bringing a snowball onto the floor of the U.S. Senate, apparently to debunk the fact of rising temperatures. "I went back, read the speech, realized that there's little to no science behind Inhofe's arguments. In anticipation of the next time we get together, and the next batch of climate-denial arguments from my father-in-law, I started researching the issues. Building a list of climate myths, assembling all the scientific research relevant to each myth. Basically, a competitive son-in-law wanting to make sure that he didn't get beaten in an argument with my father-in-law."

But when Cook presented his findings, they didn't work. His father-in-law rebutted him with all the familiar objections: that the data were rigged, the science unclear; that, from his father-in-law's fundamentalist Christian vantage point, scientists were the enemy; that the government was just trying to take away your freedom and maybe your land. Cook had similarly frustrating conversations, echoing the same beliefs, with his own father and other relatives.

Because of the certitude of these older men, Cook didn't typically challenge them live. "If you start pushing back against this information, it's World War III," he told me. "I would just file it away and then go and research. But being that über-nerd that I am, my approach was to start building a database of 'Here are the different talking points. Here are the different arguments against climate change,' then collecting peer-reviewed science relevant to each."

But this amassing of evidence didn't help. "I learned that the climate dismissives are immune to scientific evidence," he told me. "It's either unproductive presenting scientific arguments to them, or it could even be counterproductive." Trying to debunk false beliefs by offering truer replacement beliefs could push someone further down the rabbit hole of disinformation.

But Cook's compiling of evidence had a side benefit. As he trawled sites for this material, he realized that vast swaths of the internet basically *were* his father-in-law. This was not just an annoying family issue. It was among the great obstacles to solving the climate problem. And that insight inspired him to ask whether he could find a solution to the challenge of people like his elders. "I guess my lightbulb moment was realizing that I'm not the only person with a cranky uncle or father-in-law or family member who denies science," he told me.

Eventually, in 2007, he launched a new website called Skeptical Science. On it he would debunk the denial of science with information that drew on peer-reviewed studies. He would counter the rejection of facts with . . . even more unrejectable facts! The early posts tended to follow a basic format: Cook would present the false belief at the top, in the headline, and then repeat it in a colorful box, and only then, further down, would he debunk it, with links to the raw evidence.

One day, he received an email from a cognitive scientist named Stephan Lewandowsky. His correspondent informed him that "debunking" myths in the way that Cook was on his site risked reinforcing the myths. In particular, his way of making each myth the headline and putting it in a colorful box effectively promoted the false belief and buried the truth down below. "What I was doing," he said, "was pretty much what almost every fact-checker does, which is lead with the myth—the headline is the myth—and then there's a long debunking after that. But that communicates the myth in a much simpler and stronger way than it's communicating the facts. The danger of that is that people can come away from a debunking just remembering the myth, because the details fade over time." He realized how much he had to learn. "I was kind of horrified by the realization that I could have been making things worse," Cook told me. Had his attempts at persuasion been backfiring? How could he persuade more effectively?

The bookish Cook who wasn't like other Cooks would go seek another degree to find out.

The email from Lewandowsky changed everything. Until that moment, Cook had thought a great deal about science and what it uncovered, but he had barely thought about how science is communicated. His mode of persuasion had been "Just the facts, ma'am." Counter lies with facts; counter disbelief with facts; counter skepticism with facts so good that doubts will melt away. Sadly, the peddlers of lies understood very well the importance of seductive communication. It was the people with truth on their side, perhaps smug about the facts speaking for themselves, who were less focused on *how* they made their case. Cook realized he had to change his ways.

In 2012, he returned to university and began work toward a doctorate. He reached out to Lewandowsky and asked if he might supervise Cook's research. He agreed. They also began collaborating on a handbook of best practices for debunking disinformation.

Cook began to plug away at the question. One day, while ruminating on a drive from an academic conference in Italy to another one in Germany, he had a breakthrough. He had just published the results of an experiment that showed that communicating a scientific consensus to a group backfires among a small fringe of far-right deniers. The message that virtually everyone was on board with the science made that narrow group *less* on board than they were before. Cruising through the European countryside, Cook had the following thought: What the study really showed was that communicating the truth to people didn't work if people were already skeptical of the source—perhaps in turn because they were skeptical of the people who believed the source. Indeed, this skepticism made it such that communicating the evidence *reduced* their level of belief in it. "I was thinking about that dynamic," Cook said, "and thinking, 'Could you make it go the other way? Could you make misinformation backfire by priming people with "Here are techniques used to deceive you"?' "

Until then, Cook, like many others, had focused on discrediting the fake facts. What his study had found was that climate deniers succeed by discrediting the source. Why couldn't the opponents of misinformation do the same? Instead of answering disinformation with better information, try to discredit the disinformers! It was in keeping with what Benscoter had experienced when the efforts to replace her beliefs with truer beliefs had failed, but then the warning that she had been deceived by unscrupulous people using unscrupulous methods worked.

Cook got to work designing a new experiment. The disinformation in question was the Global Warming Petition Project, which claims to feature more than thirty-one thousand "scientists" who believe the evidence of man-made climate change to be inadequate and the most commonly proposed remedies to be damaging to the environment and to human societies. Cook, the longtime cataloger of false information and its underlying fallacies, would today slot this one under "fake experts." Some of the signatories might well have been scientists, but very few of them were scientists with any expertise on climate. They tended to be ideologues with often tenuous connections to other sciences. Cook's task was to see if he could stave off the effect of this piece of disinformation.

He divided his experimental subjects into three groups. The first received no information. The second received the petition and only that. The third group—this was the heart of what was being tested—

received a distinct intervention before being exposed to the dubious petition. The intervention was an account of how mid-twentieth-century cigarette ads used fake medical experts to cast doubt on the expert consensus about the risks of tobacco. The intervention was not directly related to the issue of climate science, but it primed one to think about the idea that expertise could be faked, because in this case the faking of expertise was obvious and familiar. And it worked. While the second group, exposed solely to disinformation, showed a loss of faith in climate science, the third group stayed put. Being primed with the general idea of fake experts fortified these subjects against a specific instance of fake expertise.

Cook was excited by these new findings. Before long, he was presenting them at a psychology conference in Sydney when a professor took him aback during the Q&A. "What you're describing sounds a lot like inoculation theory," he said. "I was like, 'What now?'" Cook recalled. "So I went back, found out that there's fifty years of inoculation theory research, and the thing that I thought I had discovered on a car drive from Italy to Berlin, much smarter people than me had already done fifty years ago."

And yet the emphasis of the existing literature was on priming people with facts to protect them from fake facts. What Cook was after was different. He wanted to vaccinate people's minds by showing them the *moves* disinformers make, the fallacies they employ to distort the facts, so that he might undercut their manipulations not just on one fake fact at a time but across the board. As Cook has written, "When we're exposed to a weakened form of a disease, we build up immunity so that we don't get infected by the real disease. Similarly, when we're exposed to a weakened form of misinformation, it builds up our resilience so that we don't get misled by real misinformation." He wanted to help people build up a general-purpose resistance to the disinformation around them. "Inoculating people against a denial technique in one topic has the potential to neutralize that form of misinformation in other topics also," he wrote in a 2017 paper on the study. "Inoculation researchers call this the 'umbrella of protection.'" In parallel, though they would only discover each other later, a social psychologist named Sander van der Linden was publishing similar findings, summarized thus:

> A threat is introduced by forewarning people that they may be exposed to information that challenges their existing beliefs or behaviors. Then, one or more (weakened) examples of that information are presented and directly refuted in a process called "refutational pre-emption" or "prebunking." In short, attitudinal resistance is conferred by pre-emptively highlighting false claims and refuting potential counterarguments.

Cook's idea about how to fight disinformation on a larger scale had resonances with Benscoter's vision: Don't fight disinformation with better information. Counter it by showing people how they're being conned. Perhaps it was no accident that more than one thinker was testing these waters in 2017, as Donald Trump came to power and Brexit charged forward fueled by lies and the Russian social media posts came to light and it began to seem that disinformation was not a problem here and there, from time to time, but potentially a defining feature of the age.

Like Benscoter, Cook believes that the disinformation and manipulation problem is a shared social crisis, one that demands a collective answer.

One basic shift he advocates, in laypeople and institutions alike, is in the attitude shown to those who take in disinformation. "The general avenue of approach I take is that people have been misled," he told me. "That if you've been exposed to this misinformation, you're a victim more than a malicious actor." Those in the reality-based world can be somewhat contradictory on this point—on the one hand, arguing that big, powerful institutions are abusing their power by aiding and abetting and spreading lies by exploiting victims and then, on the other hand, blaming citizens for falling prey to them.

Whether interpersonally or at the level of the system, Cook argues, the rather common practice of making manipulated people feel stupid is a terrible way to fight these forces. "Most people like to think that they are critical thinkers," Cook told me, "especially people who do, ironically, deny science or are conspiracy theorists." Never mind that they have allowed themselves to become the opposite of critical thinkers. Here, too, Cook was finding what Benscoter had observed with her work on cults: To make people feel stupid is to play back to them a version of themselves they don't recognize. But to appeal to them instead as critical thinkers who deserve to know how they are being misled—this has the potential to work. And it works by harnessing one part of them—the deeply human desire not to be anyone's fool—against another part of them that has succumbed to manipulation. If you convey a blanket contempt for a person as a person, you are not in a strong position to harness some good, useful part of them against another part.

Cook also advocates a wholesale change in how scientists communicate with the public. For many scientific experts, their self-image of seriousness and sobriety is deeply important to them, and it keeps them persisting at their fruitless countering of lies with facts and refusing to employ novel, unconventional, and proven methods. Humor, for example, has been shown to be an effective way to reveal the moves of science deniers, lowering the stakes of changing one's mind. Simplification can be effective, too, because it can reduce the shame many feel in not understanding, a feeling that can foster proud resistance to changing one's mind. "As my boss, Ed Maibach, says, 'If you don't simplify your own research, someone else will,'" Cook said. He also thinks scientists need to grow more comfortable bringing personal revelation, story, and emotion into their communication. "One of the principles of debunking is you need to fight sticky myths with stickier facts," Cook told me. "We need to make our facts even more sticky, more compelling, more catchy than the myth that we're debunking." In public presentations to scientists, he said, he often goes through a series of ways to make your facts more sticky. "Some of those techniques include appealing to emotion and telling stories. And when I say appeal to emotion, you can just see the tension in the room go up." It's not how his fellow scientists see their jobs.

Yet Cook's focus, like Benscoter's, is systemic rather than personal—on building up the society's resistance to deception through education. And in recent years the appetite for that project has grown. A few years ago, he braided together his multiple talents and wrote a cartoon-and-text book called *Cranky Uncle vs. Climate Change.* The book catalogs the various myths that have been spread on climate and systematically debunks each one. At the same time, it embodies the generosity of spirit that drives Cook's approach. It relentlessly calls out the disinformers and their modes of conning, but it never demonizes those they con. It guides you on how to call them in with care.

Cranky Uncle takes you through the five principal techniques of science denial, which fall into the acronym FLICC:

—Fake experts
—Logical fallacies
—Impossible expectations
—Cherry picking
—Conspiracy theories

Myth by myth, Cook explains why each myth is a myth. The tone throughout is humorous and light. Many of the arguments are by analogy. "It's cold . . . global warming doesn't exist" is a common technique of denial, as incarnated by Senator Inhofe and his snowball. So alongside a cartoon illustration of that line of denial Cook adds another: "It's dark . . . the sun doesn't exist." Here the false belief itself is being mocked. But the people who succumb to these false beliefs are never mocked. Indeed, throughout the book, Cook uses a sleight-of-handy but well-meaning "we" for those who deny or minimize climate change: "We think of something as psychologically distant if we're not directly experiencing it." Or, "Like frogs in a pot slowly coming to a boil, we find the severity of global warming difficult to grasp."

When Cook turned the book into a game, he had a breakthrough. In game form, educators felt they could incorporate the inoculation against lies into their curriculum in an easy, engaging way. "Cracking echo chambers is one of the big challenges that I've been trying to figure out for the last decade, and not really had an answer to until just recently. Because if inoculation is the answer, and I've been doing research into developing effective inoculations, how do you deliver those into communities that are siloed and within their echo chambers? I really had no answer until I started working on a gamified version of this critical thinking smartphone game." As he began to share it publicly, he heard from "educators in red states just as much as in blue states who were keen to use the game in their classes." The game began to spread in school and college classrooms.

A player of the game is first invited to pick one of the FLICC denial techniques and learn more. Say you pick fake experts. You have a few practice rounds of identifying the fake expert out of three choices. And then you're at bat. Choose the argument that involves a fake expert:

> "Scientists weren't afraid to look into the strange physics behind lasers and semiconductors, so I don't think we should be afraid to look into telepathic remote-viewing."
>
> "Celebrity Jenny McCarthy says vaccination causes autism."
>
> "Boris Johnson has funny hair so he's a terrible Prime Minister."

If you said Jenny McCarthy, you won! Cook's idea was that students could challenge other students, compete on score, classes could compete with other classes, and you'd end up with what he called "basically a critical-thinking matchup."

With this gamification, Cook was trying to level the unfair playing field that disinformation tends to exploit. Human beings are understood to have two principal modes of thinking, fast and slow, as the psychologist Daniel Kahneman famously called them. Fast thinking is reflexes. Slow thinking is reflection. Disinformation often appeals to the fast-thinking system. It plays to the gut, and the gut does as directed. The challenge for fact-based people is, as Cook puts it, that "trying to get people to be critical thinkers and think logically through misinformation is really pushing upstream." What the game does is give people enough practice at spotting disinformation and its underlying fallacies that their skills of bullshit detection move into the realm of the reflexive.

What had begun as Cook's pursuit of in-the-moment climate talking points for tense family dinners had evolved. What if these methods could train a new generation to recognize the moves and signs of disinformation and be guarded against them? What if illustrating those moves on a single issue, climate, offered that "umbrella of protection" against disinformation on topics far afield, as some early research suggested it did? What if, as Cook seemed to believe, it was futile to hope that Fox News or Facebook or anti-vaxxers or anti-maskers or microchip truthers would go away? What if you grudgingly accepted their lies as here to stay and sought to forge citizens resistant to them?

7

MEANING MAKING AT THE DOOR

The drive from Phoenix to Flagstaff cut through stunning Arizona desert, greening as you went north. Cacti gestured toward the plain azure sky like fingers making Hindu mudras. Bushes and shrubs pixelated the land without filling it. Forests of ponderosa trees blurred past. Mesas appeared tinily on the horizon and then swelled as you approached, their flat tops almost unnatural, diamond cut. The exits along I-17 North told their own story of Arizona's land and its people. Indian School Road. Cactus Road. Sonoran Desert Drive. Carefree Highway. Pioneer Road. Bumble Bee/Crown King. Cottonwood. Mormon Lake. A sign warned that there would be no civilization, no gas, no food, no water, for dozens of miles, and it wasn't kidding. Everything disappeared for a long stretch. And then, all at once, a settlement appeared, a camp town carved into the unforgiving landscape.

I switched on a podcast as I drove—*The Daily,* from *The New York Times.* To my surprise, the day's episode was of particular local relevance:

> As congressional Democrats dramatically scale back the most ambitious social spending bill since the 1960s, they're placing much of the blame on moderate Democrats, who have demanded the cutbacks.
>
> The holdup on this massive plan is Democrats Joe Manchin and Kyrsten Sinema, who say we don't need to spend this kind of money—this is way too much money.

Today, the story of one of them, Senator Kyrsten Sinema of Arizona.

The podcast recounted the saga of Arizona's most mysterious politician. Sinema had once been a member of the Green Party and a leftist leader protesting the Iraq War. She ran for the state legislature as an independent and lost. Then, in 2004, she ran as a Democrat and won. She established herself as a movement leader who went inside: one day she was defending the cause of immigrants in the legislature; the next, she was marching on the state capital alongside undocumented people in the Arizona summer heat.

Then, several years into her tenure, something turned. Chasing dreams of political elevation, to the U.S. House of Representatives and then the Senate, Sinema reinvented herself as a political moderate who took pleasure in thwarting her own party and would vote with President Trump's position most of the time in his first year in office. "I'll work with anybody" became her new brand mantra.

When President Biden took office, with a fifty-fifty Senate standing between him and most elements of his agenda, Sinema, along with her colleague Joe Manchin of West Virginia, became a pivotal figure in Washington. It was she who famously thumbsed-down, with a performative curtsy, a chance to raise the federal minimum wage. Will-they-won't-they became a national guessing game as two senators who often seemed closer to corporate donors than to their own constituents held up most of Biden's agenda during a historic crisis.

Toward the end of the podcast, the host played audio of the Bathroom Incident. With the fate of Biden's Build Back Better proposal still in the air—a package of rare ambition that, if put into law, would transform the social safety net from cradle to grave, fight climate change, and, potentially, create a pathway to citizenship for millions of undocumented people—the fates of many rested on two senators. Sinema was engaging in her usual obstinacy and dangling and withdrawing of hope at that time, which infuriated many on the activist left. And so a group of protesters had followed her into the bathroom after a class she taught at Arizona State and filmed themselves confronting her.

"We need citizenship for seven million. We need the Build Back Better plan right now," one activist said. "We knocked on doors for you to get you elected, and just how we got you elected, we can get you out of office if you don't support what you promised us," called out another.

"Wow," the podcast's host said, reacting to the idea of a protest following a senator into the bathroom. After a long recounting of what had made Sinema so rage inducing to so many, this tactic seemed to strike the host as a bridge too far.

The local group that confronted Sinema was known for its uncompromising defense of undocumented immigrants. It was called LUCHA, or Living United for Change in Arizona. Its priority at that moment was pushing Sinema to support a pathway to citizenship for the undocumented as part of Biden's big legislation.

As it happened, I had arrived in Arizona that morning for the purpose of witnessing LUCHA's work, not out of any interest in bathrooms, but because LUCHA's organizers pursued multiple and contradictory modes of persuasion. On one front, they were attracting attention to a form of protest that very visibly and confrontationally called Sinema out, while on another front they engaged in the work I had come to see: a promising experiment in persuasion by door knocking, grounded in increasingly hard-to-muster behaviors of empathy, curiosity, and nonjudgment, fueled by an almost mystifying faith that people can change.

My guide to the process known as deep canvassing was Cesar Torres, whom I found at LUCHA's offices in Flagstaff. Out in the corridors were posters of inspiration ("Leaders: Leadership is action, not position," accompanied by a bald eagle). Inside was the managed chaos of activists working against the clock—an array of folding chairs, a bottle of Febreze, hand sanitizer, packets of sugar, water bottles, alcohol wipes, Ziploc bags, Gatorade, bug repellent, bags of Doritos, printer toner, Stayfree pads, and a microwave above a mini-fridge.

Cesar was wrapping up a video meeting with leaders of other deep canvassing projects around the country, each with its own goal: in one state, they might be working to raise the minimum wage; in another, to strengthen gig-worker protections; in another still, to redirect funding from the police to social services. Cesar was wearing an

Under Armour baseball cap, which throughout the day he swiveled 180 degrees around, backward to forward, forward to backward; a blue Adidas hoodie; and rectangular glasses that underscored his image of earnestness, sincerity, and calm.

Cesar, now a leader of LUCHA's deep canvassing operations in Arizona, had come to the work rather by accident.

He was born in Mexico, the son of a carpenter. His family was neither rich nor poor. "We had it good in Mexico, but my parents always wanted the best for their kids," he told me. His father ventured north alone to get a job in the United States. A year and a half later, when Cesar was seven, his mother led him and his two sisters, then two years old and six months old, north as well. The children crossed illegally, with the help of a coyote.

The family reunited and settled in Richmond, California, a largely Latino community just north of Berkeley in the Bay Area. "It was super Latino, so to me it was normal," Cesar told me. It was only when he left the area for higher studies that he realized that he lived in a country full of people wanting to be rid of people like his family.

Cesar didn't know he was undocumented until he was fifteen or so. He wanted to get a job, which forced his parents to tell him the truth: "That was a little shocker to me." His mother worked as a nanny, and his father as a handyman and a welder. Both parents applied for residency and citizenship long ago, but Cesar said their applications have been frozen since September 11, 2001, and the clampdown on immigration. "We've been waiting for something for decades now," he said.

His parents had come to America with dreams of their children going to college. But being undocumented made that dream elusive. The Deferred Action for Childhood Arrivals, or DACA, program had yet to come into effect, and so financial help with college was out of the question. Instead, Cesar enrolled in a local community college. He joined student government. At a conference one day, he heard someone say they were hiring political canvassers in Riverside. He signed up for the gig, and the organization looked the other way about his status.

He went to work as a canvasser for Mi Familia Vota, a national civic organization that registers and educates Latino voters. The director took a shine to Cesar and showed him the ropes. "Being undocumented, you feel like a second-class citizen sometimes," Cesar said, "where you don't really think you have a say. He showed me the power of organizing and how I can have a voice without necessarily having one."

After a few years of doing that work, Cesar was advised by his mentor to go and study some more. He went to get a bachelor's in political science. Then it was back to canvassing. He became an accomplished campaigner, working for campaigns directly as well as firms that offered organizers for hire. He traveled the country and managed teams.

If what he would later do was called deep canvassing, it was in reaction to the traditional kind of canvassing being comparatively shallow. For Mi Familia Vota and other campaigns, he generally knocked on the doors of friendly voters, confirming that they were voting for the desired candidate, ensuring they had a plan to vote, or registering them if need be. Changing minds wasn't the mission, and it turns out there was a reason for that.

The Democratic Party, and much of the left in general, was migrating from a fixation on persuading moderates and Republicans to a fixation on turning out and energizing their own diehards. The journalist and television anchor Chris Hayes has described the shift well. For years, he said, "there was this kind of dominant ethos among Democratic Party operatives, which was the obsession with the swing voter." The party's sages were "prophets of the swing voter," who "almost always coded as white, suburban voters, who went this way and that, and you could appeal to them if you were a Democrat and you were fiscally responsible and tough on crime and you checked all these boxes that made them not worry that you were too much of a lib." This thinking still very much exists in the party firmament, and when losses happen, the prophets will rise from the dead.

But in recent years, Hayes continued, "newer-school thinking about the Democratic coalition" was ascendant. It was a "product of a number of things—post-Obama, the demographic changes in America, and the vanishing swing voter, where the idea is the country is polarizing, the number of people that bounce back and forth between the parties is shrinking, people have these tribal affections and loyalties, the parties stand for incredibly distinct visions of existential truths about people, like who is an American—basically, who counts." The emerging view was "mobilizing your coalition, getting people enthusiastic," Hayes said, echoing Anat Shenker-Osorio.

Hayes set up this schema before launching into an interview with an organizer named George Goehl, a major figure in the deep canvassing movement. And Hayes made plain his own feeling about these approaches and the change of strategy in recent years. "I am generally sympathetic to this latter model, which I think is in the ascendancy, which I think is about mobilizing your coalition," he said. But there was one thing about the emerging model that gave him pause: "There's a kind of thing that happens when this 'mobilize your people' idea gets taken to its most extreme logical conclusion, which is a kind of writing off that happens."

It was one thing to make the best use of an organizer's time by focusing on shoring up those in your in-group whom you could most effectively mobilize instead of those who seemed less likely to move. But the "writing off" Hayes feared went beyond that simple calculus. Somewhere down the line, it risked becoming a habit of mind to assume people can't change, won't change, that you don't need them anyway, that they'll never get that vaccine, that they'll always vote for the racist, that they're beyond the reach of persuasion.

In his first years of traditional canvassing, Cesar's work was more or less entirely in this ascendant mobilizing mold. He didn't think much about the writing-off issue, about what was *not* being attempted, until he heard about, and then landed, a job managing campaigns at LUCHA. At first, it seemed pretty similar to other canvassing jobs he'd done. But he knew he was in strange new waters when he was told at a training session that the goal was to spend thirty minutes per door. It sounded like a spoken typo. Coming up in political canvassing, he had absorbed the mantra "If you're spending more than five minutes at a door, you're wasting your time. You are not going to convince somebody."

This new deep canvassing method, by contrast, was about staying long enough to surface something different. Cesar was trained by his new employer to knock on doors, get people to start talking and keep talking, and begin a protocol designed with scientific rigor to change minds. It was live-action persuasion built on an approach that felt quaint and somewhat contrary to the culture's drift toward confrontation and fatalism about others. Cesar learned that the deep canvasser had to listen, truly listen, and keep listening, then listen some more, as the person on the other side of the door explained why they felt some kind of way about transgender people or undocumented people or minimum-wage workers. He had to listen without judgment and with visible curiosity even when they were criticizing or degrading people like him. He had to refrain from calling the other person out. Instead, Cesar was trained to probe for the person's experiences around the group of people or topic under discussion. In the hope of changing their political preferences, he learned to help people process those stories and reflect on their own dissonances—the way they deplored immigrants because they were lazy but did love Manuel, who worked in their yard, because he worked so hard, and come to think of it, everyone in Manuel's family worked hard, too.

As Cesar trained in deep canvassing, he found it super intriguing. When he went out in the field for the first time, he said, "I saw the effect it had on folks. And it was like, 'Whoa, this is dope.'" Though it flew in the face of his prior training, it rhymed with his deepest orientation. "I've done it my whole life," he told me. He was always the guy in the bar who realized some of the other guys were right-wingers and who sought out a conversation with them about immigration and, at the perfectly chosen moment, revealed that he was among the undocumented people they feared. He was the guy who tried to tell himself what John Cook had argued: that the crazies weren't perpetrators so much as victims of a society awash in mis- and disinformation.

The method Cesar was learning was built on assumptions that pushed back against widespread cultural beliefs: that persuasion in politics doesn't work; that people can't and won't change; that calling out every chauvinism everywhere is a moral duty, and failing to is complicity; that the views of the other side are deep rather than superficial.

"One of my most memorable canvass stories," Cesar said, "is that I went to talk to a person, and they were like, 'No, I don't know any immigrants.' And I still kept digging in there, and she was like, 'Oh, well, yeah, my sister's husband is undocumented, and he got hurt at work. He had an accident. He's in the ICU, and they have no health care, they can't get worker's comp, and they're struggling.' And I was like, 'Yeah, he would definitely benefit from making sure that we pass a pathway to citizenship.'" What struck Cesar was how her hostility to immigrants lay on the surface but, right below it, was the seedling of another view. Yet it wouldn't sprout on its own. It needed watering. The woman needed help making meaning of her experiences. Though she had, in her own brother-in-law, a source of dissonance with her view of immigration, "she doesn't see him as an immigrant guy," Cesar said. "She's like, 'Oh, this is my sister's husband. This is my brother-in-law. He's just a regular person.' And the message that I was able to get across to her was, 'When you think of immigrants, sure, you're thinking of the border crisis or gangs or whatever the media wants to bring up that week. But it's not that. It's people like me.'"

Cesar's parents worried about him doing this work. "You don't want to be a mechanic or something?" they sometimes asked, partly because it was a job they didn't understand, partly because what they did understand concerned them. "I would be on Telemundo or Univision doing Spanish interviews," Cesar said, "and they're like, 'Why are you on there? Why are you putting our family at risk of deportation?' They were just scared, because all you see on the media is, ICE is deporting this many people, ICE raids. My parents are like, 'If you're supporting immigrants, they're going to target you.'" How reckless it might have felt to his parents for their boy, whom they had lovingly smuggled across a border, to go to people's houses and tell them he was undocumented. But for Cesar his work was not a betrayal of their struggle but a fulfillment of it. What better way to resist living in the shadows, fearing a knock on the door, than to be the one who does the knocking?

At 3:00 p.m., Abby and Dakota, the two other canvassers working that day, reported to LUCHA's offices. Cesar had been taking stock of where the campaign was. LUCHA was on week twenty-nine of a thirty-week marathon of deep canvassing. By the latest numbers, the canvassers had hit 49,250 homes, attempted to speak to 70,945 distinct people, sometimes speaking to couples or adult children living with parents. Of those, 8,067 people had answered their initial question of how strongly they support a pathway to citizenship on a scale from one to ten, and 97 percent of those who answered the first question kept the door open long enough to answer the same question at the end of the conversation. The difference, if any, between the opening answer and the closing one was how the canvassers measured a changed mind.

Cesar handed his colleagues "turfs," maps of the neighborhoods and homes they would be hitting. Those, paired with the voter database they had on their phones, would guide them. Then he gave Abby and Dakota a pep talk.

"The pressure is working," Cesar told them. "Sinema feels it. And we need her to know that we are not stopping until the Build Back Better Act gets passed."

Respectfully but skeptically, Dakota, a newcomer to LUCHA, asked, "Just to confirm, the pressure is, in fact, working?"

It was a reasonable question. Every day came another story of Sinema hosting fundraisers, jetting off to Europe to court donors, and dutifully shutting down some corporation-hindering provision of the legislation under debate. Meanwhile, there were phony "audits" of the 2020 election vote ongoing in Arizona, funded by mega-donors across the country hoping to reinstate Trump a year after he lost the election. There was something touching about LUCHA's theory of change—that going to people's doors and urging them to make calls to pressure Sinema to support a pathway to citizenship could counteract the shadowy dance of special interests and dark money.

Cesar was at pains to tell them that, yes, it was working. He seized on any bit of evidence he could to make the point. Take, for example, all the donor events Sinema was doing. To Cesar, this was proof that she was scared. Would a senator confident in her reelection prospects a full three years in the future be fundraising as if there were no tomorrow? Then there was the fact that her voice-mail box was full days earlier but had been cleared again. Someone had to be listening. When you invest so much time and energy in working the levers of bottom-up democracy, you need to believe it works. Whether or not it does is another matter.

Then the three canvassers went their separate ways. I followed Abby to the east side of Flagstaff, where she would be canvassing. Though it was still in the three o'clock hour, the late October air was crisp and chilling fast. Abby constantly found herself calculating how much time she had before it got dark, around six. She would keep going for another hour or hour and a half after that, but it got a little hairy walking dark streets, turning into shrouded properties, knocking unexpectedly.

This was one of the harder-up neighborhoods they worked. The cars tended to be missing parts—hubcaps, grilles. Houses often sat beside empty lots with metal fencing, inside of which ferocious dogs barked—the local alarm system. Mostly the neighborhood was quiet, but there were some signs of communal life. In the front yard of one home, a man sat shirtless in the cold air having his hair cut by another man with clippers. Halloween decorations were popping up. Sandbags encircled many of the lots, sometimes stacked two or three high, to absorb the flooding that came with the summer monsoon season. Many of the bags had burst after a recent flood, the sand erupting into the street. It was one of those once-in-centuries floods that seemed to happen all the time now, caused by forces that other canvassers in other states were knocking on doors about.

Abby first approached a ranch house and found a mother whose two small children hovered at her knee, one of them sucking on a lollipop. Her partner was the one in the voter database, and he wasn't home. Abby asked if a conversation about a potential pathway to citizenship might be something he'd be interested in. The woman was pretty certain it was not. Move on. Then Abby came upon a short-haired, incredibly pleasant progressive woman who wanted her to know she was a progressive and was totally on board with it all, the immigration, the everything. She wasn't sure why Abby stuck around, barreling through her script. But one of the many things that distinguishes deep canvassing from other approaches is that you don't rest on the laurels of a self-professed ten, as the progressive woman was on the pathway to citizenship. What you don't want is an unreflective and tribal ten, someone saying what they think they are meant to say because they're on Team Blue. Such a person might be with you now, only to blow in the wind the next time a charismatic leader with a different view comes along. So whereas another kind of canvasser might speed along, Abby tried to stay as long as she could, even as the progressive woman made clear she needed to get back to things, working from home and all. Abby got her to verbalize some of why immigration was important to her, got her to talk about some of the immigrants she knew, her personal stakes in the matter. Then, having secured a promise by the woman to make a call to Sinema's office, Abby left.

Soon Abby was standing outside a small house, knocking on the door of an older white woman with flowing white hair. She asked if the woman would be willing to have a conversation "about immigration reform and stuff."

"Will it take long?" the woman asked.

"Usually like ten-fifteen minutes," Abby said.

"I really can't stand that long," the woman said. "I have a medical condition." And where many traditional canvassers might have respectfully yielded, Abby tried to find a solution. Could the woman come outside and sit on one of her plastic Adirondack chairs? Could she maybe wear an extra layer to brave the chill? The woman went back inside, grabbed a woolen poncho, and sank into the plastic chair, the fading sun warming her face.

Abby went through the early motions. How is your afternoon going so far? Then she introduced the matter at hand, semi-reading from a script that seemed to perpetuate some of the problems with communication on the left that Shenker-Osorio railed against, above all selling the recipe instead of the brownie.

"We're just going around specifically talking, as an organization, about the process of reconciliation through the federal budget as well as the Build Back Better Act. Are you familiar with either of those things?" Each time I witnessed the opening of these exchanges, the canvasser seemed on the verge of losing someone who had agreed to talk to them, only to regain their footing momentarily. A flood of earnest, alienating words washed over them—"reconciliation," "budget," "allocated," "reform," "parliamentarian." For the canvasser, these words were the stuff of life, the object of their aspirations, but for many people on the other side of the thresholds, they were words that created distance, reminding them of pin-striped people far away who didn't see them, didn't help them, and kept thriving as the country wilted.

Now, having gotten through the preliminaries and the declaration of her purpose, Abby moved in to gauge the white-haired woman's support for a pathway to citizenship. She was a ten. "For people who want to become citizens, yeah, they need an easier time doing it," she said.

Again, Abby stayed, having been trained not only to gauge and strengthen support for a policy but also to assist the subtler process by which people organize their ideas and experiences into opinions. The white-haired woman gave reason to pursue this path. She seemed at once supportive of immigration but not especially versed in it, not as sure of herself on the subject as the progressive woman before her had been. This was the kind of faint allegiance that could evaporate, that the canvassers wanted to deepen through talk.

At this point in the conversation, whether facing a skeptic or a die-hard supporter or someone in between, the canvasser is trained to ask the subject if they know any immigrants in their own life. If the answer is no, there is another, more complex conversational path to follow. But, fortunately for Abby, the white-haired woman said yes.

"I know some that became citizens," the woman said. "Some of them don't want to. They just want to make enough money to go back to Mexico, and they tend to do that. There's all different kinds. Some of them were illegal here. And that was really sad, because a lot of them, where they were, they were going to die if they didn't leave. Their kids just didn't have a chance. So if they want to stay and be citizens and vote and everything, and be part of this country, I say, 'Yeah.'"

Cesar had met up with Abby by this point, and the white-haired woman's words inspired him to share his own story. "Myself personally, I came to the United States when I was seven years old," he said. "My parents brought me. Obviously, I had no choice at the age of seven. And it's been a struggle trying to figure out—"

"The DACA," the woman offered.

And so Cesar told the woman his DACA story—the expiration of his status, the delays wrought by Trump's gutting of the program. He talked about the $495 fee he has to pay every two years, the background checks and fingerprints he must do, just to continue living in the only country he has really known. This was another important aspect of the deep canvassing process. After getting the subject to reflect on people they know affected by the issue, you share your own experiences, whether personal or those of people you love. And I saw now how the concrete details of a life can make things even clearer for a voter than the moral appeals that may stir the kinds of people who become canvassers (or journalists). The white-haired woman's ears perked up when she heard Cesar say he had to pay his fee every two years, and additionally pay for getting his fingerprints.

"On top of the $400?" she asked.

"Every two years, yeah."

"You have to pay for fingerprints?" she asked. That particular point really stuck with her.

Cesar now moved into the ask phase. Would she make a call to Senator Sinema? Inserting a pathway to citizenship into the Build Back Better bill would make these troubles go away for Cesar. The woman said she would call. Then, with the questions still washing around in her mind, she came back to the one about whether she knew any immigrants personally.

"I used to work at a Walmart after the recession," the woman said as Cesar stood in front of her, helpfully shadowing her face to keep the sun out of her eyes. "And most of the kids there—they were brought over. They were in college; they were going to school while they were working. And the other kids, they weren't. They were just messing around and stuff. And it really impressed me that a lot of people that come here really do want a better life, and they're willing to work for it. They ought to get it."

This memory hadn't seemed to occur to her in the first moments of the conversation. It took having the conversation. At first, she had had a position: they deserve a life here if they want it. But with a little help from her canvassing friends, the opinion had struck deeper roots. She had seen immigrants up close at Walmart. And they weren't just decent people, same as everyone else. They put her own fellow Americans to shame, as she remembered it. Yes, that was it. That was why she felt the way she did. And now, hearing what she hadn't known, just how hard it is for many people in that boat, even having to pay for their own fingerprints—can you believe that?—her conviction grew sturdier.

And so the LUCHA team moved through the area, asking how afternoons were going, soliciting these personal stories, sharing their own, helping people process their experiences and opinions, and the rhymes and sometimes the dissonances between them. What had occurred with the white-haired woman was the relatively easy case—

a supporter of the cause from the outset who did have personal relationships with immigrants. Other encounters that evening illustrated the more forbidding path when such relationships are lacking.

Abby knocked on the door of a white house, outside of which human-sized ghosts had been hung as decorations for the Halloween festivities looming that weekend. A grizzled woman named Lily opened her front door but remained behind a wrought-iron outer door, scowling.

What's it all about? Lily wanted to know.

"What we're talking about right now is the Build Back Better Act that's trying to be passed right now," Abby began, "and the reconciliation budget, which is going to allocate money toward immigration reform. So that's just, like, the main thing."

"What do you mean, immigration?"

Abby said she was advocating for "the undocumented community, specifically within Flagstaff." This did not have the effect she hoped.

"Oh, we're citizens," Lily said. Abby hadn't suggested otherwise, but it was revealing that what Lily took from her spiel was that Abby was going around trying to help immigrants and that was of no use to Lily, since she wasn't an immigrant.

"Yeah, no, for sure," Abby said. "We're talking to folks whether they're an immigrant or not."

At this point, despite her evident hostility toward Abby and the topic, Lily, like a surprising number of people at the door, signaled she would stick around for a conversation. She turned halfway around and yelled at somebody inside to pause whatever they had been watching.

Now Abby asked Lily how supportive she was of a pathway to citizenship.

"I don't know nothing about immigration. Nothing," Lily said. It seemed important to Lily to separate herself from immigrants. So even as Abby made clear that she wasn't assuming Lily was an immigrant, Lily kept making clear that she wasn't.

Abby asked Lily to quantify her position on a scale from one to ten. "Knowing me, I would say no," Lily said. Okay. Put her down for a one.

It was time for the personal-relationships gambit. "Do you know anyone that has immigrated into the United States?"

"Nope." It was somewhat hard to believe for someone living in the middle of Flagstaff. But this not knowing, this total lack of association, seemed important to Lily. Abby wasn't sure of Lily's background, but she knew the neighborhood was heavily Native American, and she had gotten this kind of reaction many times in the community: people who quite understandably resented the idea of helping newcomers to the United States when their own community, here before the rest, had never gotten a lick of help.

In the choose-your-own-adventure that is deep canvassing, the personal connection road had proved a dead end. So it was time to attempt the detour, a route the experts called analogic perspective taking, which, luckily for them, is a phrase the canvassers don't use at the door. The idea is that even if you don't have a personal stake in the issue, in this case the lives of immigrants and undocumented people in particular, the issue reflects some more universal dimension of the human condition to which you may be able to relate. So to the person who knows no immigrants, you might ask, "Have you ever struggled in your life? Have you ever wanted to do right by your kids but been hindered from doing so?" To the person who doesn't really know what transgender means, you might say, "Have you ever been counted out or disrespected just because of who you are?"

The appeal of the personal-connections route is that it is easier to go from people you know, certainly people you care for, to embracing a politics that would ease their lives. But the power of the perspective-taking detour is that it universalizes. It takes the particular struggle of one group and de-exoticizes it. It makes it a timeless human struggle, almost the Hollywood version of a political fight. And it asks you to see yourself in Others.

"Was there a time in your life when you have had to help someone through a particular struggle, maybe taking care of a family member or something?" Abby asked Lily.

"Oh, I donate a lot, but I'm against the immigrants," Lily said. "I'm not just talking about from Mexico. I'm talking about all over."

"Gotcha," Abby said, abiding by her training to bite her leftist-college-student tongue.

"We got our own families," Lily said. She noted that she did take care of her boys, so that counted as helping people.

Abby came back for another swipe at the perspective taking, this time the other way around: "Was there a time in your life where someone has helped you through some sort of challenges, struggles, and then what was that like for you?"

"Nope."

"Cool. Awesome," Abby said unsinkably. The conversation ended.

Minutes later, in an apartment building just around the corner, a conversation with many of the same rudiments went in a different way.

Kyle surfaced from inside wearing a 2014 Winter Chill NBA sweatshirt, Nike slippers, and a blue metallic chain. Abby began her ritual, and from the outset Kyle seemed curious and interested, even if his eyes kept falling to his phone.

At first, during the spooning out of the reconciliation-allocated-facilitates-reform jargon soup, Kyle was polite but monosyllabic—yeah, uh-huh, yeah.

When asked to register his support for a pathway to citizenship, though, he immediately pronounced himself a ten.

Abby proceeded into the personal-connections question. But here, as had been the case with Lily, Kyle claimed no connections with immigrants.

"Me? No. No, I don't know anybody," he said. But then something unexpected happened. Before Abby could get to the perspective taking, Kyle went there himself and argued for the logic of that method with plainspoken eloquence.

"Well, I'm a Native American," he said. "So, either way, it still applies to me the same way as the immigrants, you know?"

Now, without prompting, so as to explain the commonality he saw, he went into the particulars of his situation. He worked construction, and these days his big problem was that he made too much money to qualify for government-subsidized health care but too little money to afford health care on the open market. "I can't even pay for my son's health care," he said. "I can't pay for my wife's health care. They say I make too much money, so it puts me at a loss at the same time. So I'm in the same boat."

There it was in that last sentence—that analogic perspective taking, though this time achieved without Abby's prompting. His first three sentences had simply been about his hardship, his difficulties making a life in working-class America. But then, in his concluding thought, where Lily saw such hardships as a reason to forswear help for others, he had said, "I'm in the same boat."

Abby went into the analogic questions meant to stir the kind of reflection that had already begun. Had Kyle ever had to support anyone through hardship? He had. "Even when I was in high school," he told Abby, "I still had to try to find a way to provide for my fiancée and her little sister and everything like that. So it's been pretty hard for us, but I mean we're getting through it right now."

Inversely, had he ever been helped?

"No. I do it all on my own since I was seventeen. I'm thirty now," he said. "My family didn't have my back or anything like that. So I had to do everything on my own, and I had to provide for my own. So that's all I got to say on that."

And, again, what Kyle took from this was that he was duty-bound to stand up for people who also hadn't gotten help. He spoke of how much he admired immigrants working in construction who do the jobs others wouldn't be willing to do. "There's nobody else that's going to do it," he said. "It's just immigrants and us Native Americans. That's it, pretty much."

Now Abby asked Kyle for his score of support once more. "I'd make it an eleven," he said.

Would he make a call to Sinema?

"Can I cuss on the line if I have to?"

He placed the call right there, reading from LUCHA's sample script. He kept it polite.

After hanging up, he asked if he could take a photo of the script with his phone, "just in case I call back again tomorrow."

"Those immigrants are my skin color," Kyle said. "So they're also my brothers. And, back in the day, we learned a lot from each other."

"Absolutely," Abby said.

"I respect them."

He spoke now of the reservation where he had grown up. "We really don't have a lot out there where I come from. No running water, barely electricity. And so when they come in, they have an opportunity to at least try to get a job." I wasn't entirely sure what he meant. I took him to mean that given how resource starved his people had been, he was happy to see that many immigrants have one thing going for them that his people hadn't: access to a market hungry for their labor.

One way to understand the deep canvassing process is as an attempt to turn Lilys into Kyles, to help people extrapolate from their own experiences and own pain a politics of wider solidarity. That wasn't what I had witnessed that day, because Lily was immovable, and Kyle was, without prodding, already there. But in the space between them I glimpsed the hope of the project.

Before Abby left the apartment, Kyle thanked her and, unbidden, armed with the script he had saved, said, "I'll give a call every day if I have to."

On Election Day 2008, Steve Deline was full of optimism—and then suddenly of despair.

Most people who remember that night will remember it as the moment when Barack Obama won the American presidency, breaking a forbidding barrier. Deline celebrated that victory as avidly as anyone. But that night a second thing happened as well, and had it occurred on any other night, the event might be better remembered: a slender majority of Californians approved Proposition 8, a ballot measure to abolish same-sex marriages, which had become legal in the state just that year.

In the next days, as millions celebrated Obama's victory, Deline was crushed. "I would walk around the grocery store and look at the people around me and just have this overwhelming feeling of 'Did you vote against me? Do you believe my love is less worthy than your love?'" he told me. "I suddenly had this profound sense of alienation from people around me, in my community and in everyday life, that I had never experienced before."

What especially devastated him was that it wasn't some distant others who had voted against his freedom. The proposition had won Los Angeles County, for crying out loud. It had won parts of the Bay Area, of all places. And the loss was, by his count, the twenty-eighth straight loss on marriage equality at the ballot box across the country. It was one thing to be able to tell yourself that some right-wing Christian fanatic on the Supreme Court had taken your rights away, or senators representing the state of Alabama had voted against you. It was another thing to know that the people walking around with you at the store, the people filling your gas tank, the people you waved to in the neighborhood—many of them were against you. "It's people around me," Deline said, "people who know a lot of people like me."

A few months later, Deline, still in his funk, heard about a canvassing experiment being developed by a local organization called the Los Angeles LGBT Center. The goal, as he understood it, was, "Let's go try and talk to the people who are voting against us. Let's go into the neighborhoods where we lost heavily and knock on people's doors and find out (a) if we can have a conversation with the people who voted against us; (b) if we can talk to each other honestly; and (c) if that's possible, if there's anything we can do to change those minds." It struck him as unusual, because so much of the canvassing he had experienced was focused on turning voters out, not confronting disagreements. "It just ran against all the conventional wisdom," he said, "to the extent of being considered folly, I would say, in a lot of circles." But if it was folly, it wasn't a folly rooted in airy hope, but rather, Deline told me, in terror. "It came from a place of desperation and feeling like I had no other choice but to try to talk to the people who I didn't think I could talk to," he said.

As a gay man himself, Deline felt that the movement was winning in the courts and legislatures. "But," he said, "if we cannot switch something in the hearts and minds of a significant number of people around us, we are blocked." As David Fleischer, who ran the Leadership LAB at the L.A. LGBT Center, has said, "People were open to saying, 'Yeah, we do not know enough about our neighbors who voted against us, and the tools that we have to gain insight into them are woefully inadequate, so we better go to talk to them.'"

After attending some protests, Deline signed up for training with the center's canvassing project. On the drive over, he pulled over and called his then boyfriend. "Remind me why I should go ahead with this," he said. "Remind me why I shouldn't just turn around and come home right now." Still, he took the training. And, before long, he was hitting the streets, testing out early prototypes of what would become deep canvassing.

On his first day of actual canvassing, the first door he knocked on was opened by a guy clutching an In-N-Out burger who gave him an "I don't want to talk to you, move on." On his second door he addressed a highly religious family eating dinner outside. The wife politely declined to talk, and then the husband began screaming at Deline. But then came the third door, and from that knock Deline was hooked.

"I talked to this average dude, mid- to late-forties Latino guy, and just asked him how he voted and why," Deline said. "And he told me that he voted for the proposition, and I explained a little bit. The experience of just getting to talk about it with him and focus on it being not an argument but a conversation about what's going on for you, what's going on for me, just allowed me to shed my sense that he was the enemy, and that he was this bogeyman that I needed to be afraid of, and it was fundamentally different for me. And I think he got to shed his sense that I was this enemy and this bogeyman—whatever framework he had in his mind for what a radical gay activist was."

Something in Deline flipped as he began to have more such conversations. "It just completely changed my sense of agency and ability to rightsize the world, and rightsize my understanding of people around me," he said. It made him think, "I'm not surrounded by bogeymen. I'm surrounded by people who are working hard, and they made a bad choice, and they had a huge impact on me, and I have to hold that pain and be honest with them about it. But I also can feel that they are not fundamentally out to get me, and we can talk about it, and we can work through it. And, actually, if I take the time to do that, that's what makes it possible for them to reach a different conclusion."

As deep canvassing developed into a more rigorous and formal method, it became a bigger and bigger part of Deline's professional life. Eventually, he became one of its major champions and practitioners. He began to see in its emphasis on listening and story sharing, non-judgment and vulnerability, an alternative to what he saw as the predominant approach to persuasion in his progressive circles—a combination of giving people the best arguments and information and shaming them for failing to come around.

"When I look at the progressive movement and people on the left, there's this sense that we just know better," he told me. "Like, 'Oh, if they just had the information or the education or the facts or the knowledge that we had, they would think the same way we do or believe the same things we do. It's just this question of education, knowledge, information.'"

But in the early experiments that became deep canvassing, that approach did little. "One of the things we tried was going out with talking points and facts. Like, 'Hey, guess what? Your church is never going to be required to marry anyone it doesn't believe in marrying. This big, giant fear you have is just not true.' And over and over again, that just fell flat, and people didn't react.

"Over time," Deline continued, "it became clear that, 'Oh, all of these answers we're trying to give aren't helping.' We can try to answer people's concerns with facts and information. And their fears about gay people, and about their church being forced to do something, and their righteous indignation about lefties pushing things on them—there's no answer we can give that dispels these fears. They're actually in a place where they're wrestling with some deeply seated emotions. The thing that actually made a difference was inviting them to talk about their lives, and then things they've experienced and their stories, and sharing our stories."

What many of his ideological allies ignored, Deline came to believe, was how emotional the process of opinion formation could be. "We are all beings who are in the hands of warring emotions, really powerful emotions. Those emotions are what lead us in a direction around politics. And what do we do when we feel like something emotionally feels right? We go out and seek out facts and information that validate that feeling we're having, that make us feel like reasonable, rational people." The scholars call it motivated reasoning.

"When we are disagreeing with someone," he continued, "and we say, 'Your facts are wrong. Here are the correct facts,' without intending to, what we are doing is telling people that what they are feeling is wrong, which is threatening on a much more deeply emotional level than telling someone that their facts are wrong." That is when people lapse into defensiveness and shut down.

The L.A. LGBT Center's deep canvassing approach began to invert this process, by providing a script and a protocol by which people could face those they disagreed with in ways that opened them up. "What we learned," Deline told me, "is changing your mind on something is about navigating a sea of conflicting emotions. Not only is what we have going on driven on an emotional level for most people, most of the time, but they also don't actually feel completely one way or the other. They feel a lot of *conflicting* emotions. They feel cognitive dissonance. So changing your mind is not actually about flipping a light switch: one second you think one thing, and the next second you think another. Changing your mind is about navigating through this morass of conflicting emotions and trying to pick your way through it and come out somewhere that makes you feel a little bit more resolved."

Deline and his fellow canvassers didn't think of themselves as being divided against their targets on the other side of the doors so much as they thought of their targets as being divided against themselves. They saw them as being lost, grasping. It was another way of saying what Shenker-Osorio had described about the swing voter being confused, not centrist. (She would eventually advise deep canvassing efforts around the 2020 elections.) The canvasser's opportunity wasn't to implant something of their own, something foreign to the target, into them. Rather, it was to pit some things going on inside them against other things going on inside them, to get them to re-rank these things.

Yes, you don't like immigrants, but you like *that* immigrant you know. Or you don't favor a pathway to citizenship, but you know what it means to be overlooked and shut out, and you think of yourself as standing up for the little guy. For canvassers, these dissonances were something to work with. They were grist for the persuasive mill.

"My discovery in doing this work was that most people are sixty-forty around most things," said Deline, who continues to do deep canvassing work through an effort called the New Conversation Initiative. "If we ask them to plant their flag on one side or the other, if we approach them that way, they're going to do so, because that's what makes us feel like rational, thinking humans—having an answer to a tough question. But if we approach people with the idea that it's normal to have complicated feelings, even if they have a Trump sign on their front yard, even if their public face expresses one thing—if we approach them with the assumption of 'There's something more going on underneath,' oftentimes we find out that there is."

In one of the early canvasses the L.A. LGBT Center did while shaping the method, captured on video, an older man stands at his door, wearing a baseball cap and greeting a canvasser who has come knocking. The man is welcoming but guarded. The canvasser, Jackson, asks how the man voted on Prop 8. The man says he didn't.

"What would you say is on the side for you that's holding you back from supporting it?" Jackson asks. "You know, I'm just trying to understand better."

"Basically, I kind of didn't want to get involved. I didn't want to make the wrong choice."

"Sure, you want to do the right thing," Jackson says.

But the question has an effect on the man. "Well, now you're making me think about this," he says, stroking his face reflectively.

And then the man begins to tell the story of his cousin, Jill, a lesbian who has been in a relationship for twenty years. She is having financial troubles that the legal institution of marriage would ease. She can't fully tend to her partner of forever when it comes to health issues. And now the man at the door begins to cry. A moment earlier, he could not be bothered to vote on this issue—who knows what's true, both sides, and so on. Now the faintest intervention has rejiggered his whole view of the matter, and he assures Jackson that next time he will be voting yes.

What the canvassers learned at doors like that one was soon codified into a methodology that I had seen practiced by LUCHA.

First, the canvasser was to make contact.

Second, the canvasser was to create a "nonjudgmental context." This didn't mean concealing the purpose of the outreach. In fact, canvassers were supposed to declare the issue they had come to talk about up front, and only then ask the resident their opinion on the topic. As the answers poured out, the canvassers were meant to keep poker-faced, "not indicating they were pleased or displeased with any particular answer, but rather to appear genuinely interested in hearing the subject ruminate on the question," as one report on the method put it. In this phase, and beyond, curiosity was among the canvasser's sharpest tools. In some versions of the protocol, after getting the subject's initial thoughts, the canvasser was to "come out" with their own rating on the issue, before saying they were interested in having conversations with people regardless of whether they agree, and moving on. (The "coming out" language hearkened back to the origins of the work, when canvassers might literally come out at that moment if they chose.)

In this early phase of listening to subjects on the door justify their opinions, grace was essential. As a report on deep canvassing on the news site *Vox* put it, "The new research shows that if you want to change someone's mind, you need to have patience with them, ask them to reflect on their life, and listen. It's not about calling people out or labeling them fill-in-the-blank-phobic. Which makes it feel like a big departure from a lot of the current political dialogue." The article quoted David Broockman, a Berkeley political scientist, even more bluntly: "In today's world, many communities have a call-out culture. Twitter is obviously full of the notion that what we should do is condemn those who disagree with us. What we can now say experimentally, the key to the success of these conversations is doing the exact opposite of that."

Third, the canvasser was to exchange personal narratives, as Abby had done in Flagstaff when she asked people if they knew any immigrants. Whether or not the subject does, the canvasser would then share their own story or that of someone who gave them cause for doing this work.

Fourth, the canvasser was to invite analogic perspective taking. Was there a time *you* needed support? Was there a time *you* needed health care but struggled to access it? Was there a time *you* were counted out because of factors beyond your control? The goal of this stage, according to the report, was "to end with individuals self-generating and explicitly stating aloud implications of the narratives that ran contrary to their previously stated exclusionary attitudes." In other words, to sow cognitive dissonance of the highly generative kind.

Fifth, the canvasser was to make an explicit case. Here, after doing much listening and eliciting, the canvasser spoke more openly of their own feelings about the subject at hand. Depending on the topic, this was the place where canvassers were encouraged to make use of the Race Class Narrative framework that Shenker-Osorio had developed and that the deep canvassing methodology made use of.

Sixth, the canvasser, having sown some cognitive dissonance, was to seek to help the subject wrestle with it out loud. Having first listened nonjudgmentally, the canvasser now could point out contradictions in what they had heard. The report gives an example of what a canvasser might say: "It sounds like, on the one hand, you think that immigrants do a lot to benefit this country, and, on the other hand, you think it is more important to take care of our own citizens first. What is on your mind now that we have been talking?"

Seventh, and only seventh, the canvasser was to respond to the subject's concerns with talking points and facts. As Deline had observed, this seventh step was step one for many amateurs. *No, Dad, the earth really has warmed!* But in deep canvassing this kind of refutation and fact-checking and responding was back-loaded, and what preceded it was a significant amount of listening and trust building. "Canvassers were trained not to address concerns until this point in the conversation so that voters would not feel threatened by this section," the report says. "Only after rapport had been established and stories shared would canvassers address concerns." To be fact-checked, in other words, had prerequisites. It helped first to feel heard, cared for, respected, seen in the fullness of one's complexity and even, yes, confusion.

Eighth and finally, the canvasser was to ask the subject to rate their support for the policy in question again. Has our conversation changed your opinion? the canvasser asks. The scholars who helped build up the method call this the "rehearsal of opinion change," with the subject often lured into "active processing" of their own ideas and stories and background and the cognitive dissonance that might have surfaced. The theory is that political opinions are often hastily formed from scanty information. Following a substantive chat at the door, the subject is encouraged to think more slowly about whether their view comports with their deepest values, with what they know to be true, with their sense of themselves, with their experiences.

Soon a method developed in one corner of the country was spreading far and wide. In 2012, it aided a victory that brought it full circle from its origins. A group called Minnesotans United for All Families, advocating against a constitutional amendment to ban same-sex marriage, undertook 222,693 phone-based deep canvasses with voters in that state and claimed 20,353 people had moved their opinion somewhat. A corresponding ad campaign reinforced the message of the canvasses: that the proposed constitutional amendment would hurt real people who lived in your community, and that you, the voter, had the power to make their lives harder—or easier. When Election Day came, the fight for marriage equality won its first victory after thirty-three straight losses in ballot initiatives. In a retrospective on the campaign titled "Eighteen Months to History: How the Minnesota Marriage Amendment Was Defeated—Money, Passion, Allies," Minnesota Public Radio called the "massive, one-on-one conversation drive" the "secret weapon" of the effort. "In the past, our side of the fight has focused on rights and equality and that this is discrimination," a deep canvassing trainer named Alison Froehle told the radio station. "But that frame of mind does not move voters. So what we're doing on this campaign is, we're having conversations from the heart. We're taking it from an abstract frame of mind and into the personal, reminding people that this is going to hurt real people." A 2008 funk in California had, just four years later, fueled a triumph in Minnesota.

A conversation conducted by the L.A. LGBT Center in 2015, also captured on video, illustrated the method in its maturity and its vast potential. A woman stands at her door in Los Angeles wearing a do-rag and two necklaces with heart-shaped pendants. The question at hand is whether to include transgender people in nondiscrimination laws. The canvasser, Steven (not to be confused with Steve), asks where the voter is on a scale from one to ten. She stares at the scale on his sheet and vigorously wipes her nose as she thinks.

Six, she says.

"Six! Okay!" the canvasser says, as excited for her as if she had said the cookies she was baking were chocolate chip.

He asks for a reason she would vote to include trans people in these laws and a reason she wouldn't.

Why she would: easy. She isn't judgmental. Why she wouldn't: "I wouldn't want that around children." She adds, "People could pretend to be . . . and go after our kids. That's something big to think about."

All this while, Steven is cool, levelheaded, betraying no hint of judgment. He moves into the next phase: Does she know anyone trans?

Yes, she does. "It's my nephew. Niece. Nephew. Whatever! He was born a boy, but he wants to be a girl."

Okay! Steven won't take the bait. But while the woman continues to call the relative in question "he," Steven now uses "she." He is patient and openhearted about the woman getting to a place of greater tolerance at her own pace, but he is clear on the destination.

Steven asks how much the niece has talked to the woman about her situation. Well, that's funny, the woman says, because they don't talk at all anymore. Her niece sensed the woman was uncomfortable with her, and she pulled away.

The woman says her niece's transition was hard for her. The lipstick, the hair. She had helped raise her niece as a baby, and back then the child was being raised as a boy. She didn't get it. But she keeps interlacing these statements of outright prejudice with a contrary point that is important to her: she is not a judgmental person.

Steven tells her a story of a friend of his, a trans guy, great guy, who felt out of place in his own body. So he got his chest flattened and was beyond excited and sent selfies of the new him to a high school friend, who responded with shock.

The woman at the door listens to this story carefully. You can see her recoil at the high school friend's reaction. What kind of person . . . And then you could see her realize that she *was* the high school friend for her niece. "Maybe that's the way I kind of reacted toward him—without saying it, but the way I guess I was acting. As if, don't come around me, that's really weird," she says.

Soon she is saying that Steven is making her feel bad, because she is realizing what she has done. And here Steven's answer is revealing and counterintuitive: "No, no, no, I'm definitely not trying to—I think it's really complicated." She is coming his way and growing apologetic for how she has been, and his concern in that moment is to give her the feeling that it's okay to struggle over these things as she now is. He is giving her Ernesto Nieto's golden gate of retreat. He stubbornly resists making it a matter of right and wrong, even though for him, doing this work, it must be.

Having had success with the "do you know anyone?" phase, Steven moves into the analogic perspective taking. Has she ever been on the receiving end of that kind of mistreatment or discrimination? Has she ever felt different?

She scrunches her nose and thinks. Not really, no. She is a Black woman living in America, but she doesn't profess to relate to the idea of discrimination—which could have something to do with the white canvasser in front of her and could have something to do with the fact that regular voters often don't see their lives in the politicized terms that activists and pundits and professionals use. Or perhaps she didn't connect "that kind" of discrimination encountered by trans people to whatever she had experienced in her life.

The woman thinks more on the question. Well, when she moved to L.A. a couple years earlier, she got some bad vibes from people. It made her feel alone. At the place she works, some of the women picked on her, nick-nacked on her, for being from somewhere else. She should, it was said, go back to where she was at.

Steven empathizes with her and tells his own story of being different. He is gay, he now reveals. In high school, he was the only one who was out. He started a gay-straight alliance in defense pretty much of himself. He won an award for it senior year. As he left the gym after receiving the honor, a bunch of guys came up to him, telling him he didn't deserve the award, he was just a fag, he only got the award because he was gay and the administration felt it had to give it to him. "It's all kind of that same feeling of 'They see you and you're different,'" he says, trying to weave his story, her story of moving to L.A., and her niece's story together. The woman nods along.

And now he tries to bring it all together. That feeling of isolation that he had felt that day at the gym—it sounds to him as if that were the feeling the woman at the door felt at work, being picked on like that, and it sounds as if that were the feeling her niece is feeling, too. "So that's why it's really important to me that something like this law is on the books," Steven says, "so that people don't have to go to work and feel like they're going to be fired because everyone's looking at them differently." He has wrapped the three experiences into one, but also subtly universalized them into the woman's anecdote about her workplace.

The woman's eyebrows perform a high jump. "That's true," she says. She hadn't made the connection before, but now she recalls that her niece had gone to work in her wig and everything, and she had been fired.

"And that's exactly what this law is doing," Steven says, meaning preventing.

"Okay," the woman says, seeming genuinely interested in new information, in the opening up that was happening. "That makes a lot more sense."

Again, Steven does something surprising here. Instead of consolidating his success, he elects to bring up the earlier hesitation that the woman expressed—about people pretending to be trans and preying on children. It might be more intuitive in that moment to let the sleeping dog of bigotry lie and go deeper into what the woman seems to be feeling now, but the canvassers believe that those kinds of objections risk flaring up again if not properly addressed and dismantled.

Steven now explains, kindly but more forcefully than before, that trans people and sex offenders are two distinct groups of people that she is conflating. "I don't have no problem with that," the woman now says. And she reflects out loud that that was probably what her niece, whom she still calls her nephew, was going through.

"I never really thought about all that like that," she tells Steven. Shortly she gives her new score of support for including trans people in discrimination laws.

Ten. "It's only right," she says. "Let a person be who they are. Hiding it is worser. So let 'em out. I believe that. Everybody should have the right to be who they want to be."

That fall, the governor of California, Jerry Brown, signed SB 703, a piece of legislation tightening restrictions on the state doing business with any company that discriminated against employees based on gender identity in providing benefits.

These various victories continued to raise deep canvassing's national profile. But it took a stinging loss in 2016 to give it its broadest reach yet.

After the surprise victory of Donald Trump, a veteran progressive organizer in Chicago named George Goehl found himself in something of the same boat as Steve Deline back in 2008: wondering how so many around him—including so many of the people he had grown up with in small-town Indiana—could vote for this madness. But also not wondering, because he knew the places where the factories had closed and the Walmarts had come in and the xenophobia and racism were never far below the surface, waiting for enterprising cynics. The organization Goehl led, People's Action, launched a rural organizing program to listen and talk to voters. "I don't think it's a high bar in the U.S. to build the biggest progressive organizing event in rural communities, to be honest. But I think we might've done it," Goehl told me. And then, in 2019, People's Action decided to apply the deep canvassing method to its organizing work, launching a three-state experiment to test its power.

The experiment was a huge success. For every hundred voters the campaign spoke to about establishing universal health care, including for undocumented immigrants, it moved around eight of them, according to the resulting research published by the scholars Joshua Kalla of Yale and David Broockman of Berkeley. The findings added to a growing body of research that was finally putting to bed concerns that surfaced after a since-retracted study in 2014. Back then, a graduate student in political science named Michael LaCour had elected to study the L.A. LGBT Center's deep canvasses and had published, in the prestigious journal *Science,* an eye-popping finding: that twenty-minute conversations at the door could change minds on gay rights, and, even more strikingly, that only gay canvassers could create these lasting shifts in view. But LaCour's study collapsed when Broockman and Kalla tried to replicate his results, and LaCour was accused of faking evidence and lying about his funding, and *Science* eventually retracted his research. Broockman and Kalla then did their own research on deep canvassing in 2015, studying a follow-up project by the L.A. LGBT Center and a grassroots organization called SAVE in Miami aimed at reducing prejudice toward transgender people. They found that the power of canvassing was real, whereas the identity-of-canvasser thesis was not. And then came the 2019 study by the same duo, which lent further credence to the hard-to-fathom notion that spending just minutes on a door with people could move the mean attitude of the targeted group as much as years of diffuse social change.

Armed with these results, People's Action began to train more and more of its member organizations, which work on the ground in local communities, in the method of deep canvassing. One of them was the group in Arizona called LUCHA.

On my first day with LUCHA, I had watched Cesar gamely reassure his two canvassers that, yes, the pressure to get a path to citizenship in Build Back Better was working! But the next morning, unbeknownst to pretty much anyone, there was a development. It was announced that, after months of negotiations, President Biden had a framework for getting his double-barreled agenda passed. The program he soon went on TV to tout was pared down, eliminating vast areas of ambition—from dental and vision coverage for senior citizens to free community college. But guess what seemed to make the cut? That pathway to citizenship. It appeared Sinema had gotten on board, along with every other Democratic senator, for Biden to be able to announce a "deal."

At the 3:00 p.m. staff meeting, Cesar was pumped. "There is some good news that came out this morning," he told a slightly bigger group of canvassers and visitors from a partner organization. "There was a really bad joke this morning in our meeting about how this process is like *Squid Game*. It's unfortunate: a lot of people died, like paid family leave and free college and a lot of other really useful things that we need as a nation, as a community. But immigration reform, which is what this campaign is about, is still there."

There were some murmurs about his comparison of slimmed-down legislation to avoiding murder by robotic snipers in a Korean Netflix drama.

"It's a little too accurate," Cesar said. "But hey."

The cause wasn't out of the woods yet. What appeared to be in this newly announced compromise was a "registry" through which undocumented people could come out of the shadows and live more normal lives and get on a pathway to citizenship. But there remained the risk that moderates would object once again and that the plan would regress to the idea of immigrant "parole," which had fewer protections and no path to citizenship and sustained the paying of fees and the permanent insecurity that Cesar knew well.

The news affected the day's canvassing plan. On the doors today, it would be less about pressuring Sinema to support a pathway and more about getting her to do what she had supposedly committed to. "A lot of this has come from the work that we've been doing the last twenty-nine weeks here, and from decades of work before that," Cesar said, speaking to himself as much as to the team. "Right now, it's the time to continue and not let up." Cesar had no way of knowing that the "deal" announced that day would collapse in acrimony, killing the Build Back Better Act's chances that year.

The team fanned out across the city. Cesar was soon walking through a private development covered in "Neighborhood Watch" signs. He mused that he had been kicked out of neighborhoods like this before. Clutching his turf sheet in one hand and the app in the other, he moved from house to house, going through his routine, finding rabid agreement in some cases but also a right-wing guy who refused to talk and a higher-than-usual proportion of unanswered doors. The Arizona Cardinals were playing at that moment. At one point, he marveled at the size of the garages around him. He said they were bigger than his childhood home.

That was in the tonier part of the neighborhood. Soon we began to see trailers in the driveways and more outdoor storage of possessions. And we found ourselves at the door of a man named Matthew.

He came to the door glowering and skeptical, wearing a long-sleeved T-shirt adorned with a dog howling at the moon and an orange knit cap. Cesar stood across from him, a "Welcome Friends" doormat between them.

Cesar, sensing wariness, sprinted through his opening, before asking Matthew about his level of support for the pathway to citizenship, one to ten.

"As of lately, down to, like, one," Matthew said, seemingly both pissed off by Cesar's arrival and wanting to make use of the platform it afforded.

"And why is that?"

"Just all the BS that's going on," Matthew said.

Did he care to elaborate?

He did.

Matthew launched into a diatribe whose sub-diatribes had sub-sub-diatribes. As it happened, "all the BS that's going on" was a fitting summary.

Why did he oppose a pathway now? Because he knew people who had come here as immigrants, busted their butts for years, were still fighting for status, and all of a sudden other immigrants got approved before them. That wasn't right.

"Yeah, no, for sure," Cesar tried. "Definitely, the system is broken. Me personally—"

But Matthew wasn't done.

The mass migrations happening under Biden. What was that about?

Cesar tried to talk about the root causes of migration. But Matthew pressed on. "I don't mind a neighboring country like Mexico, but now we're absorbing further south countries. Yeah, they're having a bad whatever. That's their country. That's three or four countries away."

Though his last name was Hispanic, Matthew wanted to make something clear: "I was born and raised here. Again, born and raised here."

Cesar tried to explain the nuances of what the pathway to citizenship would actually do. He was struggling to meet Matthew where Matthew was.

"The problem is everybody in the government just needs to get their butts kicked out and they have some new blood in there," Matthew said.

Matthew continued his monologue, teetering between somewhat accurate criticisms of the American political establishment and batshit-crazy theories and lies. The politicians keep telling us X is going to happen, and then they slip in Y, and they don't tell their constituents. Obama bowed down to Mexico's president one time. ("You never do that if you're supposed to be a superpower.") There were opinions of presidents: Trump "did some decent stuff and then did some dishonest stuff"; Nixon was a "decent president, dirty"; Biden was "the joke of the Hill." Matthew's view of the Biden administration's agenda of physical infrastructure and social spending was that "nothing is going to get done except for them wanting to pass whatever money that they want to get."

Standing beside Cesar, I saw Matthew through the deep canvasser's eyes. He was a fount less of political opinions than of political emotions. He felt betrayed, lied to, ignored, condescended to. Many of those feelings were grounded in the realities of American political life. But he then felt a need to assign ideas to those emotions. It was Cesar who was coming to his door inviting him to do that. And here Matthew faltered. Sometimes he knew what he was saying; sometimes he didn't. Fox News or its equivalents seem to have done some of the work of helping him array his feelings into a rudimentary politics. Cesar's hope was that those feelings might be organized in other ways.

"I don't even care—Democratic, independent, or otherwise, they need to clean out the White House. They need to clean out the Senate. All that old blood just needs to be flushed out," Matthew said. "I'm not saying to riot the Capitol or anything, but that'd show them how pissed off people actually are." With that, he seemed to worry even himself: "I'm not cheering those people on. That was wrong to do that. There's a legal way to do it.

"Everybody has just failed at their job in the government, period—from the city level lately, with the floods that happened around here, all the way up to the federal level," Matthew said.

There was another thing, too. Biden wasn't doing anything on the border, so the policy, Matthew said, was effectively, "Hey, come here, come in." Then, he added, Biden had finally responded to the border crisis Matthew had, seconds earlier, condemned him for ignoring and abetting. "Now Biden is finally trying to fight that, but he switched positions, reversing on that a little bit. Do you want a person in office that's switching his opinion so much to popular opinion?" So it was wrong not to attend to Matthew's concern and wrong to change your mind to attend to it.

Cesar tried again to speak to these roiling emotions. "No, I understand your sense—I mean, I think, you know—"

But Matthew just barreled on. He didn't like immigration. Didn't favor that at all. That said, he did favor people who come and work hard and accomplish things. Matthew knew people who had to move because the immigration cops came to their door. He now made an aside about how he could personally show you where to cross the border, if you wanted to know.

Soon Matthew talked himself into another sentiment. Think of the Border Patrol agents. "What about those guys?" he said. "They get hurt, they get killed, they get injured. Do people care about them? No. They're like the Man."

And in short order, Matthew had a new worry he wanted to raise while he had Cesar. So you have this open border, people just flooding across, not from a neighboring country, but three or four countries away. What was to stop some terrorists from more of the Middle Eastern part of the world from sneaking in along with the legions of migrants? Matthew claimed he had been in the military, so this was coming from a place of knowledge. Surely the Taliban or whoever has some guys among their ranks "that look like a Mexican or Hispanic—Latin origin." Were those guys pouring across the border, too? "We've already dealt with one 9/11," Matthew said. "Do we want to invite something else like that in this country now?"

He was talking himself into further stress. How did those hijackers even get in the country on 9/11? You're telling me no one thought it was a *little strange* that some Middle Eastern guys were taking flight lessons here in the United States of America? Were they even pilots? How come no one asked these questions that Matthew was asking?

Now Matthew said something honest and moving: "I had a buddy die over in Afghanistan. That's where the aggression is coming from. They screw up everything. They can't get nothing right." This show of vulnerability was an opening, perhaps, but by this point Cesar had given up.

As he walked away from the house, Cesar said of Matthew, "He's in a dangerous place of misinformation mixed with truth."

A short while later, just after 6:00 p.m., with the sun gone and the cold night air of the desert blowing and Matthew still on his mind, Cesar knocked on a door in a sprawling apartment complex.

For the longest time, no answer. Just as he was about to leave, the door opened. A hefty, well-built man stood there, missing his left leg, hopping on crutches, wearing an Outlaw Threadz T-shirt that said "Never Forget" on the front, referring to 9/11, and "American Patriot" on the back. Cesar, though trained to talk without judgment, though proud of having the temperament to do so, was spirit tired after Matthew's filibustering and now braced himself for another round.

He launched into his script.

"You're talking about illegal immigrants?" Raymond interrupted.

Oh, no.

"Well, in a way, yes, undocumented immigrants," Cesar said, concerned. Cesar asked if Raymond was familiar with the current proposals in Congress to address the issue.

Raymond said that he was familiar with those proposals, and in fact he was familiar with the broader issue in another way, too: "My dad used to be a coyote."

"Oh, wow," Cesar said, taken aback. "That is insane."

And now Raymond gave his reasons for supporting the undocumented community. There was of course his father's work, the same work that had carried Cesar to America. There was the fact that those immigrants do jobs no one else seems willing to do. But for Raymond there was another thing, too. Like Matthew, Raymond said he was a veteran. And the way he saw it, "undocumented citizens are more than welcome to come to my country because I served for seven years. And they can come here, and I'll still protect them."

Now he pointed Cesar to the front of his T-shirt: "Never Forget." And he turned and pointed him to the back: "American Patriot." And then he said, with great self-satisfaction, "There you go." As if his position on undocumented people were self-evident given his service, given the slogans on his chest and back. It was, to him, obvious: he was a patriot. Some awful terrorists had come here and done some real harm on 9/11. He wouldn't forget. Didn't forget. Went into battle for his country. Served as a patriot would. And he served for a purpose: to make and keep the country safe. And what good was keeping it safe and wonderful if people couldn't avail themselves of its bounties? He said he wanted people to come from away and make use of what he had fought so hard to keep.

Cesar, moved by this speech, thanked Raymond for his service and for receiving him so warmly.

"Hey, I got your guys' back, man. You ever have problems, let me know."

Cesar thanked him again and went into the particulars of how to place a phone call to Senator Sinema's office.

As he left, Raymond repeated his promise, gesturing to the shadowy stairwells and alleys of the complex. "You run into any problems around here," he said, "just come back." He took a few hops and, with a smile, closed the door.

George Goehl, the organizer who ran People's Action, helped me better understand what I had observed in Arizona. I had flown in perhaps expecting dramatic, instant mind changing, a Bourne movie of door-to-door persuasion. After all, I had seen the process work in any number of videos. I had read of the results in studies. But as it happened, in the two days I was on the ground, in the fewer than a dozen meaningful interactions I witnessed, there were no dramatic one-to-ten conversions, or even more modest ones. That was partly random and partly because so many of the people we encountered were already supportive of the undocumented—one of many signs that Arizona's politics were changing, as its recent embrace of the candidacy of Joe Biden had shown.

What I had seen was subtler, a slow discourse movement that sought to insert itself in the never-ending process by which voters figure out what they think. The term Goehl used for this process was "meaning making." The way he saw things, the country was in the grips of great forces of change—demographic, economic, political, climatic. Even before voters were angry, and so many of them were, they were lost, discombobulated, unsure of how to see themselves and the world—voters of all backgrounds, all persuasions. What they were seeking wasn't to be found in thirty-second campaign ads or proposals for better health care, Goehl believed, as important as those things were. What they were hungry for was a way of making sense of it all. They were in the market for something like what Alicia Garza had spoken of as a "home." Goehl's fear was that the cruel and hateful and greedy in public life were more ready to give them that than his own allies were. "Absent positive, generative meaning makers in people's lives, the only thing that's left is the far-right preacher and Fox News and Rush Limbaugh, and, increasingly, proud white nationalists," Goehl said. "So every day we forfeit being involved in helping people make meaning of what's happening, we forfeit a chance to help move some people toward us, and that's a lot of people."

Goehl harbored an abiding faith in this meaning-making project, and it grew out of his experience knocking on doors. "Over and over, you would see somebody have something wash across their face. They'd be like, 'I never thought about that.' Or, 'I've never connected my struggles to this other person's struggles.' Or, 'I've never thought about the fact that I am focused on the wrong culprit in this story.' It keeps you wanting to come back, and wanting to figure out how you're going to reach more people. We're starting very late. This is a project that needed to start decades ago."

When Goehl spoke of meaning making and the various ways that process could go, he was explaining what I had seen at the doors. In Lily and then in Kyle, I saw two people, a few houses apart, make opposite meaning of similar underlying experiences. That Lily had been neglected meant that others should now be neglected like her. That Kyle had been neglected meant that he and others should come together in solidarity to demand an end to neglect. The next day, in Matthew and then in Raymond, I saw it again. That Matthew had served his country meant that it should close itself off to the lazy and dangerous and undeserving. That Raymond had served his country meant that it should open itself up to dreamers everywhere, because what good was a cornucopia uneaten? The churning that led to these positions was not automatic or inevitable. Asking people for their vote every few years wasn't enough. Goehl believed it was vital to be just as present in the off-season.

And for him this insight was highly personal. Before he used terms like "meaning making" or knew much about politics, Goehl had a street education in the difficulty of changing others.

He grew up in Indiana, in parts that were rural even by the standards of the rural. "We had to drive forty miles to get to a place with twenty thousand people," he told me. The family was simultaneously educated and working class, in terms of income, culture, and geography. Goehl's father sold metal crafts, and his mother worked as a social worker; both had university educations. Goehl's was a childhood full of mud-ball fights and minibikes, of catching fish in the pond and crawdads in the creek. This was the Indiana that was closer to Kentucky, physically and otherwise, than to Indianapolis.

When Goehl was ten, his parents split. He moved with his mother to Bloomington, a college town and a veritable megalopolis relative to what they had known. Suddenly he was an exotic being to many of his new acquaintances who made fun of how he said "warsh" for "wash" and "crick" for "creek." At the same time, he encountered a range of humanity that had been unfathomable before the move. Across the street from his school was the Tulip Tree Apartments, Indiana University housing that was full of international students and their families. "So suddenly I've gone from running through the woods on three-wheelers to my friends being from Zimbabwe and Malaysia and Nigeria and going over to their house to eat and smelling all this food—like my senses were alive," he once told an interviewer.

A transition that was interesting and eye-opening at first became harder in time. Goehl began to struggle with drugs. "Fast-forward to when I was probably nineteen or twenty, was deep in a serious drug culture and using like crazy and really very much a hot mess," he said. Someone told him about a soup kitchen up on Pigeon Hill in Bloomington that would feed him. After a few visits, he noticed that some who came to eat there also volunteered there—taking out garbage, mopping, wiping tables. He thought he should do that, too, and began to. A new kind of drama entered his life.

An Armenian man from Beirut who cooked at the soup kitchen did theater on the side and asked Goehl if he would act in his production of *Equus*. Ordinarily, Goehl might have passed. But a short time earlier, as he wrestled with his own demons, he had lost a close friend to suicide. She left a parting note for him that stuck: "I remember it saying something like, 'You're really talented. I'm watching you just waste away here. And if anything comes out of what I'm about to do, I hope you do something with your life.'" Perhaps because of that, Goehl said yes to the play. The cook paid Goehl part of his own $3.85 wage to come into the soup kitchen and rehearse while the cook cooked. "It was a long path to getting it together," he told me, "but that was him investing in me and seeing something in me." It was the spark of Goehl waking up, getting clean, turning his life around.

Eventually, Goehl got a paying job at the soup kitchen that had once fed him. A place that had, at first, just stabilized him now began to radicalize him. Coming in every day, seeing the same people show up again and again in line, was an education. "I didn't really have some serious political analysis or grow up with heated conversations about politics and structures at the kitchen table or anything like that," Goehl said. "So that was the beginning of me being like, 'Oh, yeah, nobody starved on my watch, but the reason people are poor is things haven't changed at all.'"

That was the seed of becoming an organizer. Early on, Goehl and some friends worked on issues of housing and homelessness. He sought out organizer mentors. He moved into immigrant rights work for a time. Ultimately, he worked his way up to running People's Action. It was there, as part of its rural organizing, that he set on deep canvassing as a new way of working.

"It is amazing what opens up when you recognize the person across from you, wherever they are at, that there's a reason they're there, and that there's probably some unmet human needs on the other end of that," Goehl told me. He wanted to make clear that the goal was not dialogue or healing or listening for its own sake. "The core of organizing is we want to create change in the world and change in structures and policies and rules," he said. "But it is a craft that first and foremost is designed to help change people, and help people shake off any limiting beliefs, whether those are about ourselves or about society, and replace them with something else."

When Goehl had been in line at that soup kitchen, it didn't look good. "I've been able to do all this neat stuff because some people decided to invest in me," he told me. "The same people could have been like, 'The guy's a drug addict and looks crazy and isn't providing any value to society and is here in line mooching off the soup kitchen,' or something like that. And people decided to do something different." Goehl changed. That inspired a mantra. He used it often: "People change."

ACKNOWLEDGMENTS

The kind of books I make would be impossible without the participation of subjects, who open their lives and minds to a writer's outside interpretation. Thank you to everyone who spoke to me for this book (some of whose names have been changed) and shared stories and fears and hopes that are not always convenient to air in public. I hope the work redeems your choice.

Thank you to Lynn Nesbit for being the best agent, phone talker, and consigliere an author can have. Thank you to Jon Segal, my editor, who is exacting, tough, and funny, and who never lets you forget what a gift and responsibility it is to be able to put a book into the world. Thank you, Madeline McIntosh, Reagan Arthur, Jordan Pavlin, and Maya Mavjee for your investment in my work and in the written word. Thank you to my whole Penguin Random House team for your dedication, including Jessica Purcell, Emily Murphy, Kim Thornton Ingenito, Tiara Sharma, Sarah Perrin, Eleanor Rummell, Dan Novack, Janet Hansen, and Ingrid Sterner.

Vrinda Condillac has been an editor, guidance counselor, dueler, and sentence-by-sentence improver of my work on all four books. I couldn't be luckier. The duels are worth it.

Julie Tate, a brilliant and assiduous investigative researcher at *The New York Times,* moonlighted as a fact-checker for this book, poring over every claim and quote and sparing me embarrassment.

Sometime during the writing of *The Persuaders*, I started a newsletter called *The.Ink*, and I'm truly thankful to every single subscriber. I am able to do the work I do without compromise because of the support you have given me. I also so appreciate my MSNBC family for teaching this writer how to do television and bringing my ideas on these subjects to a broader public.

Priya, you are my center, my adviser, and my first set of ears, followed by eyes. I am glad we met at the bar that night, with your then boyfriend. Orion and Zora, one day you will be old enough to read what I hope you already know: you give our lives so much meaning and renewal. You remind me daily of what I am writing and fighting for. And to my parents, Ruki, Tom, and Kiyan, for the mooring through it all, for the endless conversations, for the spicy group chat.

Finally, S. and H., Z. and J., M. and P., M. and J., A., and, of course, P.: you were my port in a storm in this time. In your many ways, you have taught me what so many subjects of this book already seemed to know: openness opens.

INDEX

A NOTE ABOUT THE AUTHOR

Anand Giridharadas is a writer. He is the author of *Winners Take All*, *The True American*, and *India Calling*. A former foreign correspondent and columnist for *The New York Times* for more than a decade, he has also written for *The New Yorker*, *The Atlantic*, and *Time*, and he is the publisher of the newsletter *The.Ink*. He has spoken on stages around the world and taught narrative journalism at New York University. He is a regular on-air political analyst for MSNBC. He is a recipient of the Radcliffe Fellowship, the Poynter Fellowship in Journalism at Yale, the Porchlight Business Book of the Year Award, the Outstanding Lifetime Achievement Award for Humanism in Culture from Harvard, and the New York Public Library's Helen Bernstein Award for Excellence in Journalism. He lives in Brooklyn with his wife, Priya Parker, and their two children.

A NOTE ON THE TYPE

This book was set in Janson, a typeface named for the Dutchman Anton Janson, but is actually the work of Nicholas Kis (1650–1702). The type is an excellent example of the influential and sturdy Dutch types that prevailed in England up to the time William Caslon (1692–1766) developed his own incomparable designs from them.

Typeset by Scribe, Philadelphia, Pennsylvania

Printed and bound by Berryville Graphics,
Berryville, Virginia

Designed by Betty Lew